Engaging Politics?

"It is never a question of whether or not Christians will be engaged in politics, but rather the question is always how? For Christianity is the most political of faiths because we worship a Savior who is unmistakably a threat to the powers. So it is a happy occasion to comment on this book by Nigel Oakley who draws on Augustine to provide a framework for developing a contemporary political theology to offer a constructive Christian position for the more difficult challenges facing us in our world today."
Stanley Hauerwas, Professor of Theological Ethics, Duke Divinity School, North Carolina

"This book will be an important tool for individuals and churches who are prepared to open their eyes to God's reality, their minds to his multifaceted but integrated truth, and their hearts to his compassion for a world greatly beloved but greatly afflicted."
N.T. Wright, Bishop of Durham

"Nigel Oakley binds the wisdom and practice of the past to the issues and dilemmas of the present in a most creative and stimulating way. This hugely informative book (spanning centuries and continents) will rescue Christians from simplistic or monochrome answers to the biblical, theological and ethical complexity of wrestling with political realities. Readers will discover some of the historical and contemporary riches of Christian reflection, with its dissonances as well as its common core commitments, and will be challenged and helped in equal measure to live up to the recognition that, for the Christian, 'non-involvement is a non-option'."
Christopher J.H. Wright, International Director, Langham Partnership International

"Engaging Politics demonstrates that, far from being incompatible, Christianity, social justice and political engagement are inseparable. A thought-provoking, stimulating and action-inducing read."
Steve Chalke MBE, Founder of Oasis Global and Faithworks

Engaging Politics?

The Tensions of Christian Political Involvement

Nigel W. Oakley

Paternoster:
thinking faith

MILTON KEYNES ● COLORADO SPRINGS ● HYDERABAD

13 12 11 10 09 08 07   7 6 5 4 3 2 1

First published in 2007 by Paternoster
Paternoster is an imprint of Authentic Media
9 Holdom Avenue, Bletchley, Milton Keynes, Bucks, MK1 1QR
1820 Jet Stream Drive, Colorado Springs, CO 80921, USA
OM Authentic Media, Medchal Road, Jeedimetla Village,
Secunderabad 500 055, A.P., India
www.authenticmedia.co.uk
Authentic Media is a division of IBS-STL U.K., limited by guarantee, with its
Registered Office at Kingstown Broadway, Carlisle, Cumbria CA3 0HA. Registered in
England & Wales No. 1216232. Registered charity 27016

British Library Cataloguing in Publication Data

A catalogue record for this book is available from
the British Library

ISBN-13 978-1-84227-505-4
ISBN-10 1-84227-505-4

Cover design by fourninezero design.
Print Management by Adare
Printed in Great Britain by J.H. Haynes and Co., Sparkford

Contents

Acknowledgements

Thanks go first of all to my supervisor at the University of Durham, Dr Robert Song, without whom my thesis, and hence this book would not have seen the light of day. Robert has not only read my thesis (several times) but also commented on my progress as I sought to expand my work for a wider audience. Other people have also read and commented on chapters of this book: I wish to thank particularly, the Rev Professor Walter Moberly and his wife, the Rev Jenny Moberly who have been a continual source of encouragement. I also wish to offer my grateful thanks to Professor Stanley Hauerwas, for his very positive comments on my chapter on him. Needless to say, the responsibility for any remaining mistakes rests with me.

I also wish to thank the Rt Rev Dr N.T. Wright, Bishop of Durham, who has also encouraged me to write this book. His support has been such that he has consented to write the foreword, for which I am very grateful.

Last, but by no means least, my heartfelt thanks go to my wife, Anne, who has coped admirably as I sat secluded in my study tapping away at the keyboard. She too has found time to comment on chapters of this book as they emerged from my printer. This work is therefore dedicated to her and our sons, Alastair and Jonathan.

Foreword

Bringing together theology and politics (or faith and public life, or religion and society, or however you want to put it) still seems to many people a kind of category mistake. Surely, someone will say, religion is all about going to heaven, and politics is all about this present world? What can they have to say to one another? Sometimes this objection comes from the theological side: don't compromise or corrupt "the gospel" by dragging it into the messy world of public life. Sometimes it comes from the politicians: we're running this show, and we don't want any religious types trying to tell us our business. And sometimes it comes from ordinary, puzzled people in the middle, who see the current rise in "religious" violence and find themselves inclined to agree with Richard Dawkins and other well-known contemporary atheists who have suggested that religion, faith and theology are not just irrelevant, outdated and disproved: they are actually dangerous delusions, and would be better banned altogether, or at least confined to consenting adults in private.

So many western Christians have grown up assuming this kind of split between theology and politics that it comes as a shock to discover that the question of how the two go together has been a major topic of theology in almost every century except the nineteenth. Suggesting that we should explore the interface between faith and public life isn't, then, a strange notion coming at us from the extreme Marxist left (as some British Christians assume) or the extreme "religious right" (as some American Christians assume). It is a major topic of continuing importance, and all the more so when, faced with beliefs and values that are indeed highly dangerous, Christians need urgently to get to grips with questions they hadn't considered before.

What we need to attempt this kind of task is a map of the terrain; and this is what Nigel Oakley provides so well in this book. Nigel is a young theologian based in Durham, one of the great centres of theological learning as well as worship and witness, under the shadow of its magnificent Norman Cathedral which speaks so powerfully (and, some would say, ambiguously!) of both the glory of God and the social and political context in which it was built. His book introduces us to the whole subject from two complementary angles. First he surveys four thinkers who have wrestled long and deeply with the key issues; then he walks us through the issues themselves, focussing particularly on several highly contentious contemporary questions.

The first half of the book begins by taking us back to one of the greatest Christian minds ever, that of St Augustine of Hippo. Having set out his political thought, Oakley brings us forward to three seminal thinkers of the last eighty years or so: Gustavo Gutiérrez, Dietrich Bonhoeffer and Stanley Hauerwas, three very different thinkers facing very different challenges, and each responding to them creatively from within the broad Christian tradition. This sets the stage for the second half, in which we face the massive and difficult questions of global poverty, slavery, marriage and sex, war and peace, and the challenge of environmental responsibility. In each case Oakley brings together the complex realities involved (it's no use theorizing in a vacuum!) and the nest of theological possibilities already outlined, and comes up with bracing conclusions.

This is the kind of book that everyone will disagree with at some point, but everyone will learn from at a great many other points. What nobody should do is to ignore it. There is no way back to the comfortable divided world in which Christians can pursue their private way to heaven untroubled by the harsh realities all around them. The call is, rather, to work for God's new creation both in the present and in the ultimate future; and that work will require not only compassion but clarity of thought. This book will be an important tool for individuals and churches who are prepared to open their eyes to God's reality, their minds to his multi-faceted but integrated truth, and their hearts to his compassion for a world greatly beloved but greatly afflicted.

+*THOMAS DUNELM:*
Auckland Castle
Trinity 2007

Introduction

Dear Reader,

So why have you bought this book, I wonder? An interest in theology? Politics? Or even both? Perhaps you are dissatisfied with the way your faith does, or doesn't tie in with your political environment?

This book sets out to show that non-involvement is a non-option for Christians. The Christian political retreat was, and remains, sub-Christian at best; at worst it was a deliberate denial of the gospel. Christ was political – "Christ" as a title was seen as a political, kingly title. He was put to death for sedition, treason. He was not put to death for mouthing some religio-philosophical platitudes for people to live by in their private lives. No, his was a public ministry that publicly upset the apple cart, the accommodation that the Jewish leaders made with the family of Herod and the Roman occupiers. That is why the crowds were brought together to shout for his crucifixion. Yes his message was "religious;" but religious does not mean private, or even personal. It means that we all have to repent; we all have to live in a way that the Nazareth manifesto becomes reality. The poor have good news: they will be oppressed no more. The captives will be free: justice is about restoration, not punishment for the sake of it. The blind will see, and the oppressed go free. If the oppressed go free, the oppressors have to change their ways, their lives, and accept their guilt before God. All too often we in the West – the USA, the UK, Europe – are the oppressors simply because we are "top dogs." We dictate to others: do it our way or else. Is our way so perfect . . .?

So why not a(nother) biblical book? Because there are so many out there.[1] Another issues agenda? Well, I do have five case studies in the second half of the book, but they are there to show that not every issue is totally clear-cut. But why theologians?

---

[1] One excellent one is Brian J. Walsh and Sylvia C. Keesmaat, *Colossians Remixed: Subverting the Empire* (Milton Keynes: Paternoster Press, 2005).

The Christian tradition is now two thousand years old. And we live within our tradition. How some people have interpreted that tradition tends to affect how others following after look at that tradition, how they read scripture – no one reads the Bible in a vacuum. We bring not only our own agendas, our own ideas, but also our culture and upbringing to the text. So I have chosen the Western churches' most influential theologian for my first chapter: Augustine of Hippo. One commentator has gone as far as to say that Augustine is the "default" position for theological thinking in the Latin West (that is, all the churches which do not go by the "Orthodox" label). So, even if you do not think you have met Augustine before, in fact you probably have: original sin and just war, to name but two topics, are ones in which, if he did not think of the category, Augustine's thought has profoundly influenced later generations. It is time therefore to have a brief look at this giant in theological terms and try to assess his legacy for Christian political involvement.

Next, I look at Gustavo Gutiérrez (and, to a lesser extent, Paulo Freire). This is in deliberate counterweight to Augustine. Augustine has been seen most recently as a political quietist: "as you're going to die anyway, it does not matter what political system it is that kills you" (to paraphrase one of Augustine's more cheery remarks!) Gutiérrez is the father of liberation theology, so I shall concentrate on him. His theology is seen as a political theology; not least because it takes the line that not getting involved, not expressing an opinion is involvement. It is involvement on the side of the *status quo*, the powers that be, and the injustices that exist in the current system. So we need to rethink, and rethink radically, how we view scripture.

Dietrich Bonhoeffer also faced the task of rethinking and re-reading scripture in the light of the Nazi menace that engulfed Germany in the 1930s. His notions of costly grace, and re-assessment of the Lutheran "two kingdoms" doctrine, were very radical, and very political in his time. It is perhaps not so much of a wonder that he was incarcerated by the National Socialist system, but that he remained free for so long. His vision was, however, not for a democratic Germany, but an oligarchic one – in his defense, it must be pointed out that it was the democratic Weimar republic that had led to the rise of Hitler.[2] For Bonhoeffer there were two errors that Christians could fall into, and often did, with

---

[2] The precise reasons for Hitler's rise need not detain us here, but my point is that Hitler rose in the context of the democratic system of the Weimar Republic: why people voted for him, and how much influence War Reparations imposed on Germany by the victorious allies after the First World War exerted, are questions that others will, no doubt, continue to debate.

relation to politics. One was the "monastic" error which assumed that the world was all bad and had to be ignored, or withdrawn from. But this is impossible as even the monastery is still the world with all its shortcomings. The other error is the secular-bourgeois one. This assumes that this world is all there is, so we get on with it, living our given "offices" without critiquing the world. In other words, the first assumes God's "No" to "the world is all there is;" the second assumes God's "Yes" to "the world is all there is." In fact, God says both "Yes" and "No" to the world, and Christians must live with that yes and no as they live, inescapably, in the world.

Fourthly, I look at Stanley Hauerwas. He is our radical, high-church Anabaptist – and not to be dismissed as a sectarian, for all he expects Christians to be politically involved as Christians. His is something of a prophetic voice in an increasingly militarized world. Hauerwas is a pacifist, and yet insists that he, and others, have something to say to the world (and how it is run). For Hauerwas, what Christians have to say will be said through their character, their story, and their worship. His is a controversial voice, and it is true to say that his voice has not always been welcome by those who walk the corridors of power.

I could, I suppose, have just given a brief précis of each theologian and left it at that, but how are we to compare a fifth-century African, a late twentieth-century Peruvian, an early twentieth-century German and a twenty-first century American? Different times, different places, different contexts. I propose to do it by looking at three different aspects of their theology: eschatology (especially the way they look at the tension of how much God's kingship is "now" and how far it is "not yet"), ecclesiology (the way they look at how the church exists in relation to the world: the tension of being in the world, as opposed to not being of that world), and their prophetic role (how they regard the tension between the "is" and the "ought" of the way things are in the world).

These tensions are, of course, related. How we regard one will affect how we relate to the others. Each theologian has their own "take" on these issues, but by comparing these "takes," we cannot only see where they differ, but also where they are united in their opinion in that – as far as is possible for us – we must be politically involved for the betterment of humanity.

The third tension is also problematic in that none of our theologians come at us with an Old Testament "thus says the Lord" approach. So I have chosen to examine their attitudes to the prophetic "ought" and the church's "is" by way of examining how they wished, or how they actually did, educate their congregations for political engagement with society outside the church door. Would that education be actively political, a mere subset of education for Christian discipleship, or seek to isolate them in preparation for the second coming of Christ?

For example, a pessimist about potential societal improvements, like Augustine, would have offered no political education as such (as we shall see), for his congregations were mostly the poor unlettered classes. They were to do nothing but obey – and on the very rare occasions when they were asked to do something "impious and wicked," they were to say that they feared God above their masters' swords, and submit to any punishment dealt out by authority. The theme for Augustine is the witness, the prophetic critique, of the martyrs. On the other hand, liberation theologians (especially if we look at their early writings of the late 1960s and early 1970s) take exception to this quietist attitude and insist that all from the base of society must be conscientized – made aware of their oppression so they would deal with that oppression. The prophetic challenge to the *status quo* under that system is immediate and obvious. The prophetic "ought" is to the fore here, and the embodied, realistic "is" is to the fore in the presentation of Augustine's position. There is critique, there is hope for a better society, but how it is to be achieved in concrete situations will differ.

Where that betterment comes into play we will see in the second half of the book: engaging politics is not just about the big issues, but also how we live our "private" lives: hence the chapter on "Love, Marriage, and the Church." I have deliberately not confined myself to the issues of the day, but I will look at sex, and singleness, in its Christian context. Singleness, celibacy, is often highly commended within scripture as is marriage. We have forgotten this. The church often appears to suggest that marriage is inherently better than singleness. Moreover, we do not need sexual, genital activity to lead happy fulfilled lives (Jesus, of course, is the best exemplar of this) even if gender and sexuality are profoundly part of our personhood. And while marriage is more than a way of "dissipating lust," it must not be seen as the be all and end all of Christian existence. Equally, however, we must remember that the celibate lifestyle does not require a lonely lifestyle. A dinner for one is rarely a pleasant experience. And community means more than mother and father and however many children they happen to have produced. For married and single alike, it is perhaps a pity that we have to look to the military to see any "esprit de corps" these days.

A pity because the Christian tradition does not, and should not, baptize the glorification of military might. We worship the prince of peace, so any recourse to war must be examined critically. There are two strands here: the just war tradition, and the pacifist tradition. My own position will probably become clear in the chapter, but we will examine both: and show that neither would endorse the current grandstanding by the USA and UK as they seek to justify their action in the "war on terror." The Christian position seeks to understand their neighbors, even when they resort to acts which take life.

Many of these people, our neighbors, are desperate, and desperately poor. If we do not ensure that the world's resources are shared more equitably, that there will be a good environment for our children's children to grow up in, then we must not be surprised when the "counter-violence of the oppressed" meets us in our streets and offices. Cause and effect may not, in fact, be so simplistic as the last sentence suggests: all too often, even in a reaction to oppression, it is the innocent who suffer most, but to ignore the fact that 80 percent of the world population have to subsist on 20 percent of the world's resources and a child still dies needlessly every three seconds is hardly a Christian response. The point is that we can all do something – we need to do the right (Bonhoeffer), without trying to make *history* turn out right (Hauerwas). In other words, we are to seek God's kingdom on earth, while accepting that it is he, not us, who will finally bring it about in its completeness.

The other two case studies are perhaps "issues of the day": we are at last waking up to climate change, and the degradation of our environment. There may be issues around how much global warming is our fault, and even how much we can do about it – but our profligate lifestyle must come under question while so many of our poorer neighbors suffer and starve. And become susceptible to slave traffickers – the fifth study. This year, 2007, is the bicentenary of William Wilberforce's Anti-Slave trade bill being passed by the British Parliament. Yet today there are more people being held in slavery, or in slave-like conditions, than ever before. What should our attitude be, especially given the apparent acceptance of slavery by Paul and Augustine?

Of course, all this work on how Christians should be involved in the political world would not be contentious if it were agreed how church and state should meet and mix. In the USA, the official line is that "never the twain shall meet" – in other words, no religion has a right of influence over policy. In the UK, there is an "established" church, but should the church stick to being the "prophetic" voice at the margins – concentrating on the proclamation of how things ought to be, or is it to get its hands dirty and get stuck in with real policies, real people, and really try to make an often incremental difference? The answer of this book is both, as I shall show in the link chapter between the two "halves" of this book; and that both are possible, even when government or other public money supports church community projects.

Four theologians, five case studies. My own views will, of course, become clear throughout the book. However the basic thesis is this: as far as the world of politics and social action is concerned, non-involvement is a non-option for Christians. If we try not to be involved, that non-involvement will be, in effect, an endorsement of the *status quo*. Obviously, not everyone can be involved in everything, on every issue, and there is more to involvement than "manning the barricades," but to confine one's Christian interest to Sunday services and Christian meetings is not what Christianity is about. None of the four theologians that I study advocates non-involvement, and none of them expect that involvement to be without cost. It is those who want comfortable Christianity who will be most disappointed by this book. The rest of you, read on . . .

One

Augustine

Augustine lived in the fourth and fifth centuries, from 354 to 430,[3] just as Catholic Christianity was becoming the only recognized religion in the Roman Empire. In early adulthood, he rejected the Catholic Christianity of his mother, and, for a while, embraced Manichaeanism – a dualistic heresy that regarded matter as bad, and only the soul as good (and which allowed him to live with his concubine, while in theory despising sexual relations!). Though he remained part of the sect for nine years, he was spiritually unsatisfied and started to look for a more adequate system of belief. It was through the sermons of Ambrose, Bishop of Milan, that Augustine returned to the faith of his childhood. He was baptized in 387 and felt compelled to give up his job at the Imperial Court in Milan, as he felt he could no longer teach his students the art of public speaking:[4] with his conversion his promising career in Imperial service was over, and he sought a life in retirement.

It was a very active "retirement": Augustine had started on the great output of books and treatises that would continue for the rest of his life. The classical idea of *otium* is better understood as a retreat from the world for study and prayer, rather than our idea of retirement where we expect to shoulder fewer burdens after a lifetime of activity.

A year later, in 388, Augustine returned to Thagaste, in North Africa, the place of his birth, to continue his "retirement," but in 391 made the mistake of going on a visit to Hippo, not knowing that the bishop there was looking for a priest to assist him. Augustine was recognized, and, in the manner of the time, was seized and forcibly ordained. On Bishop Valerius' death, Augustine became Bishop of

---

[3] Among the best biographies of Augustine are Peter Brown, *Augustine of Hippo* (London: Faber and Faber, 1967) and Gerald Bonner, *St Augustine of Hippo: Life and Controversies* (Norwich: The Canterbury Press, 1986).

[4] With this art, the students were meant to be able to sway an audience onto their side with their eloquence; it was not a matter of seeking after truth – it was the winning that mattered.

Hippo in his place, a vocation he was to fulfill until his own death thirty-five years later.

Even while he was a priest, Augustine was, against the practice of the time, encouraged to preach, and to play his part in church affairs. The church in North Africa was beset by the Donatist controversy – a split in the church that dated back to the time of the anti-Christian persecutions. Augustine was to spend much of his life debating with, and writing against, this sect (as well as the Manichees and, later on, the Pelagians). Passions ran high on both sides, and Augustine was the target of an assassination attempt. Across the Mediterranean, the Empire was under threat. In 410, Rome itself was sacked. Although the physical damage was comparatively minor, the damage to the Roman psyche was colossal (this may well be compared to the damage done by the 9/11 attacks). Augustine felt compelled to write an extended rebuttal, called *The City of God*, to those pagans who derided Christianity, on the one hand, for taking people away from the old gods who had protected Rome for centuries, and, on the other, for having a God who was clearly too weak to protect the center of the Empire. Augustine knew that the Roman peace was fragile, and that disaster could easily be around the next corner. He therefore sought, and encouraged others to seek, the peace of eternal life – of the city of God – which was better than any peace that the world could give.

The Two Cities

Augustine's *The City of God* is his major work on the theme of the earthly and heavenly cities. These two cities would only be separated at the *parousia* – the return of Christ in glory – until which time members of the two cities would have to live together; both seeking (for different reasons) the "peace of Babylon."

Augustine regarded the Christian as a pilgrim member of the city of God, a member of one city, whilst living among those from another city. Only at the end of time, when Christ returns in judgment, would the members of the two cities be separated and receive their reward on the basis of whether they have been guided by love of God or love of self. Both the earthly and the heavenly city, according to Augustine, have existed, and will continue to exist, throughout time. The division of the universe into the "city of God" and the "city of Earth" originated for Augustine in the prideful revolt of the (now fallen) angels in heaven. In *The City of God*, Augustine makes it clear that he does not regard members of the city of God as being "at home" in the earthly city.

> Now Cain . . . belonged to the City of man; the second son, Abel, belonged
> to the City of God . . . When those two cities began to run through their
> course of birth and death, the first to be born was a citizen of this world,
> and the second was a pilgrim in this world, belonging to the City of God.
> The latter was predestined by grace and chosen by grace; by grace he was
> a pilgrim below, and by grace he was a citizen above.[5]

From this, it seems that the earth is the territory of the earthly city,
through which the pilgrims are to pass on their way to eternal glory.
However, the situation is not as simple or as clear-cut as it might first
appear; members of both cities "make use of good things, or are afflicted with the evils, of this temporal state" and will continue to do so until
"they are separated by the final judgment."[6] In other words, members of
both cities must live side by side in the same world, and make use of the
same peace,[7] until that world ends.

For Augustine, humanity is naturally social.[8] However, it does not follow that he believes that humanity is naturally political. For Augustine,
humanity was made to have lordship over the "irrational creatures" but,
significantly, not over fellow human beings. This means that any relationship of over-lordship was not part of the creation, and so such
dominion of one group of people over another only came about because
of sin, because of the Fall. From this, the state, and everything therein,
only follows from the Fall, and not from original creation. Augustine
enjoins Christians to live peaceably under this dominion, but, as far as
he is concerned, the state suffers from all the lusts and pride that any
human being is heir to: specifically he regards people as victims of, or
under the power of, the *libido dominandi*, the lust for mastery, the desire
to dominate others. So, instead of everyone living together in peaceful,
innocent companionship, we have two cities coexisting side by side in
this world. All are required to make use of the good (and suffer the evil)
it offers, but the question arises as to how this coexistence is to be
achieved and carried on.

---

[5] R.W. Dyson (ed. and trans.) *The City of God against the Pagans* (Cambridge:
Cambridge University Press, 1998), book XV chapter 1. All quotations from
The City of God (hereafter referred to as *DCD*, after the initials of the Latin title
of the work, *De Civitate Dei*), unless otherwise indicated, will be from this
translation.

[6] *DCD*, XVIII. 54.

[7] *DCD*, XIX. 26.

[8] See *DCD*, XII. 22–3, XIX. 12.

A Common Good?

One of the major difficulties for the pilgrim members of the city of God is that "the order of their love" is so radically different from the members of the earthly city (who will always be in the majority).[9] As far as Augustine is concerned, either one's love is orientated toward God, or it is orientated toward self. However, if people are to live peaceably together, there has to be some sort of agreement over what is to be the basis of their society – what is to be "the common good." The difficulty is that Augustine believes that there can be no common good between the two cities, just as there is – and never has been – a truly just state which based its conception of justice upon a sincere allegiance to God.

However, in *The City of God* XIX. 24, Augustine accepts that all societies have cohered somehow. There is, he claims two chapters later, an intermediate concept of peace – one which members of both cities can use – and it is in this intermediate concept of peace, "the peace of Babylon," that an intermediate common good can be placed. In other words, even though at the deepest level, there is no common good, Christians are told by Augustine to make use of the "peace of Babylon," and they are to pray for "the temporal peace which is for the time being shared by the good and the wicked alike."[10] Christians are also expected to be involved with the world, their prayer is active, not a passive sitting in the corner: "the life of the wise man is a social one."[11] Further, toward the end of *Confessions*, Augustine states that

> our soul yields works of mercy 'according to its kind' (Gen. 1: 12), loving our neighbour in the relief of physical necessities . . . This means such kindness as rescuing a person suffering injustice from the hand of the powerful and providing the shelter of protection by the mighty force of just judgment.[12]

What we would call political action, action in the public sphere, is motivated by the Christian command to love our neighbor. However, such involvement was always tinged with uncertainty. Augustine, even as he

---

[9] See, for example, *DCD*, XVI. 21 and XXI. 12.

[10] *DCD*, XIX. 26.

[11] *DCD*, XIX. 5.

[12] *Conf.* XIII. xvii (21). Text from *Saint Augustine: Confessions*, trans. Henry Chadwick (Oxford: Oxford University Press, 1991). All quotations from Confessions (hereafter referred to as *Conf.*), unless otherwise indicated, will be from this translation.

allowed for correction, coercion, and even war, knew that these forms of discipline did not necessarily lead to correction, but could lead to a worse hardening of the heart of the offender. The prayer of the judge, or presumably any public official, was "from my necessities deliver Thou me."[13]

As far as Augustine is concerned, the peace of Babylon was all that could be expected from the political authorities, not least because one person cannot see into another's heart.[14] Augustine is also aware that, if a society exists by being "bound together by a common agreement as to the objects of their love," then it follows that "the better the objects of this agreement, the better the people."[15] However, true peace, a peace that did not depend on coercion, was only to be found in the city of God.[16] In *Letter* 138, we are told that "an army composed of the sort of soldiers that the teaching of Christ would require" along with others, both in authority and under it "would contribute greatly to the security of the commonwealth;"[17] this, still, is not the same as a perfect society. In *The City of God*, Augustine makes the hypothetical point that:

> If kings of the earth and all nations, princes and all the judges of the earth . . . people of every age and each sex . . . if all these together were to hear and embrace the Christian precepts of justice and moral virtue, then would the commonwealth adorn its lands with happiness in this present life and ascend to the summit of life eternal, there to reign in utmost blessedness.[18]

Nevertheless, if we read Augustine as a whole, it is safe to conclude that he held out no hope for a perfect society in this world. But, even while he was aware of how imperfect the world is (and how it will never be perfect); he never abandoned the hope that guides us toward the peace and love of God. The more we try to imitate God's love, the more we are able

---

[13] *DCD*, XIX. 6

[14] Even with the aid of torture, a judge cannot be certain he has arrived at the truth. See *DCD*, XIX. 6.

[15] *DCD*, XIX. 24.

[16] Even Christians cannot obtain true peace in its entirety in this life. See *DCD*, XIX. 27.

[17] *Letter* 138. 15, in E.M. Atkins and R.J. Dodaro (eds. and trans.), *Augustine: Political Writings* (Cambridge: Cambridge University Press, 2001). All references to Augustine's sermons and letters will be from this collection, unless otherwise indicated.

[18] *DCD*, II. 19.

to live decent lives in our societies.[19] The best we can say is that society can be "Christianized" – in that society may be composed of Christian soldiers, judges, kings and so on – and that Augustine saw that this sort of "Christianized" society would be better than other societies.[20] This does not mean that Augustine saw the (earthly) possibility of a *societas perfecta* (a perfect society). But, although there can never be a *societas perfecta* on this earth, there is an intermediate peace which all can strive to maintain. It is at this level of striving that Augustine expects his judge to sit, and the Christian king is expected to rule – even while those judges and kings are all too aware of the lack of true peace and justice in the world.

The Eschatological Question

Even in his defining of the two cities, and how they came about, Augustine is clearly thinking eschatologically. It is equally clear that members of the city of God are not "at home" in the earthly city.

> It is written, then, that Cain founded a city, whereas Abel, a pilgrim, did not find one. For the City of Saints is on high, although it produces citizens here below, in whose persons it is a pilgrim until the time of its kingdom shall come. Then it will call together all those citizens as they rise again in their bodies; and then they will be given the promised kingdom, where they will reign with their Prince, the king eternal, world without end.[21]

How, therefore, are we to understand the role of the pilgrim in what we must assume to be a hostile environment?

Eugene TeSelle, in his book *Living in Two Cities: Augustinian Trajectories in Political Thought*, devotes a whole chapter to the nature of the pilgrim. I have already noted the pilgrim nature of the Christian's journey through this life, but this does not mean that Christians should despair of "attempts to transform the world," or be people who react against the "occupied territories" language of liberation theologians. As TeSelle says:

> Both moves are Augustinian only as a *first step*, a clarification of one's primary values and commitments. When they become the last word they are

---

[19] See *Letter* 138. 15.

[20] *Ibid.*

[21] *DCD*, XV.1.

un-Augustinian in their indifference to relative judgments about better or worse in the temporal sphere. Augustine . . . was not prepared to abandon the world . . . in the same manner.[22]

Even as they are pilgrims, Augustine expects that Christians who are truly "fathers of their families" create a household that "ought to be the beginning, or a little part, of the city;" and therefore "domestic peace has reference to civic peace."[23] However, there is a difference between "true fathers" and "earthly fathers":

> But a household of men [*sic*] who do not live by faith strives to find an earthly peace in the goods and advantages which belong to this temporal life. By contrast, a household of men who live by faith looks forward to the blessings which are promised as eternal in the life to come; and such men make use of earthly and temporal things like pilgrims: they are not captivated by them, nor are they deflected by them from their progress towards God.[24]

Though the world has to be traveled through, it is not, therefore, abandoned. It is clear that Augustine viewed Christians as pilgrims through the earthly city, with their sights set on the eschatological city of God. In the end, for Augustine, all political life is relativized: the Christian was to make use of the peace of Babylon, and to pray for that peace even while knowing that this earthly peace was not, and never would be, perfect peace. For Augustine, the peace of Babylon is something that the Christian can make use of, but for different ends than members of the earthly city for whom this peace is the only peace they know. However, Augustine also saw that Christians had a responsibility to love their neighbor and were therefore required to be involved in civil society. While not setting out to transform society, the pilgrim had a different ethos of life, which could affect society – hopefully for the better.

For Augustine, true justice will only occur in the city of God, but Christians, as pilgrims on their way to their homeland, are to offer their talents to be used in the earthly city in order to secure and maintain the peace of Babylon. In other words, even if the eschaton is the first word – that in the end very little matters in terms of what civil customs and laws we follow,[25] or under what authority we live – it does not mean it is the

---

[22] E. TeSelle, *Living in Two Cities: Augustinian Trajectories in Political Thought* (New York: University of Scranton Press, 1998), 61.

[23] *DCD*, XIX. 16.

[24] *DCD*, XIX. 17.

[25] Provided that "there is nothing indecent or immoderate about it" (*DCD*, XIX. 19).

only word Christians offer to the world. For Augustine, political involvement is a necessary part of life. Therefore, I shall consider how the Augustinian church should relate to civil society.

The Church and Civil Society: The Ecclesiological Question

The balance between looking to the infinite and living in this world is, of course, difficult to achieve. And as we look at Augustine's writings, at times one aspect is emphasized, then the other. On the one hand, he clearly tells his congregation not to be disobedient to anyone (not even to tyrants)[26] – after all we are all going to die sometime anyway.[27] All of this points to a very quietist approach to life. And yet, we also see Augustine vigorously defending himself when taken to task by a Roman official, Macedonius, who suggests that religion should be kept out of politics (or, in this case, the justice system).[28]

When any examination is undertaken of Augustine's political involvement, we see that it is Augustine himself, or his fellow bishops,[29] or Christian imperial officials[30] who are urged to take some form of action in civil society. This tendency can be seen in both Augustine's more theoretical (even if polemic) writing,[31] as well as when he is dealing with practical, up to the moment, issues in his letters and sermons. This action depended upon the authority which had been given to various bodies by Rome: Augustine himself "was a much sought-after arbitrator" in his own Episcopal court.[32] Conversely, the ordinary people are encouraged *not* to act – and certainly not to take part in a lynching. In *Sermon* 302 [302.13], Augustine rages against his congregation for their part in the death of an unpopular Roman official:

---

[26] *DCD*, II. 19. "Christ's servants, therefore . . . are commanded to endure this earthly commonwealth, however depraved and wholly vile it may be, if they must."

[27] *DCD*, V. 17. "As far as this mortal life is concerned, which is spent and finished in a few days, what difference does it make under what rule a man lives who is soon to die, provided only that those who rule him do not compel him to do what is impious and wicked?"

[28] *Letters* 152–5.

[29] See for example *Letter* 10* to Alypius.

[30] See for example *Letter* 220 to Boniface.

[31] Such as "The Mirror to Princes," in *DCD*, V. 24.

[32] Bonner, *Life and Controversies*, 123.

"But," you might say, "think of the things that crook did . . ." He has his own judges, his own authorities. There is an established government: *all that there are established by God* [Rom 13.1]. Why are you so violent? What authority have you been given? But, of course, this isn't public punishment, it's simply terrorism in the open.

In the same sermon, the only people encouraged to act, as they were the ones with the legal authority, are the heads of households who should have prevented their families (and anyone else under their authority) from taking part in the disturbance.[33] It is clear that Augustine does not approve or advocate mob violence of any description. Of course, Augustine is more concerned about how this action may turn Christians from wanting to live justly into people who envy those with power, and that they may seek that corrupting power which those in public office possess. For Augustine, if they truly wish to create a more just society, they should first renounce the use of violence. If they do not do that, then they simply become indistinguishable from those they seek to oppose. Their only example and model is that of the martyrs, and the only true way to reform political society is to oppose injustice through nonviolence.

At first, we may wish to question this nonviolent approach as it sits strangely with Augustine's advocacy of the just war and coercion (which I shall discuss below). But there is a difference in Augustine's mind between the actions an "ordinary" Christian can undertake, and, for example, a Christian emperor. For Augustine, motivation is key, and the Christian ruler should only engage in *just* wars.[34] Ordinary Christians are, in many ways, expected to follow their elders and betters.

However, Augustine is not totally averse to political action by his congregation – when they release slaves from a slave ship docked in port, there is no condemnation similar to *Sermon* 302. In his letter to Alypius, Augustine notes that his congregation, being "aware of our practice of performing acts of mercy in such cases," released 120 people either from the docked ship or "from the place where they had been hidden before being put on board."[35] Augustine pleads with Alypius to do what he can so that the illegally enslaved people can and do remain free, and

---

[33] *Sermon* 302.11. Heads of households were seen as a mediating authority between household and state (see *DCD*, XIX. 16).

[34] See *DCD*, V. 24.

[35] *Letter* 10*. 7.

Augustine's congregation is no longer harassed by the slave traders demanding the return of their "goods." Augustine's lack of condemnation here shows that quietism in all circumstances is not the end of the story.

So, from this, it must be concluded that for the ordinary Christian, direct political action is not an option unless it is within the realms of legitimate authority,[36] and is done with the correct motive: that is, action is undertaken for others (like those on the slave ship) rather than themselves.

Augustine himself, as I have noted, defends the right of the church to argue in supplication for the guilty. "In short, the Lord himself interceded with the men to save the adulteress from stoning, and by doing so he advocated the duty of intercession to us."[37] Augustine may be aware that his efforts will not necessarily succeed, but this does not mean that he wishes to abandon the right to argue his case.

Coercion, Punishment and Just War

Of course, what Augustine was also doing, in dealing with imperial civil servants, was accepting that, as I have already said, that both the heavenly and earthly cities must cohere somehow. One of the ways in which they must cohere is in the maintenance of peace. Here we come to one of Augustine's most debated "accommodations" with life "as it is": his acceptance of coercion and of war. For Augustine, only the city of God will be free of coercion. So, all of us on this earth, including the pilgrim members of the city of God, must accept the need, and the use, of coercion. Even within the family, and Augustine both accepts and defends the authority of the Roman paterfamilias over his household, there will be the need for coercive discipline. In *Letter* 104. 7, Augustine asks:

> If, as little boys, or even as bigger ones, we had been let off by our parents or teachers whenever we pleaded for pardon after committing some sin, would any of us have been bearable as an adult? Who would have learnt anything useful? These things are done out of care, not cruelty.

---

[36] *Letter* 10* makes clear that Augustine wishes to use the appropriate laws to keep the "slaves" free. He is not interested in a clandestine "free the slaves" movement.

[37] *Letter* 153. 11.

Augustine is aware of the ambiguity of punishment, and guards against cruelty (where he can), but he insists that even the most war-like brigand is merely seeking to impose a better peace on his surroundings. Such a peace may merely be one which allows the brigand to enjoy their ill-gotten gains, but the general point is they are striving for peace even as they wage war.[38]

Augustine was well aware of the downside of war, but still expected wars to happen, and he expected Christians to take part in such wars, (even when ordered into battle by "an infidel Emperor").[39] For Augustine, all leaders were obliged to act in ways that Augustine would clearly object to if he met similar action in ordinary members of his congregation. It is the motive with which a Christian goes to war that exercises Augustine: "if they resort to punishment only when it is necessary to the government and defense of the commonwealth, and never to gratify their own enmity." So, the Augustinian Christian ruler would only engage in just wars.[40] Of course, this leaves us with the problem of what a just war is (and how to distinguish it from an unjust one),[41] but the theme is at one with Augustine's idea that God imposes punishment on people. In *Confessions*, Augustine affirms that there is a beneficial side to Divine punishment: "you 'strike to heal,' you bring death upon us so that we should not die apart from you (Deut. 32:39)."[42] If God is prepared to punish, Augustine is therefore prepared to accept the fact of both punishment and coercion in church and in civil society.

For Augustine, external coercion could and should lead to internal, motivational change. However, he is also aware that there is no guarantee that punishment would work: "I don't know whether more people are reformed than slip into worse ways through fear of impending punishment."[43] Augustine is caught between the ideas that punishment could lead to a person's destruction, but that leaving that person unpunished could "lead to someone else being destroyed."[44] Therefore, we can see that while Augustine is clear in his approval of the official use of force, he clearly also has his misgivings: not least because power of coercion can so readily convert itself into a tool for selfish interest, a means of exercising the *libido dominandi*. This, in turn, is merely another sign of how far fallen we are.

---

[38] *DCD*, XIX. 12.

[39] See *Enarrationes in Psalmos*, CXXIV. 7.

[40] *DCD*, V. 24.

[41] See the chapter on just war and pacifism below.

[42] *Conf.* II. ii (4).

[43] *Letter* 95. 3.

[44] Ibid.

Broadly speaking, it seems that Augustine accepts that all leaders will use coercion in civil society, but the means and motives for the use of coercion will be different for Christians than for others. Coercion is to be used to set people on the right path, not as mere retributive punishment. For Augustine, the person best equipped to create that order and resist imperial grandiosity, is the person who has been educated in the Christian *paideia*. Rowan Williams points to Augustine's eulogy of the (almost) ideal Christian emperor

> whose motive in all he does is love and not the lust for glory. Theodosius I is regarded ([*The City of God*] V, 26) as a ruler well on his way towards this ideal . . . [W]e should note what exactly it is that Augustine picks out as the marks of good government – law and coercion employed for the sake of the subject by one who is manifestly not in thrall to *libido dominandi* or vainglory, because he is capable of sharing power and accepting humiliation.[45]

Augustine was, however, always concerned that leniency should be applied, and he always wrote against capital punishment; in one case telling the proconsul of Africa (called, confusingly, Donatus), that if the latter were to put Donatists to death in his court, he would "deter us [Catholics] from bringing any such case by our own efforts before your court."[46] He still wished for the Donatists to be brought to trial, but then "be persuaded and informed" rather than "led through force alone" to "bend their will to a better course." This is because, even when he advocated coercion, Augustine still realized that "when people are led through force alone and not through teaching even to abandon a great evil and embrace a great good, the efforts expended prove burdensome rather than profitable."[47]

The coercive nature of life in civil society is the most difficult part of Augustine's thought to come to terms with. If Christians are to "get involved in politics," how do they cope with the apparently arbitrary use of force? Augustine's only answer seems to be that Christians are involved unhappily. Augustine ends *The City of God* XIX. 6 with a description of a judge who may have to torture the innocent and act in ignorance against justice:

---

[45] Rowan Williams, "Politics and the Soul: A Reading of the *City of God*," *Milltown Studies* 19/20 (1987), 64–5.

[46] *Letter* 100. 2.

[47] Ibid.

we certainly have an instance of what I call the wretchedness of man's condition . . . [though the judge] is not guilty . . . is he also happy? Surely, it would be more compassionate, and more worthy of the dignity of man, if he were to acknowledge that the necessity of acting in this way is a miserable one: if he hated his own part in it, and if, with the knowledge of godliness, he cried out to God, "From my necessities deliver Thou me."[48]

Christians are in the invidious position of trying to live a Christian life and practice the Christian faith while at the same time struggling to maintain the shadowy "peace of Babylon."

Augustine clearly has a pessimistic view of human nature and therefore of the amount of progress that can be expected in civil society, but he does not want his congregation frozen in inaction. If Christians are called to love their neighbor as well as their God, then the attempt to improve their neighbor's political lot must be made by all those in a position to do so; and all must do what they can: in one sermon, Augustine asks his congregation for money so that he can pass it on to a poor man who has "not received over-much from you." It seems that, as ever, Christians must be exhorted to do their bit!

Augustine's life and times were violent and unstable. He regarded the world as a dangerous place, but where Christians must live, where they must pray for the "peace of Babylon," but from which they do not take their final authority. Christianity, certainly Augustinian Christianity, supplies the believer with standards of judgment that are ultimately independent of the regime and the pervasive influence of its principles. If you were a true Christian, you could not be a true Roman. This will always create tension. The earthly city – because of the foundation of its love (on itself and not on God) – will seek the ultimate in loyalty, dedication, and even worship, from its citizens. It will not, therefore, appreciate anyone who – however obedient to its laws – has in the final analysis, a different loyalty.

There is no evidence that Augustine ever supposed that any commonwealth would be perfect – and *The City of God* is a total attack upon the value system of Rome, which leads, according to one commentator, to three conclusions:

1. Neither pagan nor Christian religion ensures a state against the temporary and military vicissitudes common to states as such.
2. As regards religion, the Roman empire can do nothing better than to be a Catholic Christian empire and thereby further among men the worship of the true God.

---

[48] *DCD*, XIX. 6.

3. The ultimate destiny of Catholic Christianity is not in the slightest degree tied to the fortunes of the Roman Empire.[49]

The political therapy that Augustine issues is much stronger medicine than most of us would realize, and takes account of the possible (or, eschatologically, definite) destruction of the state – any state. In the end, although according to Augustine the state would do best with saints in office (and anywhere else in society),[50] the earthly city will fall, so even as the church seeks to do what it can for its neighbors, it must continually look to the *parousia* of Christ.

Education

The education of the individual, or any group of people, and the influence of others over them (especially in their formative years), is vital for the relationship between the developing individuals and their social environment. Augustine was aware of this – we have already noted his comments in *Confessions* about divine discipline. Education in its broadest sense is, of necessity, "pre-political."[51] This is because, whether for good or ill, our education – whether it is formal schooling or the more informal influence of our home life – lays down our attitude toward involvement in public life. Whether we accept any plausible leader who promises us more in the way of "bread and circuses," or whether we look for leaders who offer less selfish and more public inducements, depends more on our background and education (in the broadest sense) than on rational thought at the time the decision is required.

Augustine's own attitude was to expect more of those who had a classical, liberal education than those who had not: in this he was a man of his time (and one who had himself benefited from such an education). To further the education of his priests, Augustine had set up monasteries in Hippo, but the problem was that these monasteries became recruiting grounds for the elite priesthood, rather than centers of general education for the populace: what the African church produced therefore was a

---

[49] See TeSelle, *Living in Two Cities*, 20.
[50] See *Letters* 138.15, 91.3, *DCD*, II. 19.
[51] By "pre-political" I mean education that prepares people to be involved in public life, to engage in social action or welfare, which in turn could easily lead to political engagement with society. I regard a political education as an education toward specific views and actions. The latter type of education can easily become political indoctrination.

highly educated elite, but a general populace who had much less under-standing about their faith (which may, or may not, be a factor in the change of religious allegiance of North African people in the face of bar-barian and Islamic invasion over the next couple of centuries).

While Augustine's church in Hippo provided sanctuary to slaves and others in times of need, and while he preached to a congregation of mainly poor people, his own writings on education are aimed at those who are already educated. Indeed in *De Doctrina Christiana*, he tells his readers to look elsewhere for teaching in the study of rhetoric,[52] though he expects the rhetorical styles to be understood and used by those read-ers when they come to put his words into practice.[53] It is, however, inter-esting that Augustine assumes a high level of intelligence on the part of his reader,[54] and he clearly assumes that the best "performances" are from those who "can argue or speak wisely, if not eloquently."[55] Therefore, though Augustine is not theoretically averse to someone who is not eloquent in expounding the scriptures, it is clear that he prefers the speaker to be both wise and eloquent.[56]

This dichotomy is evidence of Augustine's tension between his past, but still enduring, educational and intellectual formation, and his present identity as a Christian bishop. Perhaps the best way to describe the ten-sion is to suggest that Augustine thinks that Christian truth *ought* to be able to stand by itself without human embellishment, but he *knows* that human beings are perfectly capable of following an eloquent speaker – whether or not that speaker propounds the truth,[57] and the same attitudes

---

[52] Text from *Saint Augustine: On Christian Teaching*, trans. R.P.H. Green (Oxford: Oxford University Press, 1997). All quotations from *On Christian Teaching* (hereafter referred to as *DDC*), unless otherise indicated, will be from this translation.

[53] "The general function of eloquence, in any of these three styles [of rhetoric], is to speak in a manner fitted to persuade . . . and if he fails to persuade he has not achieved the aim of eloquence." (F. van der Meer, *Augustine the Bishop* [trans. Brian Battershaw and G.R. Lamb; London: Sheed and Ward, 1961], 143).

[54] Ibid., 7.

[55] Ibid., 17.

[56] Ibid., 22. Augustine, against pagan criticism, also states that the scriptures are naturally eloquent (ibid., 25).

[57] "But the speaker who is awash with the kind of eloquence that is not wise is particularly dangerous because audiences actually enjoy listening to such a person on matters of no value to them, and reckon that somebody who is heard to speak eloquently must also be speaking the truth." *DDC*, IV. 17.

will prevail when it comes to reading the written word. Augustine himself, as a young man before his conversion, regarded the scriptures as "unworthy in comparison with the dignity of Cicero."[58]

In *De Doctrina Christiana*, Augustine changes Cicero's priorities of eloquence from saying that the "teaching and delight were subordinate to the ultimate goal of persuasion,"[59] to the idea that teaching, or instruction, "is a matter of necessity."[60] Delight, for Augustine, is part of (Christian) eloquence, merely because "the disdainful kind of person . . . is not satisfied by the truth presented anyhow"[61] and persuasion, or moving people cannot occur, unless they have been taught.[62] However, if the use of rhetoric is what will allow them to learn, to perceive delight, and be moved to action, then so be it. Given that Augustine's "overriding emphasis [is] on teaching the truth,"[63] it is unsurprising that he would wish to make use, and recommend others to make use, of a skill that had served him so well in both his civil and his pastoral careers – even if he has to considerably adapt classical rhetoric before it can be deemed suitable for Christian use.

In sum, we can conclude that, although Augustine does not require everyone to be eloquent in propounding the scriptures, he is fully aware of his culture and his time. That culture meant that, all too often, the eloquent rather than the wise would win any argument. Augustine's own education was elitist and this elitist thought can still be seen in works such as *De Doctrina Christiana*.

Leading Us into All Truth

For all practical purposes, as I have noted, Augustine expects his congregation to be obedient to those in power. While this does not mean we can dismiss the idea of Augustine teaching the congregation on how they should approach political matters – even in *Sermon* 302, as I have noted, he tells the congregation that their remedy is through the laws of the state[64] – Augustine does not set out a political program, nor does he

---

[58] *Conf.*, III, v (9).

[59] van der Meer, *Augustine the Bishop*, 73.

[60] *DDC*, IV. 76.

[61] Ibid., 78.

[62] "People may either do or not do what they know must be done; but who could say that they must do something which they do not know they must do?" (Ibid., 76).

[63] Ibid., 73.

[64] See *Sermon* 302. 13.

give a political *paideia*. This is because the subject of *paideia* for Augustine is not politics, but truth.

Also for Augustine, it is the church that guides us all to the truth – and no political authority (however good in secular terms) that ignores the truth of God is truly just.[65] From this Rowan Williams tells us that "Augustine assumes that a person nurtured in the church and in the ordered *caritas* it inculcates is uniquely qualified to take responsibility for wielding political power."[66] Whether Augustine would accept that any Christian was so qualified is open to doubt. What we do know[67] is that Augustine is happy to refer to the idea of Christian leaders in civil society even though he does not expect there to be a perfect society.

This is not to say a Christian leader would have an easy time as he tried to balance the conflicting interests of the earthly and the heavenly cities. Not only does a Christian leader have "the alarming task of discerning the point at which what he is defending has ceased to be defensible,"[68] but also there is the tension of knowing, more generally, that wise leaders will be sensitive to the dichotomy that Augustine points to in *The City of God*.[69] This dichotomy is based on the fact that, on the one hand, ignorance is unavoidable – as we cannot see into each other's hearts – and, on the other, judgment is unavoidable because human society compels it. This inevitably leads to tensions, and to the realization that the only certainty is that mistakes will be made. Hence Augustine's praise of Theodosius, whose penitence (very much against the norm for Roman emperors) over the massacre of the Thessalonians is commended in *The City of God*, V. 26.

So we can see that Augustine's thinking meant that he expected there to be leaders both in the church and in civil society. The leaders in the church should guide the rest toward the Christian truths. Also, Christian leaders in civil society would face an almost impossible task in their uncomfortable role. In the light of his hierarchical thinking, it is unsurprising that Augustine did not advocate political action on the part of his congregation. However, in spite of the difficulties facing leaders, the only education Augustine offered was the informal Christian education of the church which had no directly political content.

---

[65] *DCD*, XIX. 21.

[66] Williams, "Politics and the Soul," 68.

[67] For example from Augustine's insistence to Boniface (*Letter* 220) and to Christian judges (*DCD*, XIX. 6) that they should continue in public office.

[68] Williams, "Politics and the Soul," 66.

[69] *DDC* XIX. 6.

Of course, if we assume that people come into church flawed (and, given Augustine's views on human nature, this is a safe assumption), then people need to be reformed, as Augustine himself needed to be after his conversion. *Confessions* stand as witness to the fact that Augustine believed that personal change was possible. The theme of reform was expanded in *The City of God* to emphasize that congregations of the Christian church could be reformed toward the true public service of neighbor-love, and it was the job of Christian leaders in the church to act as the intermediaries, the prophets, recalling the congregation to its founding principles. In other words, a Christian statesman takes it as his or her moral task to strive to contribute to the *quality* of the earthly or secular peace just as individual Christians can intervene in the education (and correction) of people who are in his or her charge on the model of the Roman *paterfamilias*.

There is no suggestion that the ordinary congregant sitting under Augustine should, or could, seek power – even if they (and Augustine) could be sure that they would use that power correctly in the service of the church and their neighbors. Whether this suggestion is not forthcoming from Augustine because he failed to consider the possibility for theological or practical reasons is a question that remains open. Theologically it could be argued that Augustine thought the seeking of political power so open to *cupiditas*, to the self-love upon which the earthly city is based, as to risk a soul's salvation. Practically it could be argued that Augustine did not live in our contemporary democracy where political power can legitimately be sought, so the problem of "ordinary people" seeking political power just did not occur to him. Any answer to this debate would, of necessity, have to be both tentative and speculative. What we can conclude is that Augustine never advocated turning our backs on society however it was construed or governed. Nor did he, as I have noted, advocate revolution. He sought to do what he could, within the law, to assist people, to increase social justice (if only incrementally), but for his congregation – for all they were to help to alleviate the plight of the poor, and to love their neighbor – they were to regard themselves as pilgrim members of the city of God; to live, as best they could, under the dictates of their society, and remember that it was the martyrs who were to be their political examples when that society commanded them to do anything "impious or wicked."

For Augustine, we must be aware of the final destiny of both the earthly and heavenly cities, we must also do what we can in obedience to the commandment to love our neighbors, and, as far as possible, live quietly among our fellow human beings. Awareness of the city of God, for Augustine, also meant awareness of the earthly city and the sinfulness of the humanity that inhabited the latter. Even the pilgrim members of the city of God were tainted by the Fall. For Augustine, the prophetic vision must have seemed very far away at times: all he could do was try to promote those small steps that might move Roman society toward being a better "Catholic Christian empire and thereby further among men the worship of the true God."

Two

The Power of the Oppressed

Gustavo Gutiérrez and a Theology of Liberation

Introduction

Liberation theology takes a very different view to the "powers that be" from Augustine, and seeks to "conscientize" the poor, so that they become aware of their oppression and begin to seek ways to combat it. Again in contrast to Augustine, liberation theology emphasizes the sinfulness of structures, not just of the individual. It is these structures – and those who use these structures to oppress the poor – that are to be opposed and overcome if the oppressed are to be liberated.

Liberation theology has, therefore, been criticized for reducing salvation to the political.[70] Certainly in its base communities and in its conscientization of the poor, it can be said to be providing a pre-political (if not a directly political) education for the poor. It is the ordinary person who, according to this theology, needs to be made aware of his or her situation in order to be able to overcome it. It must also be said, as we shall see, that liberation theology does not view itself as a political theology in this reductionist fashion, but opposes "apolitical" theology on the ground that this is self-deception – if the church does nothing, it is simply giving covert support to the *status quo*.

In this chapter I have chosen to concentrate on the writings of Gustavo Gutiérrez as he is the best-known liberation theologian[71] – *A*

---

[70] Not least by Cardinal Ratzinger (now Pope Benedict XVI) of the Vatican's Sacred Congregation for the Defence of the Faith.

[71] Alfred T. Hennelly describes him as such in his "General Introduction" to *Liberation Theology: A Documentary History* (Maryknoll, NY: Orbis Books, 1990). He notes "[t]he very title of the liberation movement is taken from his book, *A Theology of Liberation*" (xxiii).

Theology of Liberation, is still regarded as one of the best expressions of what he calls a *"new way* to do theology"[72] – and because of the influence that Paulo Freire had on his work, I will also look at the life and work of this Latin American educator.

Before we examine the theology, a brief word about Gutiérrez and Freire: Gustavo Gutiérrez is a Peruvian priest who lives and works in a world where the majority of the poor and impoverished, those he terms "the oppressed," are Christian. He himself works in the *favelas* (slums or shanty towns) of Lima, the capital city of Peru. His theology is born out of praxis – what Christians do and practice in the world – and reflection on God's word in his Latin American culture. Gutiérrez is insistent that he deals first and foremost with his own culture and situation, though he notes with approval in his introduction to the revised edition that "the liberation perspective" has been adopted across denominational, cultural, and religious boundaries. His original, and remaining, purpose is to seek a response to the plight of the oppressed which would compare with the biblical presentation of "liberation – salvation – in Christ as the total gift, which . . . gives . . . liberation its deepest meaning and its complete and unforeseeable fulfillment."

Paulo Freire, who died in 1997, had a seminal influence on liberation theology because of his approach to education. The key for Freire is conscientization: it is only by this process of moving the learner toward his (or her) own "critical consciousness" that real education takes place. Freire is not interested in what he calls "banking education" or "domestication," where the students are treated as mere objects to be filled with requisite facts, and thereby conditioned to be content with their allotted place in society – a place allotted to them by the dominant class. Freire's conscientizing approach, of course, requires a different attitude from the teacher: on the one hand, the teacher is to be a learner in dialogue with his or her students – an authoritarian approach is not one Freire would approve of, as it denies the students the status of "subjects" – but, on the other hand, the teacher does have an authority, and is expected to lead the class toward their critical consciousness. In Freire's later works,[73] the authority of the teacher has come more to the fore, perhaps to counter the

---

[72] Gustavo Gutiérrez, *A Theology of Liberation: History, Politics and Salvation* (revd edn; London: SCM Press, 1988), 12, emphasis original.

[73] See, for example, Miles Horton and Paulo Freire, *We Make the Road by Walking* (Philadelphia: Temple University Press, 1990), 186–9, where the "difference between having authority and authoritarianism" is discussed.

impression given in the early work, *Pedagogy of the Oppressed*, that the teacher was to be just a fellow learner with the students.[74]

However, Freire did not just gather a group of poor people together and teach them how to be revolutionaries. His job was to teach them how to read and write. The problem was that he was successful in both doing the job and in the methods employed in doing that job. In a sense (and in a sense only) any "revolutionary" action on the part of the people was incidental. For Freire did not see directing the form of action that the conscientized people undertake as part of his remit. But how does a literacy program conscientize the poor?

In order to "read the word," Freire believes, one has to "read the world." To use an example given in *Cultural Action for Freedom*, the sentence "Eva saw the grape"[75] makes no sense to the poor – being taught to read such sentences becomes a meaningless exercise divorced from their reality: they cannot afford to see, buy and eat grapes! On the other hand, words such as *"favela"* ("slum"), do make sense as it represents "the same social, economic, and cultural reality of the vast numbers of slum dwellers in those [Brazil and other] countries."[76] So it is words such as this that allow the poor to read both the word and the world.[77] It is once the poor can read the word and the world that they begin to reject the image of themselves that has been imposed on them by their oppressors.

The Assumptions of Conscientization

The process, begun by a literacy program, of conscientizing the poor, starts with an assumption on the part of the educator: that the poor person is indeed an illiterate "oppressed within the system."[78] This is opposed to the assumptions of other literacy programs whose authors

> do not recognize in the poor classes the ability to know and even create the texts which would express their own thought-language at the level of

---

[74] See Paulo Freire, *Pedagogy of the Oppressed* (Harmondsworth: Penguin Books, 1972), 53.

[75] Paulo Freire, *Cultural Action for Freedom* (Harmondsworth: Penguin Books, 1972), 24.

[76] Ibid., 38–9.

[77] For a detailed account of how Freire teaches the poor how to read using "generative words" (words generated from the poor's own context), see ibid., 85–8.

[78] Ibid., 29.

their perception of the world. The authors repeat with the texts what they do with the words, i.e., they introduce them into the learners' consciousness as if it were empty space – once more, the "digestive" ["banking"] concept of knowledge.[79]

The effect of this lack of recognition is that the students are domesticated; that is, they are prepared "for a life of political alienation in society,"[80] rather than empowered. Given the above dichotomy (that either the teacher assumes that his or her students are to be filled with the required knowledge so that the students become "good" passive members of society, or the teacher assumes that the students are to be conscientized – to recognize how the *status quo* treats them, and *not* to be content within that system) then it is unsurprising that Freire assumes that education is politics. Neutrality is not an option; the educator must ask him- or herself,

> What kind of politics am I doing in the classroom? That is, In favor of whom am I being a teacher? . . . Of course, the teacher who asks in favor of whom I am educating and against whom, must also be teaching in favor of something and against something . . . After that moment, the educator has to make his or her choice, to go farther into opposition politics and pedagogy.[81]

The tragedy for Freire is that these questions and choices are not usually in the forefront of an educator's mind: the educator is also passive. Indeed, Freire found that the "banking," or "domesticating," system is so universally adopted that the biggest difficulty he faced in his adult literacy programs was training the teams of coordinators.

> Teaching the purely technical aspect of the procedure is not difficult; the difficulty lies rather in the creation of a new attitude – that of dialogue, so absent in our own upbringing and education. The coordinators must be converted to dialogue in order to carry out education rather than domestication

---

[79] Ibid., 26.

[80] Ira Shor, "Education is Politics: Paulo Freire's Critical Pedagogy," in Peter McLaren and Peter Leonard (eds.), *Paulo Freire: A Critical Encounter* (London: Routledge, 1993), 25.

[81] Ira Shor and Paulo Freire, *A Pedagogy for Liberation: Dialogues on Transforming Education* (Massachusetts: Bergin and Garvey, 1987), 46. Freire makes a similar point in Paulo Freire, *Pedagogy of Freedom: Ethics, Democracy, and Civic Courage* (Lanham, MD: Rowman and Littlefield, 1998), 73.

. . . The period of instruction must be followed by dialogical supervision, to avoid the temptation of anti-dialogue on the part of the coordinators.[82]

Freire's methods face criticism, often from those it is intended to help, because they have "internalized" their oppression so effectively that the poor assume that they are totally ignorant.[83] The students are so indoctrinated with how education ought to be done to them, that they find it difficult to visualize how a different approach to their schooling could be appropriate. Under this new cooperative system, the teacher has (as Freire admits in *Learning to Question*) a difficult balancing act to complete:

> I have never said that not having a truth to impose implies that you don't have anything to propose, no ideas to put forward . . . Educators cannot refrain from putting forward ideas, nor can they refrain either from engaging in discussion with their students on the ideas they have put forward. Basically, this has to do with the near mystery of the praxis of educators who live out their democratic insights: they must affirm themselves without thereby disaffirming their students.[84]

If people, in other words, are to be conscientized, they have to have *their* own consciousness raised, and not a pseudo-consciousness that merely reflects how the educator thinks the popular masses ought to react to their situation. Here we move into a difficulty of Freirean education: the many requirements of an educator. In his fourth letter to those who dare teach,[85] Freire lists the following "indispensable qualities" that progressive teachers need to develop in order to carry out their work. He lists humility, which is the understanding that "[n]o one knows it all; no one is ignorant of everything." Then there is courage, tolerance, decisiveness, security, "the tension between patience and impatience" and the joy of living. The tension between *patience and impatience* as one quality is intriguing, but Freire insists that:

> Neither *patience* nor *impatience* alone is what is called for. Patience alone may bring the educator to a position of resignation, of permissiveness that

---

[82] Paulo Freire, *Education: The Practice of Freedom* (London: Writers and Readers Publishing Cooperative, 1974), 52.

[83] Freire discusses this "'self-depreciation,'" in *Pedagogy of the Oppressed*, 38–9.

[84] Freire and Faundez, *Learning to Question*, 34.

[85] For the following, see Paulo Freire, *Teachers as Cultural Workers: Letters to Those Who Dare Teach* (Oxford: Westview Press, 1988), 39–46.

denies the educator's democratic dream . . . Conversely, impatience alone may lead the educator to blind activism, to action for its own sake . . . Isolated patience tends to hinder the attainment of objectives central to the educator's practice, making it soft and ineffectual. Untempered impatience threatens the success of one's practice, which becomes lost in the arrogance of judging oneself the owner of history. Patience alone consumes itself in mere prattle; impatience alone consumes itself in irresponsible activism.[86]

Apart from this tension between patience and impatience, there is a further, more basic, tension for the progressive educator. On the one hand, there has to be a (political) assumption on the part of the educator about the people he or she is educating, but, on the other, these same people have to be free to make their own choices without dependence on the educator. This seems to require an almost impossible juggling act on the part of the educator – who is required to conscientize the students without directing the action that those students should take once they are conscientized (except as one member of the conscientized group).

Also, educators, who were generally not poor themselves, but who wished to assist in helping the oppressed, are, according to Freire, to commit "class suicide." They need to do this in order to integrate themselves with the reality of their country and people.[87]

This "class suicide" has, needless to say, yet to occur in any society. Professor Peter Mayo makes the point well that "so many factors" need to be rejected:

> like one's habitus (values, norms, taste for culture, "master patterns" of thinking and speaking, relationship to language and culture, etc.), one's educational background, the nature of one's everyday work . . . possibly even one's acquired coherent and systematic view of the world . . . that can distinguish the adult educator from the working class participant with whom he or she is working.[88]

This gap between educator and "educatee" is one that is extremely difficult to close. Gutiérrez himself tacitly admits that there is a problem when he talks of solidarity with the poor. Real identity with the poor will not occur in this life. "The will to live in the world of the poor can

---

[86] Ibid., 44, emphasis original.
[87] See Paulo Freire, *Pedagogy in Process: The Letters to Guinea-Bissau* (New York: Continuum, 1983), 78ff.
[88] Peter Mayo, "A Few 'Blind Spots,'" 90.

therefore only follow an asymptotic curve . . . [that] can, however, never reach the point of real identification with the life of the poor."[89]

All this reveals a certain dichotomy in Gutiérrez's thought, and one that he has yet to solve. On the one hand, he insists that "[w]ithout love and affection, without – why not say it? – tenderness, there can be no true gesture of solidarity," and, on the other, he admits to this asymptotic curve; so that the solidarity with the poor still carries a certain awareness of difference from the poor – a sort of being with the poor without being of the poor – Gutiérrez himself, having been able to choose his vocation is part of the "not poor." He may be seeking to lead the poor by showing them what he believes liberation to mean, but he is not intrinsically one of them. The very fact that he can choose to live among them, whereas the poor themselves do not have that choice, shows his difference from the poor. The question then arises as to how this difference would be perceived by the poor, especially as they become more conscientized, more aware of their need for them to take action themselves to further their liberation – when would be the moment for them to drop their teacher and become the agents of their own liberation?

It is not evident from Gutiérrez's writings, but Curt Cadorette tells us that Gutiérrez spends a great deal of time in leadership training:

> Among the poor are people [called "organic intellectuals"] with charisms of self-awareness, integrity, and a will to political change . . . Gutiérrez and the members of his team have learned from experience that without such people the processes of conscientization and social change will invariably flounder. For this reason they devote a great deal of their time in the *pueblos jovenes* to leadership training, which includes both socio-political analysis and theological education.
>
> The challenge for the "organic intellectual" and the conscienticized [*sic*] poor is to tap the power of their culture and belief in such a way that they point to "the urgency of a revolutionary process" and stimulate appropriate socio-political action on its behalf.[90]

The problem, as I see it, is how much the pedagogue inputs, or influences, the outcome of the training. Liberation theology has therefore been criticized for its willingness to impose its own "compelling belief system" on the poor. But as we have noted above, any teacher has to

---

[89] Ibid. 126.

[90] Curt Cadorette, *From the Heart of the People: The Theology of Gustavo Gutiérrez* (Oak Park, IL: Meyer Stone Books, 1988), 49.

make assumptions about those taught, and also has to make the difficult decision about when he or she should yield to the "organic intellectual." These are persons who "are committed to the cause . . . not as a revolutionary élite, but as persons of and for the poor."[91] While élitism is emphatically not built into liberation theology – it does seem that hierarchy returns by the back door in Gutiérrez's thought: there is the pedagogue, the "organic intellectual" and the more backward popular masses.

This hierarchy works against Gutiérrez's statements that only the poor can liberate themselves, as there is always the danger that the pedagogue and organic intellectual "classes" could become self-perpetuating – which would leave the poor simply having changed one set of masters for another. This is clearly not Gutiérrez's intention; and Gutiérrez himself is committed to a church of the poor, where ideally all the poor would be conscientized and there would be no difference between the pedagogue and the "organic intellectual." Liberation theology and the Base Ecclesial Communities have led to a revitalization of the church in the poor communities, and to demands from the poor to be treated as human beings, and this in turn has led to persecution and martyrdom for many as the privileged power brokers (including some of the ecclesial hierarchy) reacted against this new phenomenon.

One of the sticks used to beat Gutiérrez and his fellow liberation theologians is their use of Marxist social analysis. However, certainly in Gutiérrez's case, the use of Marxist analysis is much muted: but, like a great many Latin American thinkers, he does tend to give socialism higher marks than capitalism, not least because he sees capitalism in terms of foreign domination, exploitation of workers, and the concentration of wealth in the hands of a few. We may find such an interpretation of capitalism galling, but if we are not prepared to see that our systems (however beneficial) have downsides, then the best we can hope for is a "dialogue of the deaf" when it comes to seeking cooperation with our neighbors. For those who choose to be suspicious of any form of Marxist or socialist nuance in liberation theology, liberation theology can then be viewed with disfavor: but this negative attitude can only be sustained if the radical nature of the Bible is also deliberately ignored. Gutiérrez has no truck with any idea of a "spiritualized poverty":

> no one can deny that the Gospel of Matthew is notably insistent on the need for concrete and "material" actions toward others and especially

---

[91] Cadorette, *From the Heart*, 49.

toward the poor (see Mt. 25:31–46). This emphasis does not seem to be compatible with a supposed Matthean "spiritualism."[92]

For Gutiérrez, "[t]he practice of justice is required of the disciples of Christ."[93] This "finds expression in life-giving actions on behalf of the neighbor and especially the most defenseless: the poor."[94] These actions are to "be seen by others in order that the latter may receive the message of the Beatitudes."[95] The disciples are blessed "because by means of concrete actions they give life and thus proclaim the kingdom."[96]

Gutiérrez concludes by telling us that:

> The Beatitudes in Luke put the emphasis on the gratuitousness of the love of God, who has a predilection for the poor. The Beatitudes in Matthew fill out the picture by specifying the ethical requirements that flow from this loving initiative of God. The two approaches are complementary. Matthew does not "spiritualize" the Beatitudes . . . he "disciple-izes" them. The Matthean approach is especially demanding.[97]

In *The Power of the Poor in History*, Gutiérrez returns to this theme telling us that there is a danger of spiritualizing the Beatitudes "too soon":

> But if, instead, we take the gospel statements at face value, unflinchingly and courageously, then what we have is God's love for the poor first and foremost simply because they are poor, simply because they are literally and materially poor. Now we have no easy God at all. Now we are faced with the mystery of God's revelation, and the gift of his Kingdom of love and justice.[98]

For Gutiérrez therefore, a spirituality of liberation leads away from any received orthodoxy which separates religion from the rest of life to a *"conversion* to the neighbor" and in them, to God. This is an active – and activist – faith, but one which requires the Christian to find the way to real prayer. Gutiérrez admits this way to prayer can be difficult, but nonetheless expects the attempt.

---

[92] Gustavo Gutiérrez, *The Truth Shall Make You Free: Confrontations* (Maryknoll, NY: Orbis Books, 1990), 160.

[93] Ibid.

[94] Ibid., 163.

[95] Ibid.

[96] Ibid., 164.

[97] Ibid.

[98] Gutiérrez, *The Power of the Poor in History* (London: SCM Press, 1983), 95.

In the sense that it promotes revolutionary behavior, Marxism is a revolutionary force – in a similar way liberation theology seeks to be revolutionary. But the revolution it promotes is a very different one from, say, the French Revolution. Gutiérrez's class struggle is not the same as class warfare. There is no sense that the triumph of the oppressed (or proletariat) requires the demise of the bourgeoisie. (It is perhaps worth noting that the integration of Aristotle's thinking into Christianity by Aquinas was not universally welcomed at the time – perhaps the same might occur with Marxist analysis in liberation theology.)[99]

Whether Marxist analysis is used or not, the continuing suffering of the poor is clearly a problem: for Gutiérrez, the church must continue to seek liberation for the poor, even if at present, it can only seek to share the poor's suffering. Working for a just society does not require God to bring it about, but the poor will see and note where God stands if the church will stand with them. However, if Gutiérrez does wish to work for a just society, questions of how he expects God to act, and when, are inevitably raised: it is to these questions that I now turn.

Gutiérrez's Eschatology

Gutiérrez clearly does not regard his fellow Christians as mere pilgrims looking for a new city at some point and time in the future, he wants action now to bring about the growth of the kingdom on earth, a kingdom that brings justice for the poor, allows them to "irrupt" into history, and which challenges the current social and political establishments and their representatives wherever they may be found (including in the church). For Gutiérrez,

> the rediscovery of the *eschatological dimension* in theology has also led us to consider the central role of historical praxis. Indeed if human history is above all else an opening to the future, then it is a task, a political occupation, through which we orient and open ourselves to the gift which gives history its transcendent meaning: the full and definite encounter with the Lord and with other humans.[100]

---

[99] Although he was very circumspect in his use of what may be seen as Marxist, Pope John Paul II does appear to have incorporated liberation theology into his thought; see Pope John Paul II, "Excerpts from 'On Social Concern' (*Sollicitudo Rei Socialis*)," in Hennelly, *A Documentary History*, 521–8.

[100] Gutiérrez, *A Theology of Liberation*, 8.

Gutiérrez's eschatology emphasizes the "now" over the "not yet." For Gutiérrez, "salvation is already here" and "the prophetic perspective (in which the kingdom takes on the present life, transforming it) is vindicated *before* the sapiential outlook (which stresses the life beyond)."[101]

When he examines the history of the people of God and God's covenant with his people, Gutiérrez is concerned to show that "[t]he eschatological horizon is present in the heart of the Exodus," and (against what can be seen as an Augustinian approach),

> building the temporal city is not simply a stage of "humanization" or "pre-evangelization" as was held in theology until a few years ago. Rather it is to become part of a saving process which embraces the whole of humanity and all human history.[102]

Gutiérrez explicitly criticizes establishment Christianity, with its emphasis on an "other-worldly" eschatology, in *The Power of the Poor in History*:

> Of course [this transitory world's] unreality did not prevent those who claimed to live only for the world "up there" from solidly installing themselves in the world "down here." Such installation was necessary, it would seem, as the platform from which to proclaim to others that they ought not to become attached to anything ephemeral and corruptible.
>
> Eternal life was seen exclusively as a future life and not as present in an active and creative form within our concrete historical involvement as well. It was a contracted, partialized view of human existence, the product of a gospel carefully reduced to suitably narrow, myopic dimensions.[103]

It is worth noting here that Paulo Freire had trouble with "traditional" theology when it emphasized this other-worldly escapism. He was thankful that many Christians were "vigorously reacting" against the attitude that it is God's will for the oppressed to suffer. "But as a child, I knew many priests who went out to the peasants saying: 'Be patient. This is God's will. And anyway, it will earn heaven for you.'" Freire continues: "How could we make God responsible for this calamity? As if Absolute Love could abandon man to constant victimization and total destitution. That would be a God such as Marx described."[104]

---

[101] Ibid.

[102] Ibid.

[103] Gutiérrez, *The Power of the Poor in History*, 39, emphasis original.

[104] Freire, "Conscientizing as a Way of Liberating," in Hennelly (ed.), *Liberation Theology*, 11.

Freire goes on to reiterate the point that this sort of faith only assists the oppressor. "Whenever men make God responsible for intolerable situations, for oppression, then the dominating structures help to popularize that myth."[105] It is Freire's Christianity that leads him to espouse conscientization, and "conscientization shows us that God wants us to act"[106] and to work *with* the oppressed:

> Conscientization . . . involves an excruciating moment . . . in those who begin to conscientize themselves, the moment they start to be reborn. Because conscientization demands an Easter. That is, it demands that we die to be reborn again. Christians must live their Easter, and that too is a utopia . . . That is why Christianity is, for me, such a marvellous doctrine. People have accused me of being a communist, but no communist could say what I have just said.[107]

In *A Theology of Liberation*, Gutiérrez emphasizes the "as well" of eschatology. Gutiérrez views the Old Testament prophets as orientating present actions of God toward the future, but based on his past initiatives on behalf of his people: "The self-communication of God points to the future, and at the same time this Promise and Good News reveal humanity to itself and widen the perspective of its historical commitment here and now."[108]

Of course, the above opens the question of what is to be done if history does not improve, in spite of Christian action: but, for Gutiérrez, this is where the solidarity with the poor – and a continuing eschatological hope – enters into the equation. In *The Power of the Poor in History*, Gutiérrez is explicit:

> Building the earthly city actually immerses human beings in the salvation process that touches all humanity. Every obstacle that degrades or alienates the work of men and women in building a humane society is an obstacle to the work of salvation . . .
>
> The prophets proclaim a reign of peace. But peace presupposes the establishment of justice . . . The conquest of poverty and abolition of exploitation are signs of the Messiah's arrival and presence . . . To work for a just world where there is no servitude, oppression, or alienation is to work for the advent of the Messiah.[109]

---

[105] Ibid.

[106] Ibid.

[107] Ibid., 12–13.

[108] Gutiérrez, *A Theology of Liberation*, 95.

[109] Gutiérrez, *The Power of the Poor in History*, 32.

This working for a just world has to be undertaken without demanding that God must act – or that he must act in a particular way. For Gutiérrez, Christian solidarity with the poor is to be prepared to go as far as entering into their suffering, it is to be prepared to suffer with the poor to the point of death. Martyrdom, while not to be sought, is, like conflict, a painful reality for those who seek to stand alongside the oppressed.[110] Indeed, the years since *A Theology of Liberation* was first written have seen much blood spilled and many martyrs (of whom Archbishop Oscar Romero is perhaps the best-known example) have fallen. It can be said that the situation of the poor has not changed all that much, but this does not mean that liberation theology has failed, nor that Christians should no longer stand with the oppressed. As Gutiérrez tells us, this suffering, this martyrdom, acts as a profound witness to the poor:

> They see in the surrender of these lives a profound and radical testimony of faith; they observe that in a continent where the powerful spread death in order to protect their privileges, such a testimony to God often brings the murder of the witness; and they draw nourishment from the hope that sustains these lives and these deaths. According to the very earliest Christian tradition the blood of martyrs gives life to the ecclesial community, the assembly of the disciples of Jesus Christ. This is what is happening today in Latin America. Fidelity unto death is a wellspring of life. It signals a new demanding, and fruitful course in the following of Jesus.[111]

Due to this suffering both of the poor and those who speak out on their behalf, Gutiérrez cannot be accused of promoting "an easy optimism" in his theology, nor in his eschatology. However, he does see change taking place, and "despite – or thanks to – the immense price that is being paid, the present situation is nourishing new life, revealing new paths to be followed, and providing reason for profound joy."[112]

Liberation theology works to create a just society on earth. Therefore it espouses a progressivist eschatology, where "secular history [functions] as part of the coming of the kingdom of God"[113] – the kingdom of God is to be sought "down here" as well as "up there." This searching

---

[110] See Gustavo Gutiérrez, *We Drink from Our Own Wells* (Maryknoll, NY: Orbis Books, 1984), 117 and n. 8, 167.

[111] Ibid., 23.

[112] Ibid., 25.

[113] Robert C. Doyle, *Eschatology and the Shape of Christian Belief* (Carlisle: Paternoster Press, 1999), 274.

for, and demands for, change in society so that the kingdom of God can be brought closer must continue despite all the hardship and persecution afflicted on those who have solidarity with the poor (and on the poor themselves) by those who feel their privileged place in society is under threat. A church prepared to suffer, to act in solidarity with the poor, offers those poor a powerful witness of the God who Gutiérrez sees as having a preferential option for the poor.

The Church and Civil Society

In *The Power of the Poor in History*, Gutiérrez discusses the awareness that Christians are developing of the nature of the class structure and the injustice inherent in that structure. This in turn requires "a new understanding of politics." Gutiérrez continues by telling us that for a lot of Christians this means "taking a revolutionary, socialist option, and thus assuming a political task, in a global perspective, that turns out to be more scientific and more conflictual than it appeared in the first stages of political involvement."[114] Gutiérrez critiques the idea that only an élite has the charism of political leadership, or that it is a distinct, spare time, activity. For him "[p]olitics is the global condition . . . of human accomplishment."

> All human reality, then, has a political dimension . . . For it is within the context of the political that the human being rises up as a free and responsible being, as a truly human being, having a relationship with nature and with other human beings, as someone who takes up the reins of his or her destiny, and goes out and transforms history.[115]

From this we can see that Gutiérrez moves us from a consideration of the global nature of politics to a consideration of the power of a single person – working with others – to transform history.[116] For Gutiérrez,

> The praxis of liberation, therefore, inasmuch as it starts out from an authentic solidarity with the poor and the oppressed, is ultimately a

---

[114] Gutiérrez, *The Power of the Poor in History*, 46.

[115] Ibid., 47.

[116] Though Gutiérrez does not say how that transformation is to be achieved.

praxis of love – real love, effective and concrete, for real, concrete human beings. It is a praxis of love of neighbour, and of love for Christ in the neighbour, for Christ identifies himself with the least of these human beings, our brothers and sisters. Any attempt to separate love for God and love for neighbour gives rise to attitudes that impoverish both.[117]

Gutiérrez is interested in the personal, but not in individualism.[118] Freedom for the person is freedom in a society of "new structures," not freedom for the individual to do as he or she wills without regard for the other.[119] For although "structures always depend on concrete persons, and the latter must be involved if we want real change," any (new) society must have justice and freedom at its core.

That is why I wrote: "These personal aspects – considered not as excessively privatized, but rather as encompassing all human dimensions – are also under consideration in the contemporary debate concerning greater participation of all in political activity" . . . The requirement is a universal one that knows no exceptions.[120]

This free gift and the new social relationships can be viewed as the basis of the poor's political power – a power that the church, with its preferential option for the poor, should seek to give them.

The phrase "a preferential option for the poor" has become something of a cliché since Gutiérrez and his liberation theologian colleagues introduced it to the world. However, this preferential option for the poor is situated *within* God's agapeic love, and also explains Gutiérrez's concerns for class struggle:

[Although] class struggle is meant to fight against the oppressors' power and blindness . . . Class struggle *calls the oppressors to conversion*. But it does

---

[117] Ibid., 50.

[118] For Gutiérrez, life is social, it "implies communion" (Gustavo Gutiérrez, *The God of Life* [Maryknoll, NY: Orbis Books, 1991], 12).

[119] Elsewhere Gutierrez refers to Bonhoeffer's writing in defining freedom: "In the language of the Bible . . . freedom is not something man has for himself but something he has for others . . . Being free means 'being free for the other'" (*A Theology of Liberation*), 24.

[120] Gutiérrez, *The Truth Shall Make You Free*, 133, quoting the first edition of *A Theology of Liberation: History, Politics, and Salvation* (London: SCM Press, 1974), 51.

not and may not threaten them with hatred or death without contradicting its own principles and purpose.[121]

However, on reading *A Theology of Liberation*, we can see that Gutiérrez is keenly aware of the biblical texts that condemn those who by their unjust actions, cause poverty. Gutiérrez then gives three principal reasons why poverty is given such a "vigorous repudiation": firstly, it "contradicts the very meaning of the *Mosaic religion*;" secondly, it goes "against the *mandate of Genesis*,"

> And finally, humankind not only has been made in the image and likeness of God; it is also *the sacrament of God* . . . The other reasons for the Biblical rejection of poverty have their roots here: to oppress the poor is to offend God; to know God is to work justice among human beings. We meet God in our encounter with other persons; what is done for others is done for the Lord.[122]

For all Gutiérrez's passion about justice, some of his readers might be uncomfortable with this approach. However, it is clear that Gutiérrez has a biblical mandate for his line of attack – a mandate, moreover, that comes from both Testaments. We have already seen that Gutiérrez does not regard Matthew as "spiritualizing" the Lukan Beatitudes – and certainly not in a manner which allows anyone to shirk their responsibility for their neighbor. Gutiérrez is very aware – after all, he lives and works among the poor of Peru – that poor people are also sinful,[123] but he believes that the society he lives in is fundamentally oppressive and, to paraphrase Marx, that the point is not to interpret that sinful society, but to change it. This of course raises (Augustinian) questions about whether any new society would be any less sinful than the one that preceded it. Gutiérrez's answer comes in *A Theology of Liberation*, where he quotes a group of Santiago priests with approval:

> We do not believe persons will automatically become less selfish, but we do maintain that where a socio-economic foundation for equality has been established, it is more possible to work realistically toward human solidarity than it is in a society torn asunder by inequality . . . In other words, today the gospel of Christ implies (and is incarnated in) multiple efforts to obtain justice.[124]

---

[121] Cadorette, *From the Heart*, 111, emphasis added.

[122] Gutiérrez, *A Theology of Liberation*, 168, emphasis original.

[123] See Gutiérrez, *We Drink from our Own Wells*, 125.

[124] Gutiérrez, *A Theology of Liberation*, 66.

Gutiérrez, although he is clearly against any form of individualism, believes that an individual "in relationship with . . . other human beings" can "transform history." While I have already shown that Gutiérrez recognizes that changing history is not as easy as some of his writing may suggest, he clearly expects himself, his church and others to work in solidarity with the poor. This expectation is based on the command to love our neighbor. The poverty that the neighbor lives under is to be denounced, and the poor themselves must be empowered to be agents of their own liberation. For Gutiérrez, the church is called to stand in solidarity with the poor so that they cannot only become aware of their oppression (be "conscientized"), but also take action in order to remove that oppression.

Education

"Conscientization," as we have noted, is all about education. It is about education for a specific purpose: so that the conscientized can note, and react against, their oppression. In some ways, liberation theology is about "power to the people," except that liberation theology says very little about power and how it should be exercised. Leadership is also viewed askance. And yet, people still follow leaders, they still need leading. If people need teaching, they need awakening to their situation and their need and ability to overcome that situation by others who can see that situation. This chapter has, therefore, been discussing that education. The principal means of imparting conscientization is the Base Ecclesial Community (BEC). These communities were not initially a "liberating" idea. They were set up by the Roman Catholic bishops in Latin America as a way of circumventing a shortage of priests. Lay catechists were trained to read and repeat the church's teachings in written material, and were only utilized in the absence of a priest. They were not meant to interpret or advocate any action, nor were they meant to question the official line taken by the ecclesial authorities.

Ironically, it was the military coup in 1968 that created the situation whereby BECs became the organizations we know today. In seeking to close down all opposition to its rule, the military *junta* left church communities as one of the very few places where people could meet. This coincided with the birth and growth of liberation theology itself: a theology which sought to open the biblical message to the poor. These groups were also the place where the "organic intellectuals" could be found and could guide their fellows in studying the gospels in the way of conscientization. Although these communities (under the auspices of liberation theology and the influence of Paulo Freire) were not supposed to have leaders in the traditional sense, and were heavily indebted to lay involvement and participation, more than one commentator has noted that without the approval – at the very least – of sympathetic priests or bishops, BECs would not have got off the ground. However, this, it is also noted, has more to do with the fact that "the poor have got into the habit of self-depreciation."

> That is why each base community is founded through a gentle and gradual pedagogy, which teaches the humble . . . to *give worth* to what they have to say as they express themselves to each other.[125]

While, realistically, those involved in setting up the BECs do not seem to expect to create a new man or woman (unlike in the earlier liberationist writings), BECs "can represent the starting point for a politics in which commitment and practice seek to serve the common good and social justice."[126] Leonardo Boff, another liberation theologian, is anxious that,

> Faith is not set aside. Instead it acquires its true dimensions as a spiritual mystique, a source of inspiration, and a signpost pointing toward liberation. That liberation transcends history, but it can be seen and anticipated in history through a process of liberation that generates less inequitable forms of social coexistence within society.[127]

The transcendent element is brought back in with a clarity that is sometimes missing from other writings: the kingdom is both now *and* not yet.[128] This view of the BEC allows, even insists, that political action is taken to create a more just, more humane society; but equally it does not exercise any sort of naïve belief that this new society would be perfect. The BEC "learns to discover God in its own life, struggles, and happenings,"[129] and approaches life with "a new kind of holiness" not confined to the ascetic. It is the holiness of the militant:

---

[125] Dominique Barbé, "Church Base Communities," in Curt Cadorette et al. (eds.), *Liberation Theology: An Introductory Reader* (Maryknoll, NY: Orbis Books, 1992), 185, emphasis original.

[126] Leonardo Boff, "Theological Characteristics of a Grassroots Church," in Torres and Eagleson (eds.), *The Challenge of Basic Christian Communities*, 138.

[127] Ibid.

[128] See ibid., 143.

[129] Ibid., 138.

Rather than concentrating on the fight against one's own passions, which remains a permanent struggle, one fights politically against the creation and use of exploitative mechanisms of accumulation; and one fights for the establishment of more well balanced, communitarian relationships. The new virtues find expression in class solidarity, participation in community decisions, mutual aid, criticism of abuses of power, endurance of slander and persecution for the sake of justice.[130]

For Boff, the BECs point both to "a greater fidelity to the liberating well-springs of the gospel message, and also fidelity to the transcendent destiny of the earth with all its anxieties and yearnings."[131] For all the failings and critiques of liberation theology, it is liberation theologians who have had the best success in identifying (as far as they can) with the oppressed of Latin America, and increasingly in other places as well. Their work is heavily reliant on education, but as we have noted, there is a need also to address leaders and leadership. This is a topic that we shall also address in our discussions with another theologian. One from the upper echelons of society, but one who was martyred for his faith-inspired political actions: Dietrich Bonhoeffer.

---

[130] Ibid., 142.
[131] Ibid., 143.

Three

Political Thought and Anti-Government Conspiracy

Dietrich Bonhoeffer's Radical Patriotism

Introduction

Dietrich Bonhoeffer (1906–45) lived his life and formed his theology in the cauldron of the collapse of the Weimar republic, the rise and implementation of Nazism, and the horrors of the Second World War.

Once Hitler had come to power and the "church struggle" commenced, Bonhoeffer, by force of circumstances, played an important role in that struggle. He later joined the anti-Hitler conspiracy, which caused the arrest, and in 1945 the execution of Bonhoeffer, his brother Klaus and brothers-in-law Hans von Dohnanyi and Rüdiger Schleicher. Bonhoeffer's theological task, as he saw it, was to rescue his church from its struggle for its own survival, to, as it were, rescue Luther from the Lutherans, and to teach its people (by example as well as word) how to live as disciples of Jesus Christ, whose call "leads us to death."[132]

This chapter will first look at Bonhoeffer's life and work, placing it in its (anti-) Nazi context. I shall then look at the Lutheran doctrine of the two kingdoms and how Bonhoeffer reworked that doctrine to overcome any idea of the separation of life into two spheres. I shall then examine whether Bonhoeffer can be thought to have renounced privilege (and thereby become more egalitarian in his outlook). Then, as with the previous chapters, I shall examine Bonhoeffer's eschatology (to examine how his thought affected his outlook on his "present-day" reality); his ideas on the relation of the church to civil society; and his ideas on the education of Christians for political involvement.

---

[132] Dietrich Bonhoeffer, *Discipleship* (Minneapolis: Augsburg Fortress, 2001), 87.

Bonhoeffer's Life

Dietrich Bonhoeffer was born in 1906, along with his twin sister, to an upper-class family.[133] It was, inevitably, a privileged upbringing, but much was expected of Dietrich and all his brothers and sisters. Though not without its tragedy – Dietrich's older brother Walter, called up to fight in the First World War, died of his wounds on April 28, 1918 – this privileged situation would trouble Dietrich in later years. He felt isolated from the less fortunate, and less able to understand them. This tension eventually led him to write about "the view from below" in his 1943 paper "After Ten Years,"[134] but he was never able to deny the legacy of generations of privilege, nor his authoritarian conservatism.

Although he was aware of the political situation in Germany, Bonhoeffer had no thought of becoming politically active until he reached America. Yet, by 1932, Bonhoeffer became ashamed of his "disinterest," calling it "essentially frivolous." Although he was appalled by the "unbearably thin and disappointingly shallow" theology in America, Bonhoeffer was impressed by the way in which Union Theological Seminary students worked among the unemployed. He also attended several lecture series, including on "Church and Community" and "Ethical Interpretations." The latter required him to analyze articles in newspapers and periodicals, forming objective opinions on foreign or domestic political questions.

With the benefit of hindsight, it is easy to see the threat that Hitler and Nazism posed to civilization and the church, but, as one commentator puts it:

> In 1934, Hitler appeared to some as a paragon of virtue and a political messiah. Hitler stood for honesty, industry, love of family and country. He restored law and order, ended unemployment, and stood against communism along with building the Volkswagen and Autobahn.[135]

On the other hand, Bonhoeffer was involved with the church's resistance to Nazism from the start. This resistance centered on the Aryan legislation of April 7, 1933 – which banned those of Jewish blood from holding

---

[133] For much of the material in this section, see Eberhard Bethge, *Dietrich Bonhoeffer: A Biography* (rev. edn.; Minneapolis: Augsburg Fortress, 2000).

[134] Reprinted in Dietrich Bonhoeffer, *Letters and Papers from Prison* (London: SCM Press, enlarged edition 1971), 17. Hereafter referred to as *LPP*.

[135] Joseph S. Harvard, "The Continuing Cost of Discipleship," *Journal for Preachers*, 7:4 (1984), 3.

any political, or civil office – and the established church was considering adopting this clause into its own constitution. Bonhoeffer saw that the question of church membership for Christians of Jewish descent was for the church, not the state, to decide; and this led him into immediate and sustained opposition to the Nazi state's attempts to take and exercise control in the church. This opposition led him to accept a position as a civilian member of the *Abwehr* (Military Intelligence) just before the outbreak of war (where he was part of a Resistance cell).

As an agent of the *Abwehr*, Bonhoeffer was able to travel outside the Reich. Officially he was gathering information for the German war effort. In practice, he was engaged in smuggling Jews, or those of Jewish descent, out of the Reich. It was this that led to Bonhoeffer's arrest April 9, 1943. Throughout the early 1940s theology was not forgotten. Prior to his arrest, Bonhoeffer spent a lot of time working on his *Ethics* with its themes of Christ and reality, state and church and "telling the truth." Even in prison Bonhoeffer contrived to continue writing – much of what survives has now appeared in *Letters and Papers from Prison* – but any hopes of release were dashed with the failure of the plot on July 20, 1944 and his transfer to the Gestapo prison on Prinz-Albrecht-Strasse in October 1944. Although Bonhoeffer's only direct involvement with the conspiracy was a trip to Sweden in 1942,[136] his fate was sealed. He was summarily tried and executed at Flossenbürg, one month before the end of the war.

Bonhoeffer and the Two Kingdoms

Bonhoeffer's idea that God's command embraces life in its entirety challenges the Lutheran doctrine of the two kingdoms. Although the two kingdoms doctrine accepts that God is in control of both kingdoms, the church comes under his right hand and the state his left. Therefore, what a person may be expected, or allowed, to do as an office holder in the secular realm may not be the same as what that person may do in the spiritual realm. Martin Luther, according to W. Cargill Thompson, saw "nothing incompatible" with one person having to live as a Christian privately, but to carry out duties as a public person "which might appear to be contrary to the precepts of the Sermon on the Mount."[137] This is because, for Luther, "God has ordained the two governments, the

---

[136] He was trying to secure peace terms with the Allies if the assassination and coup d'état had been successful.

[137] W.D.J. Cargill Thompson, *The Political Thought of Martin Luther* (Sussex: The Harvester Press, 1984), 61.

spiritual [government] which fashions true Christians and just persons through the holy Spirit under Christ, and the secular [*weltlich*] government which holds the Unchristian and wicked in check and forces them to keep the peace outwardly and be still, like it or not."[138]

Whatever Luther may have intended by his idea of the two kingdoms, by the early part of the twentieth century, Lutherans in Germany lived as if religion had been confined to the private sphere, separate from the world where "one either saw radical flight from the world as one's way to God, or one lived in this world, radically open to it but independent of all relations to God."[139] According to a noted Bonhoeffer scholar, Bonhoeffer regarded religion "as something which either separates or identifies faith and the world" and overcoming it as the "chief task" for theologians of his generation. In other words, he wished to overcome the misappropriation of the two kingdoms doctrine so that the conflict "between a Christian and a bourgeois-secular vocation" no longer existed.[140] For Bonhoeffer a different conflict must remain: God's "Yes" *and* his "No" to the world, a "yes" and "no" that has remained since the Fall:

> That humankind must live in the fallen world . . . that is the *curse*. That humankind *is allowed* to live in this world and that it will not be deprived of the word of God . . . that is the *promise*.[141]

For Bonhoeffer, the curse and promise associated with the world applies everywhere. Retreat from the world is not a valid option. Jesus' call is to the world, but that call, for all disciples, leads to the cross. As Bonhoeffer puts it in *Discipleship*:

> Things cannot go any other way than that the world unleashes its fury in word, violence, and defamation at those meek strangers . . . In their poverty and suffering, this group of Jesus' followers gives too strong a witness to the injustice of the world. That is fatal. While Jesus calls, "blessed, blessed," the world shrieks, "Away with them!" Yes, away! But where will

---

[138] "On Secular Authority," in Harro Höpfl, *Luther and Calvin: On Secular Authority* (Cambridge: Cambridge University Press, 1991), 10–11. "*Weltlich*," Höpfl notes, can also be translated as either "worldly" or "temporal," see ibid., xxxviii.

[139] Ernst Feil, *The Theology of Dietrich Bonhoeffer* (Minneapolis: Fortress Press, 1985), 101.

[140] Bonhoeffer, *Discipleship*, 50.

[141] Dietrich Bonhoeffer, *Creation and Fall* (Minneapolis: Augsburg Fortress, 1997), 132, emphasis original.

they go? Into the kingdom of heaven. Rejoice and be glad, for your reward is great in heaven.[142]

Bonhoeffer notes that these people while worthy of heaven, are (and here he uses Nazi terminology) "obviously at the same time . . . unworthy of living." These same people are to be salt and light – they are to be a visible community that preserves the earth.

However, the disciples cannot judge the other person; that other person can only be viewed as one "to whom Jesus comes." Enemies must be prayed for. If the sin is to be condemned, the sinner is not. On the other hand, they cannot force the forgiving Word on an unwilling world. Like Luther, Bonhoeffer, in *Discipleship*, does not expect a large number of true Christians: "The call [of Jesus] separates a small group, those who follow, from the great mass of the people. The disciples are few and will always be only a few."[143]

Even here there is separation: profession of faith, or "confession" alone[144] does not save people. They must be doers of the word as well. The "doing" is the call to serve even the weakest and despised "brothers or sisters – be they Jew or Greek, slave or free."

In *Ethics* Bonhoeffer has nothing similar to the Lutheran idea of the separation of the two kingdoms; here the interrelation (but not interdependence) of the two kingdoms is shown. The question for us is what action should we take in the world in preparation for the ultimate?

> The hungry man [*sic*] needs bread and the homeless man needs a roof; the undisciplined need order and the slave needs freedom. To allow the hungry man to remain hungry would be blasphemy against God and one's neighbour, for what is nearest God is precisely the need of one's neighbour . . . If the hungry man does not attain to faith, then the guilt falls on those who refused him bread. To provide the hungry man with bread is to prepare the way for the coming of grace.[145]

Bonhoeffer is careful to say that these actions are not the same as the coming of grace, but for those who do these things "for the sake of the ultimate":

---

[142] Bonhoeffer, *Discipleship*, 109–10.

[143] Ibid., 175.

[144] Even in a time when "confession" (as in profession of faith) was an important means of differentiating between the Confessing and Reich churches – see ibid., 178, n. 234.

[145] Bonhoeffer, *Ethics*, 136.

this penultimate does bear a relation to the ultimate. It is a pen*ultimate*. The coming of grace is the ultimate.[146]

The penultimate is spoken of and done to prepare the way, "so that the word of God, the ultimate, grace, can come to them." Even here, however, there is no clear link between action and the ultimate; it is not the case that "values must be set in order" before people can become Christians. Bonhoeffer points to the paradox that "precisely at times when the world has seemed to be relatively in order that the estrangement from the faith has been especially deep-seated and alarming." He continues:

> The preparation of the way for Christ cannot, therefore, be simply a matter of the establishment of certain desirable and expedient conditions; it simply cannot be the realization of a programme of social reform. It is quite certain that the preparation of the way is a matter of concrete interventions in the visible world . . . yet everything depends on this activity being a spiritual reality, precisely because ultimately it is not indeed a question of the reform of earthly conditions, but it is a question of the coming of Christ.[147]

Therefore, even though we are all still sinners, because of the "approaching ultimate," the penultimate must still "be respected and validated." Christian life involves living in the world, however aware we might be of the fallen nature of that world. Bonhoeffer makes his position clear in his "Outline for a Book":

> The church is the church only when it exists for others . . . The church must share in the secular problems of ordinary human life, not dominating, but helping and serving. It must tell men of every calling what it means to live in Christ, to exist for others . . . It must not under-estimate the importance of human example . . . it is not abstract argument, but example, that gives its word emphasis and power.[148]

Bonhoeffer clearly reacted against his Lutheran inheritance in terms of the separation of the two kingdoms and argued trenchantly against "thinking in terms of [two] spheres."[149] He insisted on Christ's lordship

---

[146] Ibid., 137.

[147] Ibid.

[148] Bonhoeffer, *LPP*, 382–3.

[149] Bonhoeffer, *Ethics*, 198.

over all, including the fallen world. Therefore, "there is no real possibility of being a Christian outside the reality of the world and that there is no real worldly existence outside the reality of Jesus Christ."[150] Bonhoeffer argued for costly, rather than cheap, grace, and for the respect of the penultimate for the sake of the ultimate. Christians must therefore be involved in society as Christians, as disciples. There will be a cost to this (emphasized in *Discipleship*), but the church is only the church *not* when it concentrates solely on God's kingdom of the right hand, but when it "exists for others." This means that the church must recognize its political responsibility. As with much else, Bonhoeffer's thought developed over time. In the next section, I shall look at how his thought developed from 1933 (the Jewish question) through to his ideas on free responsibility and how disciples can operate under an "ethic of resistance" when the church itself is in danger of acting inauthentically.

The Church's Political Responsibility

Responsibility for the Jews

From the moment Hitler came to power, Bonhoeffer was involved with the church's resistance to Nazism. As noted above, this resistance centered on the Aryan legislation of April 7, 1933, but in his essay "The Church and the Jewish Question," unlike his later work, Bonhoeffer still followed the traditional Lutheran line and carefully differentiated between what the church could, and what it could not, tell the state to do:

> Without doubt, the Church of the Reformation has no right to address the state directly in its specifically political actions . . . Without doubt the Jewish question is one of the historical problems which our state must deal with, and without doubt the state is justified in adopting new methods here.[151]

But, Bonhoeffer continues, the church should "continually ask the state whether its action can be justified."[152] Bonhoeffer's attitude to the Jews, it must be remembered, was considerably more liberal than a lot of people in Germany at the time. He had to fight an often lonely battle, even as his own

---

[150] Ibid.

[151] Dietrich Bonhoeffer, *No Rusty Swords* (London: Collins, 1965), 222–3.

[152] Ibid.

thought progressed and he worked through the three options of church action and involvement laid out in his 1933 essay. Bonhoeffer had to think through (and react against) an unquestioning obedience to the state that was engendered by his culture and his Lutheran religion. The calls for political action on the part of the church were generally ignored, but had they been heeded, and had other church leaders joined Bonhoeffer "while there was time to prevent genocide," then there may have been a chance for effective resistance to Hitler before tyrannicide became the only option.[153]

Responsibility for peace

It was Hitler's antipathy toward the Jews that renewed Bonhoeffer's demands for political action on the part of the church, but his concerns were wider than that. His ecumenical work brought him into contact with many (including the English bishop George Bell) who were "fighting" for peace. This concern about the international situation was all the more surprising from a Lutheran – who was expected to "see that Christianity involved giving Caesar his due and that bearing arms for the Fatherland when required was a natural and Christian duty"[154] – and a German where there was "widespread opposition to anything savoring of 'internationalism.'"[155] However, Bonhoeffer was not a typical German Lutheran, and he was challenged by Jesus' teachings on the Sermon on the Mount not "as ideals for an ideal world," but as a concrete command to nonviolence.[156] In 1932, at the ecumenical conference at Gland, Switzerland, Bonhoeffer challenged the churches to re-examine "a world whose idol has become the word 'security' – a world without sacrifice, full of mistrust and suspicion, because past fears are still with it"[157] and to stand for a peace in which "righteousness and truth are preserved."[158] His concern remained much the same at the 1934 conference in Fanö, where his call was for a peace that "must be dared."[159] But the churches were timid and lacked the will to commit to such a risky cause. This led to Bonhoeffer's complaint that the churches spent too much time looking after their own perceived interests and survival

---

[153] See Michael Westmorland-White et al., "Disciples of the Incarnation," *Sojourners* 23 (1994), 30.

[154] Keith Clements, "Ecumenical Witness for Peace," in de Gruchy (ed.) *The Cambridge Companion to Dietrich Bonhoeffer*, 155.

[155] Ibid., 157.

[156] Ibid., 155.

[157] Bonhoeffer, *No Rusty Swords*, 186–7.

[158] Ibid., 188.

[159] Ibid., 291.

under Nazism to engage in resistance – and action on the part of those whom the regime victimized.[160]

Responsibility before Christ

So, how were Christians to behave, especially as the church (even the Confessing Church) failed to live up to the promises of the Barmen declaration?[161] From 1935 to 1940 Bonhoeffer was engaged in training candidates for ministry in the Confessing Church. Discipleship is Bonhoeffer's key to Christian behavior at this time. This discipleship, this radical living for "Christ in community," can be seen as forming an "ethic of resistance."[162] Bonhoeffer's treatment of the Beatitudes, especially his ideas on not resisting evil, forgiveness, or loving one's enemies, has to be seen not as a flight from the world, but a struggle to establish a critical church presence in the world.

This countercultural perspective can be seen in *Discipleship* when the Christian is to "expect nothing from the world but everything from Christ and his coming realm."[163] In this light any revolution against current social order is forbidden.[164] *Discipleship* was written to counter "cheap grace" where

> the world is in principle justified by [cheap] grace. I can thus remain as before in my bourgeois-secular existence . . . The conflict between a Christian and a bourgeois-secular vocation is resolved. Christian life consists of my living in the world and like the world, my not being any different from it.[165]

---

[160] See Bonhoeffer, *LPP*, 300 and 381.

[161] The Barmen declaration was politically radical "because in that situation it created a freedom zone 'in the midst of a system of terror'" (de Gruchy, *Bonhoeffer and South Africa* [Grand Rapids, MI: Eerdmans, 1984], 33). The Barmen declaration rejected the false doctrines of the Nazified German Christians, especially that the church could have any "truths . . . alongside the one word of God." This reaffirmation of Christ as Lord (and therefore Hitler emphatically wasn't), was the start of the Confessing Church, in opposition to the Reich church, in Germany.

[162] Green, *A Theology of Sociality*, 307. Green notes that Bonhoeffer criticizes ethical postures that may have served previous generations well, because they are insufficient for the present task, and therefore it is responsible action that "is in fact at the center of Bonhoeffer's ethic of resistance" (ibid., 305–7).

[163] Bonhoeffer, *Discipleship*, 239. This sentiment strikes an Augustinian note (the sojourner idea is especially clear in ibid., 250–2).

[164] Ibid., 238–9.

[165] Ibid., 50–1.

Given the difference between "cheap" and "costly" grace, it is unsurprising that this book contains mostly Bonhoeffer's "No" to the world. However, this "No" to the world also contains the radical "Yes" to Christ that Bonhoeffer wished to emphasize against the prevailing culture of accommodation to Nazism. This radical "Yes" to Christ does not diminish in Bonhoeffer's theology. As he becomes more deeply involved in the conspiracy, he still defines the Christian life as "prayer and righteous action."[166] How he conceived "righteous action" and what it consisted of may have changed over the period from *Discipleship* to *Letters and Papers from Prison*, but the two sides of faith and action (or obedience to Christ) in the world are constant themes.

This gives both people and churches responsibilities in the civil realm, responsibilities that Bonhoeffer discusses explicitly in his *Ethics*.[167] Even though he knew that the Confessing Church had failed to hold the Nazi government to account, he clearly felt that the church still had responsibilities toward the state.[168] These responsibilities consisted mainly of "call[ing] sin by its name and . . . warn[ing] men against sin."[169]

What cannot be discerned from Bonhoeffer's writings is the sort of political action (apart from prayer) Bonhoeffer would expect from the ordinary member of the congregation. Bonhoeffer has been seen as a sympathetic character by liberation theologians,[170] but he also has an élitist side. In *Ethics*, Bonhoeffer discusses the French Revolution and its inheritance, he is clear that there are (or ought to be) "strong and mentally superior personalities" over and above the masses, and is concerned that "the increasing acceptance of mass standards will . . . level

---

[166] Bonhoeffer, *LPP*, 300.

[167] Bonhoeffer, *Ethics*, 344–6.

[168] These compare with the responsibilities Luther held that the church had toward the state (see above p. 41–2).

[169] Ibid., 345.

[170] G. Clark Chapman Jr. charts several parallels with, and criticisms of, Bonhoeffer by liberation theologians, including the parallel between praxis, "the continuing reciprocity of action and reflection" and Bonhoeffer's portrayal of discipleship ("Bonhoeffer: Resource for Liberation Theology," *Union Seminary Quarterly Review* 36 [1981], 231). Chapman also criticizes Bonhoeffer for his lack of awareness of the class conflict, but this, just like the criticisms of his sexism (see H. Russel Botman, "Is Bonhoeffer Still of Any Use in South Africa?" in John W. de Gruchy [ed.] *Bonhoeffer for a New Day* [Grand Rapids, MI: Eerdmans, 1997], 367–8) is criticism out of time. There was enough conflict in the 1930s and 1940s, for anyone to cope with, without demanding that Bonhoeffer be aware – before the world around him – of other conflicts.

down mental achievements to such an extent that technology itself will cease to develop and will therefore cease to exist."[171] Later on in the same book, Bonhoeffer asserts that "it is granted to only very few men . . . to experience the hazard of responsible action."[172] However, Bonhoeffer is not content to leave it there. He is critical of a society that crushes those, outside the great and the good, who "venture to act on their free responsibility," with "the machinery of the social order."[173] He also, in the light of this "machinery," seeks to redefine free responsibility:

> every life can experience this situation [of free responsibility] in its most characteristic form, that is to say, in the encounter with other people. Even when free responsibility is more or less excluded from a man's vocational and public life, he nevertheless always stands in a responsible relation to other men; these relations extend from his family to his workmates. The fulfilment of genuine responsibility at this point affords the only sound possibility of extending the sphere of responsibility once more into vocational and public life.[174]

In this and the following paragraph, one can detect signs of the conservative aristocrat ("The apprentice has a duty of obedience towards his master, but at the same time he has also a free responsibility for his work, for his achievement and, therefore, also for his master"[175]), but Bonhoeffer has clearly opened the door toward ordinary people becoming more involved with action for others. As with his theology from below, these moves are only tentative, and have not been fully worked through – there is tension here between the author of *Discipleship* who did not see the Christian as being given the task of upsetting the social order, and the desire to see all humanity capable of exercising a free responsibility that accepts the "tension between obedience and freedom."[176]

In his discussion of the place of responsibility, Bonhoeffer reacts against "two disastrous misunderstandings"[177] of the call of the grace

---

[171] Bonhoeffer, *Ethics*, 102.

[172] Ibid., 246–7.

[173] Ibid., 247.

[174] Ibid.

[175] Bonhoeffer, *Ethics*, 248.

[176] Ibid, 249. Though, interestingly, in *Discipleship* Bonhoeffer also writes: "The rights of a man with a university education and the privileges of social standing are no longer valid for anyone who has become a messenger of Jesus . . . Let it become clear that with all the riches you have, you covet nothing for yourselves" (*Discipleship*, 189).

[177] Bonhoeffer, *Ethics*, 251.

of Christ on a person's life.[178] The first is the secular Protestant one that confuses the call to earthly duties and institutions for the whole of Christ's call on a person's life. The second is the monastic one that attempts "to find a place which is not the world and at which this call [of Christ] can, therefore, be answered more fitly."[179] God's "no," as well as his "yes," "is addressed to the whole world, including the monastery."[180] For Bonhoeffer, although he talks about recognizing a "limited field of accomplishments" that may be a person's lot, he insists that its boundary is broken both by Christ "from above," "but also in an outward direction."[181] In theory this can apply to everyone, and Bonhoeffer argues that "there can be no petty and pedantic restricting of one's interests to one's professional duties in the narrowest sense." However, Bonhoeffer's example is of a physician (like his father?) who may be called to take "public action against some measure which constitutes a threat to medical science." It would have been interesting to see how Bonhoeffer saw boundary breaking responsibility working for the apprentice (or the schoolboy, student, or industrial employee) whom he regarded as in a relationship of free responsibility, even while they held a duty of obedience to their respective masters.[182] Professionals, such as church pastors, are encouraged to go beyond the "Lutheran" idea of the limitation of responsibility and care for the neighbor who is farthest away from them,[183] even to the extent of breaking God's own law "solely in order that the authority of life, truth and property may be restored."[184] This means that acceptance of guilt is also a part of free responsibility, but, yet again, it is the professional classes who seem called to exercise this sort of free responsibility.

Bonhoeffer certainly called for, and was active on behalf of the Jews of Nazi Germany, and was prepared to go his own way in following Christ when even the Confessing Church wanted to compromise with Nazism, but he never denied that the good things in life were also gifts of God.[185]

---

[178] Ibid., 251–2. This objection is reminiscent of Bonhoeffer's attack on "cheap grace," in *Discipleship*.

[179] Bonhoeffer, *Ethics*, 252.

[180] Ibid.

[181] Ibid., 253.

[182] See ibid., 247–8.

[183] Ibid., 255–7.

[184] Ibid., 257.

[185] See Rasmussen, *Dietrich Bonhoeffer*, 124; cf. Bonhoeffer, *LPP*, 341–2 (the letter is from June 30, 1944, not June 27, as Rasmussen claims).

Bonhoeffer certainly sees the goodness of his middle-class situation even in prison, as when he wrote to his recently born great-nephew and god-son:

> The urban middle-class culture embodied in the home of your mother's parents has led to pride in public service, intellectual achievement and leadership, and a deep-rooted sense of duty towards a great heritage and cultural tradition. This will give you, even before you are aware of it, a way of thinking and acting which you can never lose without being untrue to yourself.[186]

Bonhoeffer was never interested in being untrue to himself, and would have seen no reason to deny his upbringing, even in prison. Not least because that upbringing meant "pride in public service," which in itself means consideration of others, even "the least of the brethren." When Bonhoeffer expressed any concern about his early career, it had more to do with his unease about using his theological gifts for his own ends: his awareness of "the clear contradiction between his vocational profession to be a servant of Christ, and his actual, conscious use of his vocation to serve his own ambition."[187] The Bible, especially the Sermon on the Mount, had a big part to play in his "liberation" from selfish ambition – as had his American experiences. Certainly, this change of heart put him on the road that, through discipleship and as a (very critical) servant of the church, led to his involvement with the conspiracy against Hitler.[188]

Therefore when the South African theologian John de Gruchy tells us, correctly, that a step of obedience is required for personal liberation – and that this "outward liberation" precedes the "inner liberation" – and "[l]ike Peter or the rich young ruler in the gospels, or like Bonhoeffer himself, white South Africans [among others] need to be set free from that which prevents them from hearing the good news – they need to be externally liberated from clinging to those things that are contrary to the gospel,"[189] this may not have to mean the "class suicide" that Paulo

---

[186] Bonhoeffer, "Thoughts on the Day of the Baptism of Dietrich Wilhelm Rüdiger Bethge," in *LPP*, 294–5.

[187] Green, *A Theology of Sociality*, 147.

[188] He was not the only member of his family involved in the conspiracy. Bonhoeffer's father wrote after the war about the loss of "two sons and two sons-in-law through the Gestapo." "But since we *all* agreed about the necessity of action . . . we are sad, but also proud of their straight and narrow attitude." Quoted in Bethge, *Dietrich Bonhoeffer*, 933, emphasis added.

[189] de Gruchy, *Bonhoeffer and South Africa*, 77.

Freire (for example) talks about; but it does mean the costly discipleship of following the "man for others."

Bonhoeffer's Eschatology

The attitude to the future, as I have indicated in my study of Augustine and Gutiérrez, can be seen in the attitude to eschatology: the last things. Bonhoeffer's theology, however, majors in ecclesiology (particularly in his early work) and Christology.[190] This does not mean that Bonhoeffer gives no thought to eschatology, but that his eschatology – like other aspects of his theology – must be seen in relation to his Christology. For example, in *Letters and Papers from Prison*, Bonhoeffer asserts that, against "other oriental religions," the redemptions referred to in scripture, "are *historical*, i.e. on *this* side of death." For Bonhoeffer:

> The difference between the Christian hope of resurrection and the mythological hope is that the former sends a man back to his life on earth in a wholly new way . . . The Christian . . . has no last line of escape available from earthly tasks and difficulties into the eternal, but, like Christ himself . . . he must drink the earthly cup to the dregs . . . This world must not be prematurely written off; in this the Old and New Testaments are at one. Redemption myths arise from human boundary-experiences, but Christ takes hold of a man at the centre of his life.[191]

This means that, even while one is conscious of "the constant knowledge of death and resurrection," one lives "completely in this world."[192] Or, to use the parallels noted above, in living in the penultimate, we point to the ultimate. "In so doing we throw ourselves completely into the arms of God, taking seriously, not our own sufferings, but those of God in the world – watching with Christ in Gethsemane."[193]

Following his discussion of the divine mandates in *Ethics*, Bonhoeffer tells us that "the will of God is nothing other than the becoming real of the reality of Christ with us *and in our world*."[194] Further on, we are also told that "[t]he will of God is already fulfilled by God Himself, by His reconciliation of the world with Himself in Christ."

---

[190] For much of what follows, see Feil, *The Theology of Dietrich Bonhoeffer*, 99–159.

[191] Bonhoeffer, *LPP*, 336–7 (cf. Feil, *Theology of Dietrich Bonhoeffer*, 94).

[192] Bonhoeffer, *LPP*, 369.

[193] Ibid., 370.

[194] Bonhoeffer, *Ethics*, 209, emphasis added.

So, Bonhoeffer clearly expected the church to hold a "watchman's brief": "If the Church did not [warn men against sin], she would be incurring part of the guilt for the blood of the wicked (Ezek. 3.17ff.)."[195] In Nazi Germany, if nowhere else, this warning against sin could only be seen as a radical critique of a society that victimized minorities and expected loyalty oaths to the leader.[196]

For Bonhoeffer, therefore, we must conclude that he (certainly at the end of his life, if not before) had come to an eschatological position that required involvement with the world, a desire to see a better world, because God in Christ loved that (real) world. Whether he would expect the church-community, or merely its leaders, to engage in permanent radical critique "in the public square" is open to question. I will therefore now look at how Bonhoeffer regarded the relationship between the church and the society it serves.

The Relationship of the Church to Civil Society

That there is a relationship between the Christian and civil society, is clear from Bonhoeffer's decision to return to Germany in 1939. Bonhoeffer was involved, as a German in German society, as so had to be with "his" people at this time of conflict, or he would not feel able to take part in any reconstruction after the conflict – assuming he would survive.

The first point to note here is that, although Bonhoeffer made his decision alone, he did not regard his decision as an individualist one. He is coming home to share the fate of his country and community. On the other hand, while standing against individualism, Bonhoeffer does see people as individuals. People "became single individuals for his [Jesus'] sake."[197]

> Christ intends to make the human being lonely. As individuals they should see nothing except him who called him . . . [This is because Christ] stands not only between me and God, he also stands between me and other people and things.[198]

But we are not left as lonely individuals; Jesus also is the basis of a new community. "He stands in the centre between the other person and

---

[195] Ibid., 345.

[196] As an example of this, see Bonhoeffer's "The Confession of Guilt," in *Ethics*, 110–16.

[197] Bonhoeffer, *Discipleship*, 99.

[198] Ibid., 92 and 93–4.

me."[199] So the lonely individual is given "the promise of new community."[200]

Bonhoeffer is clear that "[e]veryone enters discipleship alone, but no one remains alone in discipleship."[201] This interplay between the individual and the (church-) community is present in *Discipleship* (quoted above) and in *Life Together*. The latter book makes two stark statements: "*Whoever cannot be alone should beware of community*," and "*[w]hoever cannot stand being in community should beware of being alone*."[202] The first statement is because "[y]ou cannot avoid yourself, for it is precisely God who has singled you out." The second because "[y]ou are called into the community of faith; the call was not meant for you alone."[203]

As I have noted above, Bonhoeffer's critique of thinking in two spheres allowed "no place to which the Christian can withdraw from the world"[204] not even the monastery. The church, and the people within it as the church-community, are to be involved with the world, even if its involvement is reduced to warning people against sin. However, it may well be that the church faces the choice between the three possible ways of acting toward the state: asking the state "whether its actions are legitimate," or aiding "the victims of state action," or, most dramatically, putting "a spoke in the wheel" of state action.[205] The question remains, how the church's involvement should be taught correctly to Christians as they seek to follow "the man for others."

---

[199] Ibid., 98.

[200] Ibid. There is much discussion in secondary literature of the interplay between individual and community. See, for example: Clifford J. Green, *Bonhoeffer: A Theology of Sociality*, and "Human Sociality and Christian Community," in de Gruchy (ed.), *The Cambridge Companion to Dietrich Bonhoeffer*, 113–33; also see A.I. McFadyen, "The Call to Discipleship," *Scottish Journal of Theology*, 43 (1990), 461–83; and Jay C. Rochelle, "Bonhoeffer: Community, Authority and Spirituality," *Journal of Current Theology and Mission*, 21 (1994), 117–22 (especially 122).

[201] *Discipleship*, 99.

[202] Dietrich Bonhoeffer, *Life Together/Prayerbook of the Bible*, 82, emphasis original.

[203] Ibid. It must be noted that *Life Together* is seen to have a "wider application to laity," and its themes are not just confined to (trainee) pastors (Ruth Zerner, "Bonhoeffer on Discipleship and Community," in *Lutheran Forum*, 30 [1996], 36). Against this, we must also note that Bonhoeffer himself was writing to and for trainee pastors.

[204] Ibid., *Ethics*, 198.

[205] Bonhoeffer, *No Rusty Swords*, 222–3.

Educating the Christian for Political Involvement

From what has been said above, it should be clear that Bonhoeffer has no program for educating even the middle-class Christian for political involvement. He expects recognition of free responsibility, which in turn recognizes God's "yes," as well as his "no" to the world. This will lead to an openness toward taking action in the world outside one's immediate professional duties. Bonhoeffer's own conscious education toward political involvement began in America in 1931 – where he found "that the denominations of America are not to be understood primarily from their theology, but from their practical work in the community and their public effectiveness"[206] – and continued for the rest of his life.

This leaves us to consider the role of the Christian in political society. Following a discussion of the political responsibility of the church (which, *in extremis*, is reduced to "establishing and maintaining, at least among her own members, the order of outward justice which is no longer to be found in the *polis*, for by so doing she serves government in her own way"),[207] Bonhoeffer turns to the individual Christian:

> Is there a political responsibility on the part of individual Christians? Certainly the individual Christian cannot be made responsible for the action of the government, and he must not make himself responsible for it; but because of his faith and his charity he is responsible for his own calling and for the sphere of his personal life, however large or however small it may be. If this responsibility is fulfilled in faith, it is effectual for the whole of the *polis*. According to Holy Scripture, there is no right to revolution; but there is a responsibility of every individual for preserving the purity of his office and mission in the *polis*. In this way, in the true sense, every individual serves government with his responsibility. No one, not even government itself, can deprive him of this responsibility or forbid him to discharge it, for it is an integral part of his life in sanctification, and it arises from obedience to the Lord of both Church and government.[208]

How should this responsible life be lived? Bonhoeffer's path, according to Larry Rasmussen, is to

---

[206] Ibid., 114.
[207] Bonhoeffer, *Ethics*, 345.
[208] Ibid., 345–6.

rule out extremes as the normal and normative patterns and procedures for the use of power. But they are not ruled out as exceptional instances of Christian action brought on by hard necessity[209]

Bonhoeffer's time is so abnormal that he can "write of the guilt of his church, his nation and his class." It follows from this complicity that "not to plot Hitler's overthrow but instead attempt to save some measure of moral innocence amidst such guilt by not supporting tyrannicide only compounds the guilt."[210]

There is another tension here. Bonhoeffer experienced the "the failure of the Confessing Church and the ecumenical church forcefully and successfully to oppose Nazism, in the one instance; and the location of the most responsible anti-Nazi action among the people of the military/political resistance, in the other."[211] This meant that Bonhoeffer had to develop his theology to account for the resisters' nonreligious "participation in the sufferings of God in the life of the world,"[212] while most people – Christians included – appeared willingly to become complicit in the evils of Nazism. This folly, is produced "in a large part of mankind" as a result of "any violent display of power."[213] Bonhoeffer is convinced that this folly cannot be overcome by instruction, "but only by an act of liberation"[214] – this again points away from an idea of "a Christian political education" (apart from Christian education as discipleship), but toward an authoritarian idea of leadership responsibility. This is not to say that he allows anyone (member of the élite or not) to feel contempt for any member of humanity,[215] but the question is whether those in power "expect more from people's folly than from their wisdom and independence of mind."[216]

In spite of such realism, or even pessimism, Robin Lovin states Bonhoeffer's "advice is that the Christian acts, not out of self-interest, but to protect those who otherwise would suffer, and they are to "live by responding to the word of God which is addressed to us in Jesus Christ," and take history into their hands.

---

[209] Rasmussen, *Dietrich Bonhoeffer*, 140, quoting from Bonhoeffer, *Ethics*, "The Structure of the Responsible Life," 220ff.

[210] Ibid., 141.

[211] Rasmussen, *Dietrich Bonhoeffer*, 118.

[212] Ibid., 119, quoting Bonhoeffer, *Ethics*.

[213] Bonhoeffer, *LPP*, 8.

[214] Ibid., 9.

[215] Ibid., 9–10.

[216] Ibid., 9.

However, we still have the question of how Bonhoeffer would educate ordinary Christians for such responsible action, especially if their family background had not prepared them to place that action higher than "personal integrity or the sanctity of an oath."[217] De Lange points to Bonhoeffer's high expectations of all Christians and church-communities, and asks whether these expectations are attainable for "ordinary people as they are?"[218] Geoffrey Kelly, on the other hand, wonders whether the church, and its "bourgeois parishioners" could cope with "Bonhoeffer's dream of a renewed, Christ-orientated church,"[219] and asks, pertinently, how churches today could "relate Christian faith with concrete action to achieve peace and justice . . .?" and, very appropriately for those following Bonhoeffer's life and work, "how can Christians condition themselves to endure persecution for the cause of justice (Matthew 5:10)?"[220]

What is clear therefore, is that Bonhoeffer believes that educating Christians to be Christians wherever they are, will, or at least should, lead to responsible action in the sphere of his or her own life "however large or however small it may be." He also believes that the responsible action, undertaken to achieve peace and justice, could involve opposition, persecution, and humiliation.[221]

Conclusion

During his adult life, Bonhoeffer moved from being an unbelieving,[222] ambitious theologian (who nevertheless talks of Christ existing in community), to an ecumenical, believing pastor and seminary leader who

---

[217] Ibid., 148.

[218] De Lange, *Waiting for the Word*, 143.

[219] Geffrey B. Kelly, "Prayer and Action for Justice: Bonhoeffer's Spirituality," in de Gruchy, *The Cambridge Companion to Dietrich Bonhoeffer*, 250. Christian Gremmels notes how easy it is for a church to talk of being for others without being with them. "There is a very subtle possibility in the concept of the 'church for others,' as it is often used nowadays, that actually it is used to keep others away" ("Bonhoeffer, The Churches, and Jewish-Christian Relations," in *Theology and the Practice of Responsibility*, 299).

[220] Ibid., 252.

[221] See, for example, Bonhoeffer, *LPP*, 7; and *Discipleship*, 108–10.

[222] In a 1936 letter, he wrote: "I had often preached, I had seen a great deal of the church, spoken and preached about it – but I had not yet become a Christian." Quoted in Bethge, *Dietrich Bonhoeffer*, 205.

calls for a peace that "must be dared" and "is the opposite of security,"[223] but who upholds the authority of the state,[224] then to a conspirator and martyr for whom "being Christian today will be limited to two things: prayer and righteous action among men."[225] This, as I have noted, involves both a development in his thinking, and tension between his privileged upbringing and his wish to "do theology from below." There is enough in Bonhoeffer's writings, like his essay "After Ten Years,"[226] for liberation theologians to point to his empathy with the oppressed, but in the same essay, we still see Bonhoeffer the conservative autocrat. When he asks the question, "Are we still of any use?" of his fellow conspirators against Hitler, we must infer that Bonhoeffer's "we" referred to those who are already privileged, to those who can make informed choices. It is, for Bonhoeffer, shameful that his church, his nation, and (for want of a better word) his class, failed in their leadership responsibility to oppose Hitler. On balance, it seems that this responsible opposition is not something that Bonhoeffer expects from ordinary people.

---

[223] Bonhoeffer, *No Rusty Swords*, 291.

[224] Bonhoeffer, *Discipleship*, 240ff.

[225] Bonhoeffer, *LPP*, 300.

[226] See *LPP*, 3–17.

Four

Showing the World How to be the World

Stanley Hauerwas and Anabaptist Pacifism

Introduction

Stanley Hauerwas, not least for his robust defense of the pacifist position, has become a controversial figure in the world of Christian ethics. He has recently described himself as representing the "anarchical anabaptist" position that "the orthodox, whether they claim to be radical or not, usually think threatens the presumptive unity claimed by Christendom."[227] Hauerwas' statement in turn opens a Pandora's Box of what is meant by "Christendom"[228] and how united it may or may not be, but Hauerwas' position is often oppositional, and he, as a violent proponent of nonviolence,[229] seems to enjoy being in such a position.

From the point of view of the interface of theology and politics, Hauerwas' stance has led to the repeated accusation of sectarianism. Hauerwas himself is unimpressed by such accusations – and rightly so – but, as we shall see, he often writes in such a way that is easy to see why some people make this assumption. The difficulty for his readers is squaring the circle of how a committed pacifist can be realistically involved in a violent world. Further given Hauerwas' metaphorical image (following John Howard Yoder) of the church as a city on a hill rather than using the more comfortable and familiar idea of salt and

---

[227] Stanley Hauerwas, *Performing the Faith: Bonhoeffer and the Practice of Nonviolence* (London: SPCK, 2004), 170.

[228] Is it synonymous with "Constantinianism," or merely the "spiritual unity" all Christians have whether we like it or not?

[229] Ibid. See also *A Better Hope: Resources for a Church Confronting Capitalism, Democracy, and Postmodernity* (Grand Rapids, MI: Brazos Press, 2000), 9: "I love a good fight . . ."

light, it is easy to see that the charge of sectarianism must at least be examined before we allow Hauerwas a place at the table with our other conversation partners.

However, as I shall show, we cannot successfully charge Hauerwas with sectarianism. Therefore we must consider him as having something to say in terms of Christian political engagement. I shall examine his theology in similar terms as that already looked at in the three previous chapters. That is, Hauerwas' eschatology, his ecclesiology, and his views on the prophetic versus the embodied nature of the church's engagement with the world. I shall show that there are dangers with his ideas of "trivial" politics: although there is much to be said for what the Christian community can show the world, it is not, surely, always the case that in an overpopulated world, we should go on having children.[230] There is also the question of how his ideas would "work" in the real, violent world, where "black" is simply a slightly darker shade of grey than "white." And finally, there is the question of how Christians are supposed to live as members of a Christian community, as if a city on a hill, when for most of the time, they are constrained to live as members of civil society – whatever their "private" beliefs. This last criticism does contain some aspects of the sectarian argument, but it is more a case of Hauerwas not being careful over where there is separation between the church and the world, and where there is continuity, and as I have noted above: in other words, he does not always make clear how one is to be both a Christian and (in my case) a Brit.

The Making of Stanley Hauerwas

Before I examine his theology in relation to the three tensions outlined in chapter 1, I shall first explore his life history. Although he represents the Anabaptist position, Hauerwas is not an Anabaptist.[231] He is a Methodist who has taught at a Catholic university and now worships in an Anglican (Episcopalian) church. He continues to be influenced by – among others – the writings, and the memory, of the Mennonite John Howard Yoder. It was Yoder who opened Hauerwas' eyes to the

---

[230] See Stanley Hauerwas, "Taking Time for Peace: The Ethical Significance of the Trivial," in *Christian Existence Today: Essays on Church, World and Living in Between* (Grand Rapids, MI: Brazos Press, 1988 [reprint 2001]), 253–66.

[231] Hauerwas states "I use the lowercase 'anabaptist' . . . to indicate that what anabaptists stand for is not to be found only in those officially identified as Anabaptist" (*Performing the Faith*, 170).

importance of pacifism, and this continues to be the keystone behind all Hauerwas' thought.

"If Stanley Hauerwas is correct . . . in saying that the only interesting arguments are ad hominem, then it is crucial to understand who Stanley is in order to understand what Stanley *thinks*."[232] Hauerwas was born and raised poor, was cultivated into the protestant work ethic by fears that working for his father would be seen as nepotism, and took that ethic with him to the universities where he lived and worked: "I'm not any smarter than other people. I just outwork 'em."[233] For many years he assumed that Neibuhr was right in his Christian realism, but required "just a little more [Barthian] Christology to buttress where it sagged."[234] However, it was just after he started teaching at Notre Dame in 1970 that he encountered John Howard Yoder, and Hauerwas "began to stammer that he was a pacifist."[235] This was not a joyful conversion. As Hauerwas has himself admitted, he is not a peaceful person. On the contrary, "this ornery man" is unwilling "to step back from conflict." So the pacifist claims serve two purposes.

> In the first place, it demonstrates that Jesus' non-violence does not preclude, but rather requires, conflict with the principalities and powers that maintain the appearance of order through the threat of violence. In the second place, Stanley's public claim of pacifism illustrates the communal nature of virtue in the Christian community, for Stanley cannot claim peaceableness as his own native endowment . . . [F]ew of us . . . have exorcised the violence within. It is therefore necessary to have a community of people committed to creating peace in order to keep each other faithful.[236]

It is this commitment within the story of the worshiping community, rather than any other that has guided Hauerwas' life and thought since then.

Hauerwas has consistently argued against the Enlightenment consensus that ethics can be viewed as distinct from theology, and that either

---

[232] William Cavanaugh, "Stan the Man: A Thoroughly Biased Account of a Completely Unobjective Person," in John Berkman and Michael Cartwright (eds.), *The Hauerwas Reader* (Durham, NC: Duke University Press, 2001), 17. I am indebted to this article for much of what follows.

[233] Ibid., 18, quoting Stanley Hauerwas.

[234] Ibid., 21.

[235] Ibid.

[236] Ibid., 22.

can be seen as academic exercises divorced from the Christian community. Before the Enlightenment, such a separation would have been seen
as incomprehensible. What Christians did depended on what they
believed and enacted as a worshiping community. Christians themselves, much to Hauerwas' chagrin, have accepted the Enlightenment,
or rather the post-Kantian consensus that once the domination of
Christianity was ruptured by the Reformation, with the "interminable
warfare" that ensued between Protestant and Catholic, then "courageous thinkers sought a morality that was not based on rival perceptions
of revelation and could thus bring peace to war-ravaged Europe." These
courageous thinkers, including Kant, have left us with a morality that
supposes, even necessitates rationality to give people the peace they
supposedly crave.[237]

However, as Hauerwas and Wells note, the Kantian story just "happens not to be true" as "the modern state in fact arose prior to the wars
of religion."[238] And, both before and after Kant, religious justifications
have only been one of many reasons that people and states have found
to wage war on each other. Also, "the result of the Kantian revolution
was the increasing growth of bureaucratic states that did nothing to
eliminate war but rather made bigger wars – such as the two world wars
of the twentieth century."[239] Hauerwas therefore questions the whole
"Troeltschian" (liberal) premise of how Christians can or should engage
in or with the world. For Hauerwas, the church *is*, rather than *has* a
social ethic. However, as I shall note, the difficulty comes in trying to
discern how eschatological this social ethic may be: is this a calling, or
does Hauerwas think this "being" is, or ought to be a current reality[240]
However, if the church is to stand as a social ethic, if the church's witness is to "be the church," if Hauerwas only wants people to engage
politically as Christians, and (presumably) not as fellow members of the

---

[237] See Stanley Hauerwas and Samuel Wells, "Why Christian Ethics was
Invented," in Hauerwas and Wells (eds.), *The Blackwell Companion to Christian
Ethics* (Malden, MA/Oxford: Blackwell, 2004), 31.

[238] Ibid. Indeed, modern states arose (in Western Europe at least) under the tutelage of the church.

[239] Ibid.

[240] This has resonances with the distinction, also discussed above between
Augustine's heavenly city and the church. The latter may contain members
of the earthly city, but the former, by definition, may not. Hauerwas and
Wells may be guilty of conflating the two when they try to follow Augustine
and say that "for all its faults the Church remains the only true political reality" ("Why Christian Ethics was Invented," 44). Augustine, if he was capable

died, is no more than a return to the Christian practice of rescuing those children "exposed" and left to die on the hills around Rome in the first centuries after Christ. Again of course, and to follow Hauerwas, this shows how baptism is more important than biology; so, if we are to be part of the church, all baptized children are closer to us than they are in biological terms to their parents. Taking time with our children (as defined by these terms) would really show the world what is really important.

Nevertheless, some of Hauerwas' remarks do need some careful nuancing. He does indeed say that "[t]o speak of the significance of the trivial is to remind us that some of our everyday activities, e.g., the *birth* of a child, embody significant moral commitments."[243] I do not know whether Hauerwas was around for the birth of his own child, but the birth of a child is not an everyday activity for most of us – it certainly was not for me – especially in the North Atlantic context where the average family now has two children or less. The raising of a child is, however, an everyday activity, simply because once you have that child, he or she requires your input on an everyday basis. This is why current society's obsession with getting everyone "back to work" or "off welfare" is so economically short-sighted. The "trivialization" of childraising needs to be questioned; as does the necessity for parents to spend most of the child's formative years outside that child's environment.

Thus Hauerwas is correct to say that:

> Nothing is more hopeful or peaceful than the willingness to open our lives to children. Having children is activity in its most paradigmatic form, as the having of a child is its own meaning. Moreover, having children is our most basic full-time project, not only in the sense that children are time-consuming, but because through children our world quite literally is made timeful. Children bind existence temporally, as through them we are given beginnings, middles and ends. They require us to take time and, as a result, we learn that time is possible only as a form of peace.

He is correct, but in so far as he does not make it absolutely clear that these children do not have to be our biological children, he does not go far enough. The action of adoption may seem less trivial in one sense, but, like birth, once that non-everyday action has been undertaken, the everyday actions of child-raising take precedence over all other "political" actions.

---

[243] Hauerwas, "Taking Time for Peace," in *Christian Existence Today*, 263, my emphasis.

If we note that "Taking Time for Peace" was first published in 1986, we can see that while it was written before the collapse of the Berlin Wall, it was most certainly written before the events of September 11, 2001. Can we therefore look to a rethinking of Hauerwas' position after the soil of America itself was violated by international terrorism? The short answer is "No." In his "homily" written some months after the event, Stanley still holds that Christians are "called to be holy,"[244] and therefore the pacifist response[245] to September 11 "is to continue living in a manner that witnesses to our belief that the world was not changed on September 11, 2001. The world was changed during the celebration of Passover in AD 33.

He finishes his article with a prayer that calls on Barth's counsel that, in a different crisis time, we must continue life "as though nothing has happened,"[246] and we should therefore respond by realizing that God has given us "all the time we need to respond to September 11 with 'small acts of beauty and tenderness.'"[247] In other words, we must continue with the trivial.

The trivial is also bound by the "tactical." Hauerwas contends that "[t]he church exists today as resident aliens, an adventurous colony in a society of unbelief."[248] Hauerwas and Willimon continue:

> The message that sustains the colony is not for itself but for the whole world . . . The colony is God's means of a major offensive against the world, for the world.
>
> An army succeeds, not through trench warfare but through movement, penetration, tactics.[249]

So, for Hauerwas, the idea of a church with a strategy for the world is, in itself, alien. It is not for the church, or Christians "to write [and speak]

---

[244] Stanley Hauerwas, "September 11, 2001: A Pacifist Response," in Stanley Hauerwas and Frank Lentricchia, *Dissent from the Homeland: Essays after September 11* (Durham, NC: Duke University Press, 2003), 188.

[245] We must note that Hauerwas states, "I would not be a pacifist if I were not a Christian, and I find it hard to understand how one can be a Christian without being a pacifist," ibid., 181 (and elsewhere). I shall examine Hauerwas' pacifism along with his assertion that there can be a nonviolent politics below.

[246] Ibid., 189.

[247] Ibid., quoting Jean Vanier.

[248] Stanley Hauerwas and William H. Willimon, *Resident Aliens: Life in the Christian Colony* (Nashville, TN: Abingdon Press, 1989), 49.

[249] Ibid., 51.

as though Christian commitments make no difference in the sense that they only underwrite what everyone in principle can know" but:

> Our task as theologians remains what it has always been: namely, to exploit the considerable resources embodied in particular Christian convictions which sustain our ability to be a community faithful to our belief that we are creatures of a graceful God. If we do that we may well discover that we are speaking to more than just our fellow Christians, for others as a result may well find we have something interesting to say.[250]

For some, such an approach may sound sectarian, but Hauerwas is interested first and foremost in the church being church, in the recognition that the world is not Christian.[251] The church has to live everywhere surrounded by the world, as resident aliens in a foreign country; the church must live "tactically," by its wits.

So, if we are to concentrate on the tactical and on the trivial, what are we to make of Hauerwas' assertion that Christians must support the state, unless that "government and society resorts to violence in order to maintain internal order and external security. At that point and that point alone Christians must withhold their involvement with the state."[252]

Given that, as I have argued above, we need to follow Augustine's argument that politics was ordained following the Fall, and that therefore, the state exists to temper humanity's excesses in that fallen state, and is therefore of necessity coercive, we need, at this point to question what Hauerwas means by violence, as opposed to coercion. Indeed, Hauerwas is not opposed to the idea "of the state – even the coercive state – as part of God's 'order.'"[253]

Therefore politics can be coercive, but not violent. However, if the Augustinian earthly city is founded on the violence of fratricide,[254] this is problematic. The only place free from coercion is the (eschatological) city

---

[250] Stanley Hauerwas, "On Keeping Theological Ethics Theological," in Berkman and Cartwright (eds), *The Hauerwas Reader*, 73–4.

[251] See Hauerwas and Willimon, *Resident Aliens*, 15–19.

[252] Stanley Hauerwas, "Why the 'Sectarian Temptation' Is a Misrepresentation: A Response to James Gustafson" (originally published, 1988) reprinted in Stanley Hauerwas, *The Hauerwas Reader* (Durham, NC: Duke University Press, 2001), 105.

[253] Ibid., 107.

[254] The earthly city's foundation is by Cain who had killed his brother Abel: see the discussion of Augustine's *City of God* in chapter 1 above.

of God, and the church is tainted by the earthly city – even as it points to the heavenly one. So, when Hauerwas states that the position that "all politics is finally but a cover for violence" is "empirically unsupportable," he lets his argument go by default, simply because he does not state it. For Hauerwas, "[w]hat the pacifist must deny, however, is the common assumption that genuine politics is determined by state coercion." The word "genuine" troubles me here. Does Hauerwas mean therefore that true worldly politics is non coercive? In which case, he needs to take a long hard look at history. Even where politics was ostensibly about "discovering the goods we have in common," there was, and is, a large amount of coercion on securing the argument over what those goods constitute. If, on the other hand, Hauerwas means that *genuine* politics is non-coercive, then Augustinians would also find this difficult, because non-coercion would only take place in, and be confined to, the heavenly kingdom.

In the end, the root of Hauerwas' argument with any just war theorist, and Augustinian scholars such as John Milbank, lies not so much with violence qua violence, but with the definition and origin of politics. As I have noted above,[255] for Augustine there could have been no politics prior to the Fall. Prior to the Fall, there would have been no dispute over values – ultimate or otherwise. In more recent times, John Rawls has noted that "[a] modern democratic society is characterised by . . . a pluralism of incomprehensible yet reasonably comprehensive doctrines."[256] Nothing is more incomprehensible to a present-day liberal than the idea of Christianity (or any other religion) being a *comprehensive* doctrine – not just a private affair.[257] For all he accepts the idea of a coercive state,[258] Hauerwas clearly has problems in accepting that this inevitably means a coercive politics. If we can have "peaceable politics," then we must have had politics before the Fall, which becomes a nonsense given the Rawlsian definition of politics, even democratic politics, quoted above. Perhaps Hauerwas will accuse me of being too "realistic," or (a dreaded word in the Hauerwasian vocabulary) "Niebuhrian," but the acceptance

---

[255] See chapter 1.

[256] John Rawls, *Political Liberalism* (New York: Columbia University Press, 1993), xvi.

[257] 'So long as the expression of your views does not offend anyone else, you can believe what you like" (Grace Davie, *Religion in Britain since 1945* [Oxford: Blackwell, 1994], 76). More and more the expression of Christian views does offend – and gets a (verbally) violent response – see for example Hauerwas and Willimon, *Where Resident Aliens Live*, 81, and 91–3.

[258] Hauerwas, "Sectarian Temptation," 107.

of how things are, of how politics is done, does not imply an acceptance of how things ought to be – even if that "ought to be" will not be fully realized until the second coming. Christians need to be involved, as Christians, in society, in politics, but they need to be aware that they are also involved as sinners in a sinful world, where God has granted the use of coercive power (the one in authority "does not wear the sword in vain") to suppress the *libido dominandi* of us all.[259]

This is at the centre of the debate Hauerwas has with John Milbank in *Must Christianity be Violent?* There is, in spite of the debate, clear agreement between the two of them on many issues (including the desire for and about peaceableness), but the key difference comes in the following exchange:

> *Milbank*: . . . you [Hauerwas] are trying to get beyond even mitigated violence. But at the same time, I would say that there can be situations where a resort to violence is not necessarily wrong. I mean, there is a sense in which violence in itself is always wrong, but there can be situations where one can feel that refraining from violence would equally be wrong or very likely actually more wrong.

> *Hauerwas*: I don't know why I would want to imagine that. Why would I want, as someone schooled into the peaceableness of God's church, to invite that kind of imagination?[260]

What Hauerwas is trying to indicate here is that if you are not committed to nonviolence, you will not come up with alternatives to violent responses.[261] On the other hand, Milbank clearly can think of examples where he would say that resorting to violence is not wrong, such as preventing the stoning of an adulterous woman (see John 8:1–11). He further contends that even if such intervention results in the death of the

---

[259] See the fuller discussion in chapter 1 above.

[260] Stanley Hauerwas, "Christian Peace: A Conversation Between Stanley Hauerwas and John Milbank," in Kenneth R. Chase and Alan Jacobs, *Must Christianity Be Violent? Reflections on History, Practice, and Theology* (Grand Rapids, MI: Brazos Press, 2003), 213.

[261] "The commitment to live nonviolently is a way to challenge our imaginations to create alternatives that would not be there if we were not committed to discovering what it means to be nonviolent. Note that I do not presume, as a given, we know what nonviolence is – but that is part of the ongoing discovery we so desperately need." (E-mail communication to the author December 19, 2006).

perpetrator in the pursuit of justice, then "I can't quite see why this sort of defensive action implicitly says, 'Life can only be protected by violence.' I mean, this is an anomalous action in an anomalous circumstance."[262] However, there can also be "circumstances where it can be better to let the innocent die because life on earth is not the be-all or end-all of everything."[263] So there can be, needs to be, a nonviolent witness in the world – where Christians "have to be in the world even if that means endangering your children."[264]

So we find that Milbank's endorsement of the possibility of violence is muted, and Hauerwas' peaceableness is not identical to non-resistance. "The question is, then, what are the forms of that resistance?"[265] Hauerwas gives no direct answer, not least because he still holds to what he wrote earlier in that "there is a sense in which my position commits me finally to questioning the legitimacy of the nation-state insofar as that state arrogates to itself the right to kill."[266] This means that there will be "a profound tension between the church and the nation-state that is not resolvable in this time between the times."[267] It may be that this awareness of tension causes Hauerwas to call the assumption that Christians had a stake in the continuation of Western civilization a mistake, "since who should know better than they that the moral good is not an achievement easily accomplished by the many, but a demanding task that only a few master."[268] Indeed, the whole "liberal project" is suspect as far as Hauerwas is concerned.[269]

In his desire to stand apart, Hauerwas has forgotten the Christian legacy behind liberalism. And the sharpness with which Hauerwas distinguishes between "the (liberal) world and the Church" has "a sectarian quality." But he does not advocate withdrawal, even if his emphasis on "tactics" rather than "strategy"[270] means that we will not get a "how to be

---

[262] Ibid., 218.

[263] Ibid.

[264] Ibid. The words are Hauerwas', but Milbank is in full agreement.

[265] See ibid.

[266] Hauerwas, "Will the Real Sectarian," 93–4.

[267] Ibid., 94.

[268] Hauerwas, *Against the Nations* (Minneapolis: Winston Press, 1985), 40. Cf. Biggar, "Is Stanley Hauerwas Sectarian?" in Mark Thiessen Nation and Samuel Wells, *Faithfulness and Fortitude: In Conversation with the Theological Ethics of Stanley Hauerwas* (Edinburgh: T&T Clark, 2000),159.

[269] Hauerwas, *After Christendom*, 34–5.

[270] See Hauerwas and Willimon, *Resident Aliens*.

politically involved" book from him – not least because Hauerwas regards "everything I write, I hope, is a way to suggest what it means to be politically involved."[271] Rather, his insistence that the "Christian Church live and think according to the norms of its own story . . . [is] the basic condition of the Church's discharge of its proper political responsibility."[272]

Is Stanley Hauerwas Sectarian?

Therefore, in his own terms, Hauerwas is not sectarian, but there have often been questions raised on these lines. Here I shall argue that, far from "retreat[ing] into the private world of the church" and thereby disengaging "from public concerns and debate,"[273] Hauerwas seeks to bring the world of the church into public gaze so that the world can at least see that the church is qualitatively different, and, if it is separate in any way, it is separate because it has a different political agenda and a different, peaceable, rule to follow. Hauerwas' own definitive response to his critics was written as long ago as 1987,[274] but in an interview in 2002, he is still being faced with the same objection.[275] The basic difference between Hauerwas and his critics on this point depends on whether you accept Troeltsch's analysis of modern (liberal) society and the churches' involvement with and reaction to liberalism as "epistemologically and sociologically" coherent.[276] As Hauerwas questions the churches response to the whole liberal project (most notably in his critique of Reinhold Niebuhr), then it is axiomatic that to some enthusiastic liberal Christians, he will appear sectarian. For Hauerwas, "the eagerness of liberal Christians to be effective in shaping society-at-large has moved

---

[271] Email communication with the author, December 19, 2006.

[272] Biggar, "Is Stanley Hauerwas Sectarian?" 160.

[273] Nigel Biggar, "Is Stanley Hauerwas Sectarian?" 141.

[274] Stanley Hauerwas, "Will the Real Sectarian Stand Up?" *Theology Today* (1987), 44, 87–94. He followed this with "Why the 'Sectarian Temptation' Is a Misrepresentation," in 1988 (quoted above).

[275] Interview with Jonathan Wilson-Hartgrove of the Institute for Global Engagement, www.globalengagement.org/issues/2002/02/hauerwas-p.htm (August 19, 2004). The exact question was: "You have been labelled as a 'pacifist,' a 'sectarian' and a 'fideistic tribalist' – among other things. How would you like to define yourself?" Hauerwas answers that he is a Christian, and continues, "I have no difficulty with Christians being involved with politics. I just want them to be there as Christians."

[276] Hauerwas, "Real Sectarian," 87.

them to jettison anything that liberal secularists might find objection-able."[277] The liberal position, as Hauerwas notes, "is to try to make religion existentially intelligible to both the cultured and uncultured despisers and appreciators of religion."[278] Hauerwas, on the other hand, follows the postliberals in believing that

> religions can "no more . . . be translated into another medium than that one can learn French by reading translations." Religions, like languages, can only be understood in their own terms. From the liberal point of view such a claim can appear only as a counsel of despair since it seems to make impossible any rational account of religious convictions.[279]

Hauerwas quotes George Lindbeck with approval, in stating that "[t]he issue is not whether there are universal norms of reasonableness, but whether these can be formulated in some neutral, framework-independent language."[280] In other words, by seeking to "translate" Christianity in liberal terms, liberal Christians have subsumed any distinctiveness of Christianity into liberal rationalism, and Christianity therefore ends up having nothing to say that challenges this "rational-ism." For Hauerwas, it is vital that the church is able to stand apart, not in order to disengage, but in order to be positioned "in a manner such that the church can serve society imaginatively by not being captured by societal options or corresponding governmental policy."[281]

In other words, as noted above, he wants Christians to be involved as Christians not as good liberals who do not rock the boat.[282]

Rocking the Boat

For Hauerwas, it is obvious that Christians will end up rocking the boat because, following Yoder, he proclaims that "[t]he gospel cannot be at

---

[277] Biggar, "Is Stanley Hauerwas Sectarian?" 144.

[278] Hauerwas, *Against the Nations*, 5.

[279] Ibid.

[280] Ibid., 6. The quote is from George Lindbeck, *The Nature of Doctrine: Religion and Theology in a Postliberal Age*, 130.

[281] Hauerwas, "Real Sectarian," 90.

[282] Biggar puts this more grandly by saying that Hauerwas "recognises the possibility of properly theological apologetics" (see "Is Stanley Hauerwas Sectarian?" 144), but this all comes under the same remit of church being church and living "tactically" in the world.

home in the world, because the church that is called into existence through the work of the Spirit exists to witness to the God found in the life, death, and resurrection of Christ."[283] In other words:

> A genuine political theology must attend to the ways in which Christian truth takes form as a power in its own right. A genuine political theology must identify and explicate the *exousia* of Jesus Christ that gives density and force to the life of discipleship.[284]

We hereby return to the point made earlier: which is that Hauerwas wants Christians politically involved *as Christians* first and foremost. It is as disciples of Christ, not as good citizens, that they are to make their mark. However, Christians do not *set out* to rock the boat, but it is inevitable that the world will react against them because the Christians' agenda is so distinct from the world's. But what is it that defines a good Christian disciple as distinct from a good citizen? What is the power that shapes our Christian lives and molds us as disciples?

Hauerwas has struggled to define this "x" factor. His early work focused on character. In his discussion of Hauerwas' early work, *Character and the Christian Life*, Rusty Reno, discusses the difficulty of finding "x":

> Perhaps if Hauerwas were a Lutheran . . . [h]e would have said that the x is the Gospel. That is the word that Lutherans use when they want to emphasize the thick and weighty power of God. Perhaps if Hauerwas were a Roman Catholic, he would have said that the x is grace, for Roman Catholics often use that word to denote everything that God does for and in us. But Hauerwas is a Methodist . . . [so he] must investigate the x that . . . shapes our lives.[285]

For Hauerwas, the central theme has become the "coherent story" of our lives. It is the narrative flow that makes up our character, not which principles we bring to mind when faced with a particular dilemma. For Hauerwas, the fatal flaw of "social gospel" and all forms of Protestant liberalism, was that it sought to isolate Christian principles "from the fabric of Christian speech and practice," which in turn left

---

[283] Hauerwas, *With the Grain of the Universe*, 219.

[284] R.R. Reno, "Stanley Hauerwas," in Peter Scott and William T. Cavanaugh (eds), *The Blackwell Companion to Political Theology* (Malden, MA/Oxford: Blackwell, 2004), 303–4.

[285] Ibid., 306.

those principles "semantically underdetermined."[286] Hauerwas refuses, in other words, to accept that the world should, or ought to, set the agenda for the church.[287] Also, he (in a very orthodox, even Augustinian manner) has "refused in the name of an autonomous created order . . . to legitimate the state as an end in and of itself."[288]

Hauerwas' Eschatology

Therefore, given that Hauerwas is no sectarian, and yet he refuses to "legitimate the state," where does he think that the kingdom of God enters the frame? Given his views on nonviolent politics, does he regard the (political) kingdom of God as only arriving at the Parousia? Given what we have noted above, we would expect not. Does he then regard the kingdom of God as present with us, or is he, like Bonhoeffer, to be accused of a weak eschatology?

According to Samuel Wells, "Hauerwas' perspective on Christian ethics is profoundly eschatological," if it is understood that "the distinction between Church and world is not about living in different spaces, but about having a different perception of time."[289]

For Wells, "the area decisive for Hauerwas [is] the attitude of the Church to the existing order." This is profoundly eschatological as "belief in the catastrophic, personal, bodily return [of Christ] encourages Christians to be faithful and ready, rather than successful."

> It challenges the existing order, but avoids a triumphalist approach which might suggest Christians should seize power. Because it is sudden, it undermines gradualism; because it is personal, it keeps continuity with the ministry and passion of Jesus; and because it is bodily, it avoids versions which seek to make Christian transformation an interior event.[290]

Wells then states: "Hauerwas would profit considerably from drawing out the eschatological features of belief in God's sovereignty in these

---

[286] Ibid., 307.

[287] See Hauerwas and Willimon, *Resident Aliens*, especially 30–48.

[288] Hauerwas, "Sectarian Temptation," 107.

[289] Samuel Wells, *Transforming Fate into Destiny: The Theological Ethics of Stanley Hauerwas* (Carlisle: Paternoster Press, 1998), 142.

[290] Ibid., 142–3.

ways." Whether Hauerwas has changed his tactics in his writing is moot, but the eschatological theme is strongly implicit in his prayer at the end of his article: "September 11, 2001: A Pacifist Response":

> Life must go on . . . "as though nothing has happened" . . . To go on "as though nothing has happened" surely requires us to acknowledge you are God and we are not. That we live in the end times is surely the basis for our conviction that you have given us all the time we need to respond to September 11 with "small acts of beauty and tenderness."[291]

As I have noted, it is Passover AD 33 which changed the world, not September 11, 2001.[292] This is not to say that Hauerwas is unaware of the eschatological implications of his work, or that he does not refer to it (and nor does Wells imply this), but the eschatological implications are often muted – and thus open the way for those who are so inclined to accuse Hauerwas of sectarianism, as it seems that Hauerwas thinks of Christians occupying different space, rather than different time.[293] This lack of clarity is cleared up in Hauerwas' later work where more "time-ful" considerations appear. He does not, though, like the phrase "in-between times": Christians "live in two times." This is opposed to the secular world, whose time is no longer "interwoven with a higher time."[294]

There are eschatological themes in Hauerwas' pursuit of nonvio-lence: nonviolence means that the specter of martyrdom appears as those who pursue nonviolence refuse to resist those who act vio-lently. It is however the eschatological belief "in a last judgment that vindicates the righteous,"[295] which means that "[t]hough they kill us they cannot determine the meaning of our death."[296] The theme of martyrdom is familiar, as all three of the previous conversation partners have met, and discussed, this very theme (in different con-texts). Whenever the churches' difference from the world is noted, then the resistance begins: *Where Resident Aliens Live* is peppered with such incidents: none involving death, but all involving a

---

[291] Hauerwas, "September 11, 2001," 189.

[292] Ibid., 188.

[293] See Wells, *Fate*, 141–2.

[294] See Stanley Hauerwas, *The State of the University: Academic Knowledges and the Knowledge of God* (Oxford: Blackwell Publishing, 2007), 170–1.

[295] Ibid., 143.

[296] Stanley Hauerwas, "On Developing Hopeful Virtues," *Christian Scholars Review*, 18/2 (1988), 113, quoted in Wells, *Fate*, 143.

reaction to, and often against, those who are different simply by being Christian.[297]

If martyrdom has its eschatological significance, then Hauerwas is also convinced of the eschatological significance of the trivial.[298] I have already discussed the significance Hauerwas sees in having children, but this significance also turns on Hauerwas' ideas of church – in other words, his ecclesiology.

Hauerwas' Ecclesiology

Church is the mirror that Hauerwas seeks to hold up to the world. Hauerwas' church is very much the city on the hill: the visible manifestation of the alternative, peaceable community that seeks to show the world how to be the world. The church is the church because it accepts all those whom the world regards as valueless. As he wrote in 1975, his Uncle Charlie may not be much of a person, but he is still "Uncle Charlie." For all that the world may decide that certain people are non-persons, the church does not. For all the world may decide that particular relationships – especially sexual ones – are important, the church does not:

> From the beginning we Christians have made singleness as valid a way of life as marriage. What it means to be the church is to be a group of people called out of the world, and back into the world, to embody the hope of the Kingdom of God. Children are not necessary for the growth of the Kingdom, because the church can call the stranger into her midst. That makes both singleness and marriage possible vocations. If everybody has to marry, then marriage is a terrible burden. But the church does not believe that everybody has to marry. Even so, those who do not marry are also parents within the church, because the church is now the true family. The church is a family into which children are brought and received. It is only within that context that it makes sense for the church to say, "We are always ready to receive children. We are *always* ready to receive children." The people of God know no enemy when it comes to children.[299]

---

[297] See Hauerwas and Willimon, *Where Resident Aliens Live*, especially 15–6, 27–8, 98–100.

[298] See Hauerwas, *Resident Aliens*, 67.

[299] Hauerwas, "Abortion, Theologically Understood," in *The Hauerwas Reader*, 613.

Of course, Hauerwas has been criticized on this point. He appears to expect too much of his church, which he wishes to use as his example to the world.[300] It is as if he expects Christians to live as if the fullness of the Parousia is present, rather than just its advent.[301] In other words, sin, as Augustine recognized, is all too present within the church as well as without. We are then left to wonder whether we should regard Hauerwas' call to the church as a prophetic, rather than an embodied one: is he merely looking and wishing that how the church ought to be is the reality, or is it a call to renewal (one which has not been seen since the days before Constantine)?

Hauerwas as Prophet of the Parousia

The trouble with regarding Hauerwas as prophet of some distant dawn, is that his work is all too grounded in reality. In his article "Abortion, Theologically Understood" (quoted above), Hauerwas includes two examples of how "unwanted" children were born and welcomed within two church communities – one Methodist and one Catholic. Both the children were conceived in less than ideal situations, yet these two communities, "one with a carefully planned strategy for supporting women and babies, the other simply reacted spontaneously to a particular woman and her baby,"[302] lived out what Hauerwas looks for in his alternative community.

And yet Hauerwas often appears to stand as the voice crying in the wilderness. This is a wilderness of pacifism, of peaceableness, of a church separate from the state (he will not, for example, support saying prayers in schools – the place for children to learn about faith is not in non-Christian institutions, however benign they might be to the faith). He is still accused of sectarianism, of not being able to say anything to the world, because he rules out violence as an appropriate response. But, as he would say, if the church does not stand for peaceableness – and therefore against violence – what does it have to say that is different from what the world is already saying? If we agree with Paul Ramsey that "the use of power and the possible use of force is of the esse of politics. By this I mean that it belongs to politics very act of being politics,"[303] then is it not all the more important to show the world that there is a

---

[300] See John B. Thomson, *The Ecclesiology of Stanley Hauerwas* (Aldershot: Ashgate, 2003), 211.

[301] Ibid., 205–6.

[302] Hauerwas, "Abortion," 607.

[303] Quoted in Thomson, *Ecclesiology*, 211 n. 27. Paul Ramsey is a noted just war theologian.

different way of "being." And it is "being" that is important to Hauerwas: his church is one that builds "communities of character" which nurtures people in the peaceable nature of Christ.

In this, I suppose we should say that Hauerwas' whole argument with the church is about how it educates its people. He insists that as a pacifist he does have a voice, he does have the wherewithal to "speak truth to power," and he expects the church to do that as well, but from a position of peaceableness. He insists that he wants his students, not to think for themselves, but to think like him – only then will they be able to do any thinking on their own behalf. If the church does not think – does not engage with liberal society by living in such a way that the world with its concerns and debates is seen not to matter – then Hauerwas is unimpressed. He expects Christians to live as *Resident Aliens* in the liberal society they find themselves; and to witness – through the trivial as may be – but to witness against the Constantinian Christianity Hauerwas asserts is too close to power. In this he is close to liberation theologians, who also state that non-engagement is support of the *status quo*.

Of course, Constantinian Christianity and liberal society (parts of Hauerwas' *status quo*) has Christian parentage and this culture is part of our upbringing, like it or not – and generally, Hauerwas does not! It is the task of the church to sort out the good from the bad and to educate its people to know where good and bad is to be found.

Yet, we again have to deal with the reality of sin. The church cannot but be somewhat "undressed politically," in that as it points the world toward peaceableness, it also has to be aware that it is itself but on the way. The difference is not so much that the church, as God's community, has arrived – it is inevitable that any structure formed within the created realm is marred by sin. As such some form of coercive power (even if it is only evidenced by the power of excommunication for those who have fallen too far by the wayside) must be exercised by those in authority.

It may be that Hauerwas will come to recognize that his project has to be more prophetic in the sense of announcing what ought to be in the church as well as what might be in the world – that, if his pacifism requires the rejection of any form of violence within the church, then his church has more in common with the city of God that Augustine pointed to, and possibly less to do with the church (disunited and rent by violence) as she exists today.

Conclusion

Stanley Hauerwas is an extremely controversial figure in modern-day Christian political thinking. His output is vast and has been no more than touched on here. His stance on pacifism has occasioned much disagreement and debate, and he has engaged in many arguments with many scholars on this issue. His contribution is important, because it makes us pause: maybe there is indeed another way. Maybe the world's *de facto* ontology of violence does not need to be accepted before we engage with the world as Christians. Maybe we can engage on our terms. We may not be arguing on the terms that those who espouse "liberal values" wish to hear, but at no point did any of our four theologians expect it to be easy to get a hearing. And with Stanley Hauerwas, at least we do have something radical to say, and we would be saying it as Christians. Whether the world would wish to hear it is another question.

Five

From Theologians to Case Studies[304]

Introduction

So far in this book, I have spent a brief amount of time with each of four theologians in order to determine what a Christian approach to political involvement might be. This, inevitably, has turned out to be an interesting exercise, not least because it has not been easy to tie down what we mean by "political" – much less what we mean by "political involvement." Christian engagement with society has, though, been conflictual or oppositional; not because Christians are out "looking for a fight," but because what they do, how they behave, challenges the world in such a way that the world tends to react like a maddened elephant – having been bitten by a dog, it seeks to flatten the forest to get at the dog. However, Christian suffering, martyrdom even, has always shown that the world does not have the last word, as Hauerwas points out:

> To Rome, Christians dying for their faith, for their refusal to obey Caesar, was an irrational act. For the martyrs their dying was part of a story that Rome could not acknowledge and remain in power as Rome.[305]

In other words, Christians may be killed, but the killers cannot determine what those deaths "mean." In the previous four chapters, I have pointed to the seemingly irrelevant or trivial, I have also pointed to the conflict and suffering that has often gone with Christian political witness. I have, for the sake of comparison, looked at the theologians in terms of their eschatology, ecclesiology, and what I shall call the

---

[304] This chapter builds on my "A Summary Grammar for Christian Prepolitical Education," in *Journal for Education and Christian Belief*, 7.2 (Autumn 2003), 143–55. That article only concerned three of the four theologians (so the references to Hauerwas, at least, are new), but the points I make are similar.

[305] Stanley Hauerwas, *After Christendom* (Nashville: Abingdon Press, 1999), 38.

prophetic tension (with particular reference to their view of how Christians should be educated for political engagement). This chapter will draw together the different theologians in order to come up with an overarching set of "pre-political" tensions – so firstly, I will explain this phrase, then I will recap briefly on the previous four chapters. After that, I will show how the tensions come together. We will then be in a position to look forward to the case studies which make up the second half of the book.

By a "pre-political" tension, I mean that the tension I have discussed above, and will reiterate below, will exist before we get involved politically, and will exist whether we get involved or not (though of course, we must bear in mind the liberation proviso that not getting involved is getting involved on the side of the *status quo*). We will be, as Christians, living with both the now and the not yet of eschatology: we exist in the world, but are supposed to be not of it. We are aware both of the prophetic vision of the future, and of the difficulty of making that happen.

The other problem concerns the word "politics" in itself. As we noted in the chapters above, for Augustine, politics (at least in the pre-Fall sense of the term) is unnatural. This is because it was the Fall which introduced the tragedy of humanity's involvement with *libido dominandi* (the lust for power, or seeking power for its own sake), then "politics" – which is so often more about conflicting values, conflicting ideas of "the good" – remains a necessary part of humanity's fallen condition. In the pre-Fall situation there was no conflict over "the good." On the other hand, Hauerwas is sure that

> there was by necessity a politics prior to the fall . . . I do think that even if we were not wrapped in sin we would need to be in communication with one another for the discovery of the goods we have in common. So politics names not only the inherent sociality of our lives but also the necessity that our need for one another comes through communication which is exemplified in worship.[306]

This is clearly a broader definition of politics than the Augustinian one I have just expounded, and – as we would expect from Hauerwas – locates the best politics within the worshiping community.

Gutierrez also wrestles with a broad and narrow definition of "politics."

---

[306] E-mail communication with the author, December 19, 2006.

> The construction – from its economic bases – of the "polis," of a society in which people can live in solidarity, is a dimension which encompasses and severely conditions all human activity . . . Only within this broad meaning of the political sphere can we situate the more precise notion of "politics," as an orientation to power . . . The concrete forms taken on by this quest for and exercise of political power are varied. But they are all based on the profound aspiration of a humankind that wants to take hold of the reins of its own life and be the artisan of its own destiny.[307]

We must note that it is only in the broader dimension that Gutiérrez says that "[n]othing lies outside the political sphere . . ." However, under this definition he is prepared to have "confidence in the future," and to say of his Latin American situation that the "thrust toward the future occurs *above all* when one participates in the building up of a just society . . ."[308] Above all, for Gutiérrez, Jesus "by freeing us from sin . . . attacks the roots of an unjust order." As a result, "[t]he political is grafted into the eternal," since "to preach the universal love of the Father is inevitably to go against all injustice, privilege, oppression, or narrow nationalism."[309]

So we have to be careful over what we mean by "politics." Where politics is seen as a debate over what is the most efficient way of implementing a course of action, there may be a wish to leave the discussion to the experts. Debate in politics, however, does not just come about because people have differing views over what is the most effective means of governing society. It also occurs because people's interests differ, so what is seen as efficient or effective will differ. More importantly, people's values differ. This means that their ideas of what is *right*, not just what is efficient or effective, will differ.[310] It is at this level of values that silence by any part of the community allows others with differing values to impose their views on the whole of society unopposed. It also means that those who do seek change will assume that silent churches, and silent church people, support the *status quo*.

In his wrestling with broad and narrow definitions of politics, Gutierrez is clearly reacting against the idea that "politics" should be a clearly defined free time activity.[311] Indeed he is prepared to regard the struggles against the marginalization of unimportant people as political struggles, even if some would regard such small gestures as "having

---

[307] *A Theology of Liberation*, 30–1.
[308] Ibid., 122, emphasis original.
[309] See ibid., 134–5.
[310] See John Rawls, *Political Liberalism*, xvi.
[311] *A Theology of Liberation*, 30.

little political effectiveness.[312] Following Gutiérrez, I am using the phrases "politics" and "political involvement" with a broad definition encompassing the values by which Christians live. A command as basic to the Christian faith as "loving your neighbor" will then have a political dimension, but the practical outworking of that love will, of course, depend on time and circumstance. None of the theologians studied in this book, however, assumed that loving one's neighbors meant that they should be left alone in their troubles. Being a Christian means being involved in civil society, and that, in turn, means being politically involved in that civil society.

This is, of course, a messy business. We cannot necessarily tell what is the right course of action to take in a particular circumstance. All we can do, like Bonhoeffer, though hopefully not in such extreme circumstances, is to take the free responsibility that we have under Christ and offer that to him and trust that our actions are indeed righteous ones. There is of course a sense of "politics," namely the narrow sense of a will to power, to which the church cannot give assent, since it does not embody a pre-Fall sense of what is "natural."[313] But if the church is only concerned with staying "pure", and thereby keeping out of politics in any sense, it will in the end be divorced from the real lives that its people (and any others whom it is trying to reach) live. In this sense, the church would return to what Bonhoeffer calls the "monastic" misunderstanding of what God's call on our lives means, and tries to find somewhere "which is not the world," where this monastic call can be lived out "more fitly."[314] This brings us to a discussion of the three tensions that I have discerned in the previous four chapters.

The Tensions of Church and Politics

The kingdom: now and not yet

As noted above, this first tension arises from an examination of the eschatology of my conversation partners. If we look at Augustine's views, we can see that he clearly emphasizes the "not yet" side of the eschatological argument: "the peace of Babylon"[315] is all we can expect in this life, and he does not expect much in the way of

---

[312] Ibid., xxx.
[313] Here I follow Augustine.
[314] See Dietrich Bonhoeffer, *Ethics*, 252.
[315] *DCD* XIX. 26.

improvement in earthly justice – indeed he finds "progress" "inherently ambiguous."[316] Augustine's view is that there has never, after the Fall, been a truly just state here on earth.[317] If we stopped here, however, we would be ignoring Augustine's relative judgments about different societies,[318] and fall into the heresy of saying that salvation has absolutely nothing to do with, and gives us no responsibility for, the present, political situation.

In other words, the eschatological division of people into the two cities is Augustinian as a first step only. Augustine was clearly involved in civil society: there were his attempts through the African church councils to improve the justice of society, and his arguments for leniency in the application of the law.[319] For Augustine, the fact that members of the city of God are pilgrims while on earth[320] and "are never bona fide members of the earthly city"[321] does not remove the requirement to care for our neighbor.[322] However, it is extremely difficult to imagine where Augustine would advocate any form of civil disobedience in order to promote greater justice in society.

Dietrich Bonhoeffer makes a similar point in *Discipleship*:

> Would a revolution which simply overturned the existing order of society not obscure the awareness of God's new ordering of all things through Jesus Christ, and the establishment of his church-community? Moreover, would every such attempt not actually hinder and delay the abolition of the entire world order and the dawning of God's realm?[323]

He clearly believes that revolution is, to say the least, an ambiguous way of trying to promote God's kingdom. This does not mean a lack of involvement, but Bonhoeffer does stand accused of having a weak eschatology.[324] This side of his theology may militate against the idea of the church-community being a "community of radical critique" that saw itself

---

[316] O'Donovan, "Augustine's *City of God*," 146.

[317] *DCD*, XIX. 21.

[318] See, for example, *DCD*, II. 19.

[319] See especially *Letters* 152–5 to and from Macedonius.

[320] See *DCD*, XV. 1.

[321] O'Donovan, "Augustine's *City of God*," 141.

[322] See *Confessions*, XIII. xvii (20).

[323] Dietrich Bonhoeffer, *Discipleship* (Minneapolis: Augsburg Fortress, 2001), 238–9.

[324] G. Clark Chapman Jr., "Bonhoeffer: Resource for Liberation Theology," *Union Seminary Quarterly Review*, 36 (1981), 238.

as having "a vital public task . . . as an eschatological community . . . to communicate a purging judgment, both in the public square and in the sanctuary."[325] However, Bonhoeffer clearly expected the church to hold a "watchman's brief": "If the Church did not do this [warn men against sin], she would be incurring part of the guilt for the blood of the wicked (Ezek. 3.17ff.)."[326] In Nazi Germany, if nowhere else, this warning against sin, which included a recognition that loyalty could only be given ultimately to God (and not Adolf Hitler) could only be seen as a "radical critique."

A radical loyalty to Christ also fits in with Hauerwas' eschatology. I have already noted his "eschatological significance of the trivial" and his idea that the best response to 9/11 being "carrying on as if nothing has happened" – of course, this statement was made to make us think about what "carrying on" means. It means living differently from the world, as if a Passover in AD 33 carried more significance than any other event: it means being aware that Christians live, not in the "in-between" times as such, but in two times. The church has to be "a church whose life is governed by the reality of the new age."[327] The new age, among other things, is, of course, characterized by the peaceableness that all Christians are called to witness: if nothing else, pacifism is a call to the witness of the new age that the church is to live in, and therefore to show the world how it should live, but does not as yet.

While he never advocates violence, Gutiérrez regards civil disobedience – including the "counter-violence" of the oppressed – as understandable, and he looks to the church, and its Base Ecclesial Communities (BECs), to be involved politically in conscientizing the poor so that they can engage in a radical critique of the *status quo*. His eschatology stresses the "now" side of the kingdom of God, and he stands against any idea that eternal life can be "seen exclusively as a future life."[328] On the contrary, for Gutiérrez, Christian actions in the temporal world and the desire to see temporal progress are connected with the growth of the kingdom of God here on earth.

The danger with this progressivist eschatology is that the idea of secular history functioning "as *part* of the coming of the kingdom of

---

[325] Larry Rasmussen, *Dietrich Bonhoeffer – His Significance for North Americans* (Minneapolis: Fortress Press, 1990), 86.

[326] Dietrich Bonhoeffer, *Ethics* (New York: Touchstone/Simon and Schuster, 1995), 345.

[327] Here Hauerwas follows John Howard Yoder, *The Christian Witness to the State* (Scottdale, PA: Herald Press, 2002), 8–13.

[328] Gustavo Gutiérrez, *The Power of the Poor in History* (London: SCM Press, 1983), 39.

God"[329] is subverted to becoming the idea that secular history *is* the coming of the kingdom of God. However, this would be an incorrect reading of Gutiérrez – he looks to a future "definitive encounter with God," and is insistent that the increase of justice is a part, but not the whole of liberation[330] – but it is the potential idolatry of a liberationist approach to eschatology: a reduction of salvation to liberation in this world. This idolatry is, however, rendered implausible by the stubborn sinfulness of human nature and all the other limits of life in this world.[331] Therefore it needs to be balanced by the "not yet" nature of eschatology. But recognizing this tension opens the question of how Christians are to live in this world.

In the World But Not Of It

Following from the previous tension, therefore, yet distinct from it, is the tension of being in the world, but not of it. Augustine tells us very clearly that, as far as the world is not the kingdom of God, it comes under God's judgment; but if we look, for example to Bonhoeffer's later works (especially *Ethics* and *Letters and Papers from Prison*), we can see that the world is also loved by God. Indeed, Bonhoeffer goes so far as to reverse his original position and states that, instead of God keeping the world in being for the sake of the church, the church continues to exist for the sake of the world.[332] Withdrawal from the world is not an option. This can clearly be seen from all three theological approaches, and even Augustine, who is most clear about the world's final "end," never advocated a hermetically sealed church separated from the world. However, Augustine's "other worldly" eschatology severely limited any expectation of improving the justice and peace in this world. The world, it seemed to Augustine, was irredeemable in itself, and only the Catholic Church pointed the way for humanity to find its true "end" in God.

Gutiérrez, however, takes a much more radical approach of involvement with the world. He states in *The Power of the Poor in History* that "[f]aith has liberating potential, but it must be developed . . ."[333]

---

[329] Robert C. Doyle, *Eschatology and the Shape of Christian Belief* (Carlisle: Paternoster, 1999), 274, emphasis added.

[330] Gutiérrez, particularly in his later works, is careful to note the "spiritual" aspects of liberation.

[331] Cf. Nicholas Lash, *Theology on the Way to Emmaus* (London: SCM Press, 1986), 193.

[332] See Feil, *Theology of Dietrich Bonhoeffer*, 138.

[333] Gutiérrez, *Power of the Poor in History*, 97.

The potential of a liberating faith, and the capacity for revolution, are inti-
mately bound up together in the concrete life of this poor and oppressed
people. Hence it is impossible to cultivate the one without the other as
well, and this is what many find so unsettling. The development of the
people's political awareness and its Christian awareness go hand in hand.
The life and work of many of Latin America's new basic Christian communities have been strongly marked by the experience of this intimate
link between faith and revolution.[334]

Both "religious" and political reductionism is rejected, though Gutiérrez
accepts that "the development of the political dimension and the faith
dimension will not always be in step" as the process, and the reality on
which it is based, is complex.[335]

For this and other reasons, change may not be as easy as some
would like.[336] So, if we are to follow Augustine's lead, we must more
closely define this tension as one that advocates involvement in the
world, but which does not expect overmuch from that involvement, as
the world will never correspond to the kingdom of God. Put this way,
it sounds pessimistic, and people could refuse to get involved on the
grounds that not much will change anyway – thereby being *not in* and
not of the world. A cursory reading of *Discipleship* and *Life Together* may
lead to the assumption that Bonhoeffer takes this separatist line as he
expects Christians to face persecution simply for being Christians and
being separate from the world.[337] This, however, ignores the context in
which Bonhoeffer was writing. To take one example, Bonhoeffer was
reminding Christians that Jesus "demands undivided obedience" in
the context of Hitler's demand for a loyalty oath to him as Führer.[338] In
fact, Bonhoeffer deplored the attempts to retreat from the world, and
pointed out that these attempts lead to a situation where one is not in
the world, *but still of it*. It was for this reason that Luther had to leave
the monastery: "Luther had to leave the monastery and reenter the
world . . . because even the monastery was nothing else but the
world."[339]

---

[334] Ibid., 98.

[335] Ibid., 98–9.

[336] Gutiérrez is aware "that a social transformation, no matter how radical it may
be, does not automatically achieve the suppression of all evils." See *A Theology
of Liberation*, 24.

[337] For example, see Bonhoeffer, *Discipleship*, 169.

[338] See ibid., 135, and editors' note 112 in ibid., 130.

[339] Ibid., 48.

In *Discipleship*, Bonhoeffer's "No" to the world was a radical "Yes" to Christ. This "Yes" to Christ is also a "Yes" to involvement with and for the other for whom Christ also died. Bonhoeffer tells us that we are blessed when, not if, we are persecuted for righteousness sake.[340] This is the most difficult lesson of all. It is all too easy, as Bonhoeffer found, for the church – in its concern to be "in" the world – to bless the bourgeois mentality and so to distort what Luther (and Augustine) said about obedience to secular authority. In other words, the church succumbs to what Bonhoeffer called the "secular Protestant" misunderstanding[341] of the call of God's grace on a person's life, and becomes both in and of the world.

If the overemphasis on being "in" the world leads to the "secular Protestant" misunderstanding of what the call of God's grace is about; then an overemphasis on being "not of" the world leads to a misunderstanding in another direction where a person fails to appreciate that Jesus' call involves struggle against the world. So this person "attempts to find a place which is not the world and at which this [misunderstood] call can, therefore, be answered more fitly."[342] Bonhoeffer insists that this attempt to be neither of nor in the world fails to take either God's "yes" or his "no" to the world seriously.[343]

One way of making sure that you take God's "yes" and his "no" to the world seriously, is "to resist letting Washington DC determine what you mean by politics".[344] On the one hand, everything he writes, Hauerwas hopes, "is a way to suggest what it means to be politically involved,"[345] but, on the other, if he and his readers are not careful, the city on the hill motif risks standing for separation – and hence sectarianism – rather than an example showing the world how to be the world. Hauerwas' point, as I have noted before, is that the church is the mirror held up to the world, a mirror that values what the world finds valueless: and a mirror that values the peaceable kingdom above all.

So, as far as the church is a representative of the kingdom of God, it must (to return to Bonhoefferian terminology) be aware of God's "no," and not be of the world. However, because it is also aware of God's "yes," it must be "in" the world, and obedient to its structures as far as

---

[340] Ibid., 109–10.

[341] See Bonhoeffer, *Ethics*, 251.

[342] Ibid., 252.

[343] Ibid.

[344] Email correspondence from Stanley Hauerwas to the author December 19, 2006.

[345] Ibid.

possible – given that the church's ultimate loyalty is to God and to the proclamation of his kingdom. This prophetic proclamation is the subject of the third tension.

The Prophetic and the Embodied Church

Given that the world is both loved and to be judged, the church must work out how it is going to live alongside the world without being a part of it: how it is to "make use of the peace of Babylon" without making such imperfect peace its own goal. According to Hauerwas, this, of course, is the temptation that the church faced, and fell into many times following the conversion of the Roman Emperor Constantine, and the subsequent "Christianization" of the Roman Empire. Part of Hauerwas' prophetic call is to resist any attempt to return to the bad old days when "Christendom" ruled. This is because what Christendom led to was a domesticated gospel, where Christianity's radical ethic was reduced to an ethic that was workable for everyone. This, in turn, denied not that a Christian way of life was possible for all, but that living as a disciple of Christ requires the work of the Holy Spirit.

This Christendom temptation is one that occurs most often when things are going well. Bonhoeffer points out that it is dangerous to assume that success and prosperity will produce more people of faith. "This is refuted by the evidence of the New Testament and of Church history; indeed it has perhaps been precisely at times when the world has seemed to be relatively in order that the estrangement from the faith has been especially deep-seated and alarming."[346]

Therefore the church must continually point to God's kingdom – to how things ought to be – and how they will be come the eschaton; but it must also work for that "ought." The first part of this, I shall refer to as the prophetic call of the church, the second as its embodied role. The vision of God's kingdom is nonetheless real, and can be worked for in practical steps (however small and incremental). It is, to follow Gutiérrez, much better to do something to improve the justice in the world, than to do nothing, as this denotes acceptance of the *status quo*.[347] It is axiomatic to state that the *status quo* is never perfectly just, so there is always something that can be done to improve the justice in the world. However, as all four theologians were aware, this attempt to improve justice will meet resistance: even Augustine, while he never advocated

---

[346] Bonhoeffer, *Ethics*, 137.
[347] See Gutiérrez, *A Theology of Liberation*, 159.

active opposition to civil authority, nonetheless continually pointed to the martyrs as his example of *passive* resistance to any idolatrous demands that civil society might seek to impose on Christians.[348]

These two roles – the prophetic and the embodied – must be kept in tension: to overemphasize the prophetic call to achieve the kingdom of God will either lead to apathy on recognition that this is humanly impossible, or to enthusiastic calls for revolution which tend to lead to more destruction and hardly witness to the kingdom of God.[349]

If revolution is excluded, then an overemphasis on the prophetic call, an emphasis on how the world does not come up to God's standards, will tend to reduce prophecy to mere denunciation, and obscure the denunciation-annunciation dialectic that Gutiérrez points to.[350] Mere denunciation will lead to a church separated from the rest of society, with nothing positive to say – and therefore it runs the huge risk of its message being totally ignored.

On the other hand, to overemphasize the incremental approach to improving justice would tend to eliminate any differences between church and civil society – you do not need to be a Christian to see that there are injustices in society. Nor do you need to be Christian in order to witness against injustice. Without the Christian prophetic denunciation-annunciation dialectic, the embodied aspect of the church's work can degenerate into the merely pragmatic where power, allies or action will be sought for its own sake – where "the peace of Babylon" starts to be seen as an end in itself rather than something to be used by the pilgrim members of the city of God.

In its living with the tension between the prophetic and the embodied, the church must be both patient and impatient in the same way that Paulo Freire expected his educator to experience the tension between patience and impatience in conscientization. As I said in the chapter on liberation theology, Freire noted that:

> Patience alone may bring the educator to a position of resignation, of permissiveness that denies the educator's democratic dream . . . Conversely,

---

[348] See for example *Sermon* 302. However, Augustine did not accept that anything less than idolatrous demands should be (passively) resisted; see discussion in Herbert A. Deane, *The Political and Social Ideas of St. Augustine* (New York: Columbia University Press, 1963), 149.

[349] As I have noted, Bonhoeffer makes this latter point in *Discipleship*. See Bonhoeffer, *Discipleship*, 238–9.

[350] See Gutierrez, *A Theology of Liberation*, 136: "The denunciation [of the existing order] is to a large extent made with regard to the annunciation."

impatience alone may lead the educator to blind activism, to action for its own sake . . . Patience alone consumes itself in mere prattle; impatience alone consumes itself in irresponsible activism.[351]

If the church is too patient, it will become resigned and apathetic, and will never aspire to bring the world closer to the kingdom of God. If it is too impatient, it runs the risk of constant and unconsidered action against "the existing order of society," with all the attendant ills that could bring. Both being too patient and impatient show a church that is forgetting the "now" side of the presence of the kingdom of God. The tension between the embodied and the prophetic will not disappear: the biblical emphasis on the prophetic clearly points toward both the failure of the Israelite community to live up to the demands of the covenant and the hostile environment in which those who followed God had to live. Then, as now, they and we are to "do justice, and to love kindness, and to walk humbly with your God."[352] Just as the Old Testament community did, we have to seek our own ways of "doing justice," in our situation, guided by those who have gone before, but aware that their situation may not be the same as ours.

We Don't Do God

So said Prime Minister Tony Blair's chief advisor in 2003, when an interviewer had the temerity to ask about the Prime Minister's Christian faith. Not doing God in the public sphere has been a big problem of late, especially for those Christians who try to be involved as Christians in the world. Of course, there are two agendas here: the church's, and the world's. There has been, ever since the Enlightenment, a tendency on the part of the world, to seek to remove "religion" from the public sphere. There is a difference, however, between a "secular" state and a "secularist" one. As Nigel Wright puts it:

> There is much to commend the idea of a "secular state" where no one is penalized for their religious confession . . . The state which safeguards religious liberty can help to limit conflict arising from sectarian divisions, provided the secular state does not become the "secularist" state which, while pretending to be neutral, is itself sectarian in that it rejects the value

---

[351] Paulo Freire, *Teachers as Cultural Workers: Letters to Those Who Dare Teach* (Oxford: Westview Press, 1988), 44.

[352] Mic. 6.8.

of religion altogether. In this case the strategy of "privatizing" religion is a way of neutralizing its public influence.[353]

Of course, such "privatization" is not merely the fault of a secularizing state. Christians have certainly colluded with the idea of a privatized religion. Kenneth Medhurst and George Moyser note that within the Anglican Church, there are those who "argue that Christianity is largely a personal matter having no direct implications."[354] Looking at the wider, social context, Grace Davie notes "the phrase ['privatised religion'] gives an accurate impression of the current state of affairs, for it is true that religion has very largely become a matter of personal or private choice. So long as the expression of your views does not offend anyone else, you can believe whatever you like."[355] The danger, for the Christian, or the member of any faith community, is that the fear of giving offence will override any contribution they may wish to make.

Of course, as we have noted, Stanley Hauerwas believes that the church should "stand apart;" but for Hauerwas, standing apart does not neuter the church in terms of social critique or engagement. "Standing apart" should position the church so it "can serve society imaginatively by not being captured by societal options or corresponding government policy."[356] Even if we think for a moment in Augustinian terms and note that there is necessary conflict between church and "state" on the grounds that the state is focused on its own survival and the church is (or should be) focused on God, Hauerwas still states that he is "not opposed to trying to harness the resources of state power to alleviate the needs of people." He objects, however, when "we think *only* in those terms."[357]

Hauerwas, like all the theologians discussed in this book, also objects to a church that becomes a supporter of the powerful, with the hard sayings of Jesus relegated to a private or interpersonal world, and public

---

[353] Nigel Wright, *The Radical Evangelical: Seeking a Place to Stand* (London: SPCK, 1996), 105.

[354] Kenneth N. Medhurst and George H. Moyser, *Church and Politics in a Secular Age* (Oxford: Clarendon Press, 1988), 356.

[355] Grace Davie, *Religion in Britain since 1945* (Oxford: Blackwell, 1994), 76. For the above paragraph, cf. my "Base Ecclesial Communities and Community Ministry: Some Freirean Points of Comparison and Difference," in *Political Theology*, 5.4 (October 2004), 461 (note 92).

[356] Stanley Hauerwas, "Will the Real Sectarian Please Stand Up," *Theology Today*, 44:1 (1987), 90.

[357] Hauerwas, "The Real Sectarian," 90, emphasis added.

life being guided by Old Testament precepts or "natural law." While Europe, by and large, has retained some vestiges of state religion, the Founding Fathers of the United States of America sought to institution-alize a church/state split where no church was granted any "rights" to influence the governance of the new country. This meant the rise of the secular state and, often, a retreat for faith into the private sphere, and thereby raising the continual danger of the church being seen as giving an effective blessing of the *status quo* by its silence. When it comes to working with the state, the church's watchword needs to be "coopera-tion without compromise" – of course, such a phrase is open to inter-pretation, one person's cooperation is another's compromise. I did not say that living in tension would be easy!

This is especially true as, both in the UK and the US, there have been recent efforts on the part of government to engage the "faith communi-ties" in regeneration and other community projects, even to the extent of granting funds to such faith-led projects (always with the proviso that such money is not used to proselytize). Indeed, in both the US and the UK, the emphasis, from the governing authority's perspective, is on the project being "entirely or mainly"[358] or "inherently"[359] for the commun-ity. In this case, churches have a choice: where do they wish to sit on the collusion verses collision spectrum? Overt collusion with regeneration projects means, as I have noted above, that one takes the government's agenda on board uncritically and then the question must be asked: what is the difference between your faith community and a secular/govern-ment funded social service agency? "[O]vert collision – i.e. a rejection of the assumptions and ethos of the [government's] regeneration matrix – leads to self-imposed marginalization, self-selected disempower-ment."[360] There are, obviously, difficulties that may attend involvement with government initiatives, but if the church wishes to say to commu-nities that "God cares about what you care about, and your church wants to discover what God is doing here," then involvement is inevitable – and it will require "significant time and trouble."[361]

Of course, cooperation in regeneration projects is not the be-all-and-end-all of Christian engagement with, or witness to, the

---

[358] Local Government Association, *Faith and Community: a good practice guide for local authorities* (London: LGA Publications, February 2002).

[359] See www.whitehouse.gov/government/fbci/guidance/partnering.html (accessed February 3, 2005).

[360] William Temple Foundation, first year synopsis of *Regenerating Communities – A Theological and Strategic Critique*, see www.wtm.org.uk, 7.

[361] Wells, *Community-Led Regeneration and the Local Church*, 26–7.

world. In the five chapters that follow, I discuss five areas where governments and other authorities need challenging, exhorting, and encouraging. But before I move on to the case studies, let me look again at the church's engagement with the world and how it will take place.

The Church and the World

When the Prime Minister's spokesman tried to rule "God talk" out of public debate, he was trying to rule "out" what was on its way back "in."[362] The problem for Christian engagement with politics, or "the state" is that too many people assume that the eighteenth-century Enlightenment secularized society and constituted a clean break with a religious past. Unfortunately, many Christians have "bought" this caricature, leading to either the liberal fallacy that you should do social action, but not mention Christ, or the evangelical reaction that salvation is all about accepting Christ, but you should not dilute your gospel with social action. What would be even more dangerous would be if we continued to read the Bible as if the Enlightenment distinctions of "church" and "state" were valid: Augustine, for one, would have had none of that. The question was not *whether* God would have a role in the public affairs of humanity, but *which* God would the Empire say was the god it sought to follow.

Which God to follow does not sound much like a question for today, but as Professor John Gray has put it:

> liberal humanism . . . is established today as the unthinking creed of conventional people. Yet liberal humanism is itself obviously a religion – a shoddy derivative of Christian faith notably more irrational than the original article, and in recent times more harmful.[363]

It is salutary to remember that, despite the legend of Enlightenment "peacefulness" as a solution to the "religious wars" of previous centuries, we have had Hitler, Stalin, Pol Pot and others who claimed no religious allegiance, and yet killed, or caused to be killed, people in their thousands.

Liberal humanist beliefs have all come under severe strain in recent years. If we examine just two of the more universal tenets of its "faith"

---

[362] See Nick Spencer, *"Doing God": A Future for Faith in the Public Square* (London: Theos, 2006), 16, www.theosthinktank.co.uk

[363] Quoted in ibid., 62 (See John Gray, "Sex, Atheism and Piano Legs," in *Heresies: Against Progress and Other Illusions* [Granta, 2004], 41–8).

we can see that stress. First, its "deification of personal freedom" is now being questioned "as fears about terrorism, crime, immigration, and social cohesion are orientating governments toward ever more anti-libertarian measures, in the belief that electorates ultimately value security over liberty."[364] And second,

> the optimism about human nature, "that human nature will triumph, that human nature is a basically good thing," that has fuelled human liberalism since its birth looks unconvincing (to put it mildly) as the human race looks back over a century of genocides and ahead to a century in which our treatment of non-human creation promises to deform the planet as never before.[365]

Of course, a humanist would point to the bad bits of Christianity: there have been the crusades and the inquisitions as well as St Francis, Wilberforce, Mother Teresa. And, for all we can observe other, more worldly, motives, there were genuinely religious differences in the Wars of Religion of the seventeenth century – differences that led people to kill each other in brutal ways. (These wars in turn helped to produce the Enlightenment that Hauerwas and others now criticize).

So, Christians, and others, while accepting our history – both the good and the bad bits – do not have to accept "public reason" at face value. All my theological conversation partners have challenged what passed for public reason in their day. Therefore we should "be willing to question the presuppositions that underpin it." As Nick Spencer notes, "[w]hat is 'reasonable' is . . . far from obvious and those that claim otherwise need to be able to defend themselves."[366]

But so should Christians. If Christians cannot defend themselves in the public realm, then it is both the fault of what Stanley Hauerwas calls "the sheer prejudice of many secular thinkers . . . [that] any reflection informed by religious claims cannot possibly be serious."[367] However, it is also the fault of "the lack of attention [given] to the inability of Christian theologians to find a sufficient medium to articulate their own best insights for those who do not share their convictions."[368] This inability may well be increased for those (like Paulo Freire) who do not call themselves theologians. Indeed, Freire tells us that "I do not feel very

---

[364] Ibid., 68.

[365] Ibid.

[366] Ibid., 69–70.

[367] Stanley Hauerwas, *Against the Nations*, 26.

[368] Ibid.

comfortable speaking about my faith."[369] This is an area that the church, its leaders, and theologians, needs to address – and I include Stanley Hauerwas in this as he is most insistent that Christians engage as Christians with society.

It is because I follow Stanley Hauerwas in the insistence that Christians need to engage with society as Christians that I question the need for "religious thinkers . . . [to] be willing to accommodate their language *and reasoning* to what is currently acknowledged as the norm in public discourse."[370] After all, we have noted already that what is reasonable is not easy to define, and what is "current reasonableness" seems to change with the wind. There will often be problems in translation, indeed the tensions I have discerned (and will reiterate below) indicate that may be the case; but Christians should not be forced by a world unwilling to regard as serious "any reflection informed by religious claims" into abandoning their reasoning for one that wishes to regard "sacred" and "secular" as divided by an unbridgeable gulf; especially when (post 9/11) this is clearly not the case.

As I shall show below there are "religious" issues that impinge on slavery, poverty, environment, war and sexuality. Indeed, for the Christian seeking to engage with the world, it is so often the case that the same people are hurt most by many of these issues:

> Bangladesh, for example, is home to the third highest absolute number of poor people in the world, after China and India. It has the highest incidence of malnutrition in the world – every day 700 children die of malnutrition-related causes. It spends the same amount repaying its debt every year – about $700 million – as it spends on public health. And its total debt in 2003 stood at $18.8 billion, five times what it was in 1980.[371]

So, Bangladesh is poor. It gets worse:

> Most of Bangladesh is less than ten metres above sea level. Every year, during the high monsoon tides, the sea swallows up more land. In June 2005, Pancha Bala, 45, saw her home on Kutubida island broken apart by the waves. When she first moved there 25 years ago, the sea was nearly 1km [0.6 miles] away. But a devastating cyclone in 1991 and annual erosion during the high monsoon tides changed everything.[372]

---

[369] Paulo Freire, *Pedagogy of the Heart* (New York: Continuum, 2000), 104.

[370] Nick Spencer, *"Doing God"*, 71, emphasis added.

[371] See www.bond.org.uk/campaign/churchestoolkit.pdf

[372] See www.christian-aid.org

In other words, Pancha is one of the hardest hit by climate change. But this is not the end of the woes.

As a young girl in Bangladesh, Sabina hoped to be able to help her family escape their poverty. So, when an Indian woman visited and promised Sabina a job, Sabina left with her. However,

> when they crossed the border, Sabina's "auntie" left her with another woman . . . For the next seven days, 12-year-old Sabina was beaten and raped repeatedly by as many as 10–15 men a day.
>
> When the week was up and her will was broken, Sabina was forced to work in a brothel. "During the day I did all the housework. At night I was forced to give company to the men who came."[373]

Sex trafficking – slavery by another name – preys on the poor of Bangladesh and other places.

> Faced with such a plethora of woes, it is easy to feel powerless. Yet the lesson of the abolitionists [who fought against the slave trade two hundred years ago] is that God can use conscientious Christians who think globally and act locally to accomplish seemingly impossible things. When the philosopher John Stuart Mill reflected on the abolition of the slave trade and the demise of slavery itself, he concluded that these great events had happened not because of "any change in the distribution of material interests, but by the spread of moral convictions." "It is what men think," wrote Mill, "that determines how they act."[374]

And it is only by thinking as Christians, and as Christians seeking to engage with the world, that we will know how to act in our own situation.

Pre-political Engagement: A Summary

What I have discerned is a matrix, if you like, against which we can measure the church's approach to pre-political involvement. The three tensions identified above, along with the idolatries that follow from emphasizing one side of the tension over the other, can be summarized as follows:

---

[373] See *Inspire* magazine, October 2006, 13, and www.inspiremagazine.org.uk

[374] John Coffey, "The Abolition of the Slave Trade: Christian Conscience and Political Action," *Cambridge Papers* 15:2 (June 2006), 6.

1. *God's kingdom is both "now" and "not yet."* If the latter is over-emphasized, the church is dangerously close to ignoring the belief that God's kingdom of justice and love has arrived, and is active on earth. Therefore, it could be said that salvation has nothing to do with the present condition of the world and political involvement is irrelevant. On the other hand, if the "not yet" nature of God's kingdom here on earth is ignored, then the church runs the danger of equating liberation with salvation, and assuming that humanity can indeed save itself.

2. *The church is in the world but not of it.* Overemphasize the former, and the church will face the expectation of baptizing the *status quo*, to be part of the world and its established order. If the idea that the churches are not of the world is overemphasized, then the temptation will be to retreat into a ghetto mentality and live as a church against the world with nothing to say to it.

3. *The church is prophetic and embodied.* Overemphasis on the former will lead to paralysis as the prophetic tends to mere denunciation of the world as it is. This will deter people from attempting to make a difference, and they will therefore tend to sit back and wait for the parousia. Overemphasize the latter, and the prophetic vision is lost as differences between the church and the world are eroded – all persons of good will can see that the world is not as just or as peaceful a place as it might be, and can be persuaded to take action if they can see that the scope and target of that action is achievable.

This is not to say that one side of a tension can never be emphasized over the other. The danger of idolatry comes when overemphasis means that the other side of the tension is eroded or lost. It may be true that "where there is no vision, the people perish,"[375] but they are equally likely to perish if no practical steps are taken to realize the vision laid before them. Any political, or pre-political, engagement with the world, whether it is done by churches, church leaders, or "ordinary" Christians must show that these tensions not only exist, but that Christians (above all people) must live with these tensions as they exercise their free responsibility in seeking to work out "how the coming generation is to live."[376]

---

[375] Prov. 29:18 (Authorized Version).
[376] Bonhoeffer, *LPP*, 7.

It is now time to turn to the case studies. These are all areas where Christians are involved; these are all areas where other people are already involved. Each chapter will examine the issue and then look at that issue in the light of each of the tensions outlined above.

Six

Let Us Make Poverty History

"We can take the calls." These words from the mouth of Condoleezza Rice summed up the recalcitrant White House view of early 2005 to the Make Poverty History movement. This – possibly apocryphal – story was cited as one of the reasons for the Live 8 concerts. Apparently the George W. Bush White House had better things to do than worry about what a few pop stars were going on about, and the threat by Bono to get all his fans to ring the White House and demand action was met with a shrug: if necessary they could employ a few extra telephonists, but people were not really bothered about countries far away. But then the Live 8 concerts were announced and the rest, as they say, is history. Except that, in 2005, we didn't make poverty history. The statistics in January were not much changed by December: according to the United Nations, it still took only three seconds for another child to die of some poverty related illness.

But then, what do you need to be rich these days? It depends where you start. Steve Henry, in his book, *Change the World 9 to 5*, action 098, notes this:

- Something on the floor other than dirt puts you in the top 50 percent of the world's wealthiest people.

- A home with a roof, a door, windows and more than one room puts you in the top 20 percent.

- A fridge and/or freezer in the home puts you in the top 5 percent.

- If you or your family has a car, a microwave, a video[/DVD] player, a computer and you have a door on your bathroom – then you are in the top 1 percent of the wealthiest people in the whole world.

In other words, most people are poorer than us. So, while there is nothing wrong with attending a rock concert that supports the eradication of poverty, we need also to apply some critical, Christian thinking to many areas.

Firstly, we need to note that 2005 was not the first time people sought to eradicate poverty. "It was in the 1790s at the time of the French Revolution that there first emerged the believable outlines of a world without endemic scarcity, a world in which the predictable misfortunes of life need no longer plunge the afflicted into chronic poverty or extreme want."[377] It was Antoine-Nicholas de Condorcet who gave expression to this optimistic view on life. For all that the terror following the Revolution hounded him to his death, he insisted on arguing against "those who maintained that the gulf between rich and poor was an inescapable part of 'civilization' . . . that inequality was largely to be ascribed to 'the present imperfections of the social art.'" Condorcet thought that, "'[t]he final end of the social art' would be 'real equality.' "[378] All we can say is that this final end seems a long time coming. In the latter half of the twentieth century, his predictions about the independence of the colonies and the spread of free trade have largely come to pass, but his assumptions that Africa and Asia would "break free" of trade monopolies, racism, and "the shameful superstition" of the Christian faith have been unfounded.[379] Not only is Africa one of the places where Christianity is growing strongly, the former colonies (although there are notable exceptions) are still in the grip of trade policies, and "debt restructuring" that are imposed on them from outside: mainly by representatives from the former colonial powers, or the United States – now the global superpower.

G8, Us and the Poor

> As a result of last year's [2005] G8 [summit at Gleneagles, Scotland], 19 countries have already received significant debt cancellation, with others scheduled to follow.
>
> But low income countries still owe US$500 billion in debts and the debt of all developing countries remains a staggering US$2.3 trillion. Bangladesh, home to the third highest number of poor people in the world, is among the many countries that are yet to receive any serious debt cancellation. Servicing its US$63 billion debt is the biggest single expenditure in the Philippines' national budget – while its poor are getting poorer.[380]

---

[377] Gareth Steadman Jones, *An End to Poverty? A Historical Debate* (London: Profile Books, 2004), 16.

[378] Ibid., 18.

[379] See ibid., 18–19.

[380] Communication from Christian Aid, January 2006.

The examples multiply. But before we blame "them," we must ask how far we are a part of the system, how far we accept the *status quo* that allows for such inequality; and we must ask if we are not still part of a religious tradition that sought, and in some cases still seeks, to make the poor accept social and wealth differences as merely a part of life. How far do we think we should go for "equality of opportunity" rather than equality itself – and what do we mean by "equality" anyway? It is dangerous to limit it to some sort of "spiritual" equality: an equality that leaves us unchallenged. Paulo Freire reacts against this kind of Christianity by pointing out that "peace cannot be purchased." In other words if "I seek compensation [for my guilt feelings] by almsgiving, I send a check to build a church, I make contributions: land for a chapel or a monastery for nuns" it won't work.

> And I can't live my peace without commitment to humans, and my commitment to them can't exist without their liberation, and their liberation can't exist without the final transformation of the structures that are dehumanizing them. There is only one way for me to find peace: to work for it, shoulder to shoulder with my fellow human beings.[381]

Therefore, conscientization is not an easy process: indeed it is "a painful birth," and it "demands an Easter."

> That is, it demands that we die to be reborn again. Christians must live their Easter . . . Those who don't make their Easter, in the sense of dying in order to be reborn, are not real Christians . . . I just feel passionately, corporately, physically, with all my being, that my stance is a Christian one because it is 100 percent revolutionary and human and liberating, and hence committed and utopian. And that, as I see it, must be our position, the position of the church that must not forget it is called by its origins to die shivering in the cold.[382]

This sort of writing has obvious parallels with Bonhoeffer's work on costly, as opposed to cheap, grace. Grace, like conscientization, is a costly process: to put it starkly, we cannot get to Easter Sunday without first going through the tragedy and darkness of Good Friday. Easter brings us great hope and a new vision, but only for those who are prepared to sacrifice their selfish desires, and take seriously God's

---

[381] Freire, "Conscientizing as a Way of Liberating," in Hennelly (ed.), *Liberation Theology*, 12.

[382] Ibid., 13.

commands to love him, and to show that love in their love for their neighbor.

However, before we get carried away with Freire's utopianism, we need to exercise a little caution, as his utopia takes very little account of the darker side of human nature.[383] It often seems that as soon as people are released from oppression, they – contrary to all history – will not oppress others. This is idealistic, and not what traditional Catholicism teaches. Freire does seek to look briefly at the complexity of the oppressed who are also oppressors in his response to *Mentoring the Mentor*, but it seems that all is needed is more teaching so that the oppressed oppressor becomes less incomplete, and engages in "the search for coherence."[384]

Theology, especially liberation theology, has a difficult balancing act to perform here. On the one hand, it insists on the preferential option for the poor, and expects a "class struggle," but, on the other, that class struggle:

> is meant to fight against the oppressors' power and blindness . . . Class struggle *calls the oppressors to conversion*. But it does not and may not threaten them with hatred or death without contradicting its own principles and purpose.[385]

However, on reading *A Theology of Liberation*, we can see that Gutiérrez is keenly aware of the biblical texts that condemn those who by their unjust actions, cause poverty. "They are not merely allusions to situations; the finger is pointed at those who are to blame."[386] Gutiérrez gives three main reasons why poverty is given such a "vigorous repudiation": it "contradicts the very meaning of the *Mosaic religion*," it goes "against *the mandate of Genesis*,"

> And finally, humankind not only has been made in the image and likeness of God; it is also *the sacrament of God* . . . In a word, the existence of poverty represents a sundering both of solidarity among persons and also of communion with God. Poverty is an expression of a sin, that is, of a negation of love. It is therefore imcompatible with the coming of the Kingdom of God, a Kingdom of love and justice.[387]

---

[383] See John L. Elias, *Paulo Freire: Pedagogue of Liberation* (Malabar, Fla: Krieger, 1994), 56–9.

[384] Paulo Freire, "A Response," in Freire (ed.), *Mentoring the Mentor*, 312.

[385] Cadorette, *From the Heart*, 111, emphasis added.

[386] Gutiérrez, *A Theology of Liberation*, 167.

[387] Ibid., 167–8.

So Gutiérrez is calling for a "recovery of a more authentic and radical witness of poverty," and it is clear from the above that he has a biblical mandate for his line of attack – a mandate, moreover, that comes from both Testaments.[388]

The Preferential Option

It is uncomfortable for us to hear about a preferential option for the poor, especially when, in worldwide terms, we are so wealthy. Surely God has no favorites – no class enemies? True, but he hates and punishes injustice, even in his own people. The story of the Old Testament is the story of a people who were oppressed by another people, and so were set free to go (eventually) to their own land. But in that land they failed to keep God's commandments. Even when they did not actively oppress the poor, they were prepared to neglect and ignore them, to shove them out of the way. Ezekiel tells us that not only were the shepherds of his people at fault, but the fault lines lay even among the people themselves: "I myself [says the Lord God] will judge between the fat sheep and the lean sheep. Because you pushed with flank and shoulder, and butted at all the weak animals with your horns until you scattered them far and wide, I will save my flock . . . and I will judge between sheep and sheep" [Ezek. 34:20–22]. The poor will be uplifted, and the rich sent empty away.

> The biblical explanation of Sodom's destruction provides an illustration of this terrible truth. If asked why Sodom was destroyed, virtually all Christians would point to the city's gross sexual perversity. But that is a one-sided recollection . . . Ezekiel shows that one important reason God destroyed Sodom was that it stubbornly refused to share with the poor: "Behold, this was the guilt of your sister Sodom: She and her daughters had pride, surfeit of food, and prosperous ease, but did not aid the poor and needy. They were haughty and did abominable things before me; therefore I removed them, when I saw it" (Ezekiel 16:49–50).
>
> This text does not say that they oppressed the poor. It simply accuses them of failing to assist the needy.

---

[388] See ibid., 165–71. This chapter will inevitably concentrate on liberation theology and its approach to the poor. I hope enough has been said in the first half of the book to show that none of the theologians discussed here would be happy with the current situation regarding the poor and the Two-Thirds World.

Affluent Christians remember Sodom's sexual misconduct and forget her sinful unconcern for the poor. Is it because the former is less upsetting? Have we allowed our economic self-interest to distort our interpretations of scripture? Undoubtedly. But precisely to the extent that our affirmation of scriptural authority is sincere, we will permit painful texts to correct our thinking. As we do, we will acknowledge that the God of the Bible wreaks horrendous havoc on the rich. But it is not because God does not love rich persons. It is because the rich regularly oppress the poor and neglect the needy.[389]

So the rich have a problem. We have a problem. How do we sort it? By yet another big push? Or by piecemeal progress? Utopian dreams are all very well, but have yet to come to pass. Piecemeal progress, by its very nature, happens on a small scale, and is less "headline grabbing." Big pushes, simply by dint of the fact that it has big money behind it, is top-down ("we will tell you how you are going to improve your lives and prospects"), while piecemeal progress has to be led from the ground up. It relies on people in the situation reacting against that situation, and being determined to do something about it, that does not in itself rely on a dependency culture.

But we all depend on God. Yes, but if we are to pray "your kingdom come on earth as it is in heaven," are we not to work for it as well? This might be simplistic, but there is a grain of truth in the old adage that we need to pray as if it is all down to God, but work as if it is all down to us. Or (to be Hauerwasian for a moment), it is not our job to make history come out right; it is our job to do the right thing whatever the result.

Paternalism, Education and the Poor

It is not always going to be easy to change attitudes. If we have been trying to make poverty history for centuries, then another "big push," however well-meaning, will not turn things around. If poor countries and poor people keep being told that they must change domestic policy in line with what the World Bank, or the International Monetary Fund says (as if the Federal Reserve could or should tell California (say) how to sort out its energy crisis, or its disaster policy), each time there is a difficulty, that they must wait until the rich nations bail them out, then they

---

[389] Ronald J. Sider, "Is God Really On the Side of the Poor?" in *Sojourners on the Issues: Christians and Poverty* (Washington DC: Sojourners, 2006), 24 (see www.sojo.net).

are going to resent the situation, or shrug their shoulders and assume that the situation does not lie in their hands at all, or both.

If we return, briefly, to the work of Paulo Freire, I can illustrate what I mean. Freire's methods faced criticism, often from those they were intended to help, because they have "internalized" their oppression so effectively that the poor assume that they are totally ignorant,[390] and (in a school situation) if a teacher asks the students "to co-develop the class with her or him, the students often doubt that this is 'real' education."[391] The students are so indoctrinated with how education ought to be done to them, that they find it difficult to visualize how a different approach to their schooling could be appropriate. In the USA, there is also an education system that fails to meet the needs of the poor. While some have argued that the poor have "power" not to cooperate with the dominant structures in society, this "power" does not seem to improve the lot of the poor themselves. An example of this attitude can be found in Donaldo Macedo's article in *Mentoring the Mentor*. He tells us of a colleague who addressed a conference along the lines that

> community people don't need to go to college because, since they know so much more than do members of the university community, there is little that the university can teach them. While making such public statements, this colleague was busily moving from the inner city to an affluent suburb, making sure that her children attend better schools.[392]

This "false generosity of paternalism" ensures that any power the oppressed holds, is of a completely inferior league to the power and "cultural capital" of the better educated. In reality the power of the poor is really only power to sabotage,[393] or to drop out,[394] which, in the end only leads to a perpetuation of the oppressed state. In the first case, the "students see their future already in their present, a life of squalor, disregard, going nowhere" so they find no motivation for cooperating with

---

[390] Freire discusses this "self-depreciation" in *Pedagogy of the Oppressed*, 38–9.

[391] Ira Shor, "Education is Politics," 29.

[392] Donaldo Macedo, "An Anti-Method Pedagogy: A Freirean Perspective," in Paulo Freire (ed.), *Mentoring the Mentor: A Critical Dialogue with Paulo Freire* (New York: P. Lang, 1997), 6.

[393] For a discussion of this "power" in US schools, see Freire and Shor, *A Pedagogy for Liberation*, 123–9.

[394] For a discussion on this (again in a US context), see Michelle Fine, "Silencing and Nurturing Voice in an Improbable Context: Urban Adolescents in Public School," in Henry A. Giroux and Peter L. McLaren (eds.), *Critical Pedagogy*,

an alienating system.[395] In the second case, the students are reacting to an imposed culture of silence, but even those who fled the school system "with resistance, energy, and vision" were "silenced, withdrawn, and depressed by age twenty-two."[396] In other words, what we have from a Freirean perspective, is a self-perpetuating system where the elite, for all they may say they wish things to change, make sure that most things stay the same whether or not one lives in Latin America.

> From a democratic point of view, Freire sees society controlled by an elite which imposes its culture and values as the standard. In schooling, this imposed standard is transferred by required syllabuses, mandated textbooks, tracking, and standardized exams . . . After years in passive classrooms, students do not see themselves as people who can transform society.[397]

It would be difficult to find a more accurate, and more succinct, summary of Freire's politico-pedagogical approach. Students trained at school to be passive in class tend to remain passive as oppressed adults. As Freire has said "[a]ny educational practice based on standardization . . . on routine . . . is bureaucratizing and thus anti-democratic."[398] If people do not believe that they can make a difference, it is difficult to see how they could be persuaded to take part in the democratic process, or, for that matter, any self-improving process. And this, I assert, applies to Make Poverty History as well in so far as it tries to continue any sort of paternalism, any sort of "we know better," when we clearly do not. Despite our best efforts,

> Almost three billion people live on less than two dollars a day . . . Eight hundred and forty million people in the world don't have enough to eat. Ten million children die every year from easily preventable diseases. AIDS is killing three million people a year and is still spreading. One billion

---

(cont.) *the State, and Cultural Struggle* (Albany: State University of New York Press, 1989), 152–73. Fine points out that this "power" merely reinforces, for another generation, the lack of opportunity for the poor of the community.

[395] Freire and Shor, *A Pedagogy for Liberation*, 128. The better off students are still alienated, but "playing by the rules in an elite school can pay off in your future" (ibid.).

[396] Fine, "Silencing and Nurturing Voice," 169.

[397] Shor, "Education is Politics," 28.

[398] Freire and Faundez, *Learning to Question*, 41.

people in the world lack access to clean water; two billion lack access to sanitation.[399]

Learning from History

Clearly what has been done before and not worked should not be tried again in the same situation. On the other hand, doing nothing is not an option. For Paulo Freire, members (and leaders) of the church cannot wash their hands of the conflict between oppressed and oppressor, lest they side themselves with the oppressor. "The illusion that suggests it is possible, by means of sermons, humanitarian works, and the encouragement of otherworldly values, to change men's consciousness and thereby transform the world exists only in those we term naïve."[400] The naïve must go through an apprenticeship of "their own Easter" during which

> they die as elitists so as to be resurrected on the side of the oppressed . . . Such a process implies a renunciation of myths that are dear to them: the myth of their superiority, of their purity of soul, of their virtues, their wisdom, the myth that they save the poor, the myth of the neutrality of the church, of theology, education, science, technology, the myth of their own impartiality . . .
>
> They will also discover to what extent their idealism had confused any number of concepts – for example, "conscientization" . . . when they tried to offer magic remedies for healing the hearts of mankind without changing the social structures, or, equally idealistic, when they claimed that conscientization was a similarly magic means of reconciling the irreconcilable.[401]

Freire parallels this sort of idealism with the moralistic position Reinhold Niebuhr condemned "whether it be found in the religious or the secular domain."[402] None of us has the right to moral superiority. But if none of us can dictate the terms under which we will help the poor, are we supposed to give them the money and let them get on with it any which way they can?

---

[399] See William Easterly, *The White Man's Burden: Why the West's Efforts to Aid the Rest Have Done So Much Ill and So Little Good* (Oxford: Oxford University Press, 2006), 7.

[400] Freire, *The Politics of Education*, 122.

[401] Ibid., 122–3.

[402] Referred to in ibid., 124.

By no means. According to Professor Easterly (whose book I have quoted above), the problem with the big projects is precisely the lack of accountability – along with, all too often, dealing with corrupt governments and officials. All too often, lofty goals are set for the medium- to long-term future, with no feedback loop of accountability: who will lose their job if the Millennium Development Goals are not met? Who would lose their bonus? The Millennium Development Goals (MDGs) are very worthy.

> The eight MDGs for 2015 are (1) eradicate extreme poverty and hunger, (2) achieve universal primary-school enrolment, (3) promote gender equality and empower women, (4) reduce child mortality, (5) improve maternal health, (6) combat HIV/AIDS, malaria, and other diseases, (7) ensure environmental sustainability, and (8) develop a global partnership for development.[403]

These are indeed wonderful goals, but somewhat nebulous: how are we going to know if and when they have been achieved? If we "promote gender equality" but women are (say) still doing two-thirds of the manual labor in the Two-Thirds World, do we still say we have done our promotion so we have reached the goal? And who will "carry the can" for this if they are not met? After all (Prof. Easterly again):

> A UN summit in 1990, for example, set as a goal for the year 2000 universal primary-school enrolment. (That is now planned for 2015.) A previous summit, in 1977, set 1990 as the deadline for realising the goal of universal access to water and sanitation. (Under the Millennium Development Goals, that target is now 2015.) Nobody was held accountable for these missed goals.[404]

A Culture Shift

And yet, there has been a culture shift. In 1977, or 1990, was there a mass movement in the developed world, the West, advocating the eradication of poverty? It is not so long ago that middle-class Christians were blinded by their upbringing, their political culture (remember Thatcher and Reagan?) that, even when they were aware of the iniquities around them, they tended to assume that there was nothing to be

---

[403] Easterly, *White Man's Burden*, 8.
[404] Ibid., 9.

done about it. Research undertaken by Christian Aid in 1993 exposed a lack of interest in poverty by church members, and if church members did think about poverty "they were quick to blame it on the victim."[405] However, there has been a culture shift in Christian thinking. Following the year of Make Poverty History, in September to October 2006, there was a month of action to remind the leaders of the West that there were people (voters!) out there watching and expecting them to deliver on the promises they made during that year (and especially at the G8 summit in July 2005). For a twenty-four hour time period from 11a.m. Sunday, October 15 to 11a.m. Monday, October 16, 2006 (British Summer Time),

> there was a global attempt to set an official Guinness World record for the largest number of people ever to Stand Up Against Poverty in 24 hours. The record was smashed by 23.5 million people (23,542,614 to be exact) ... with Guinness World Records spokesperson Craig Glenday saying: "By the time we get all the figures in it will be the largest single coordinated movement of people in the history of the Guinness World Records". . .
>
> In Johannesburg, Kumi Naidoo, spokesperson for the Global Call to Action Against Poverty said: 'Ordinary people around the world have stood up to express their passion to end poverty. Together, we have sent a clear message to our political leaders that we are going to keep pushing them to deliver on aid, on debt cancellation, on trade justice and to provide good and accountable governments. The people's voices are growing louder. We will not rest until poverty is ended.[406]

In other words, for all there is criticism, rightly, of the West's often patronizing and patriarchal attitudes, there is pressure that will not go away. Tom Allen warned that "the next big collective campaigning moment for the Global Call to Action Against Poverty will be in June/July 2007, when Germany hosts the G8 and we reach the halfway point of the Millennium Development Goals."[407] Of course, what is notable about Make Poverty History, like the Jubilee 2000 campaign before it, is that the impetus came from ordinary Christians determined to make a difference. Both campaigns unite people of any faith or none, but there is a faith agenda here underlying the hard-nosed politics.

---

[405] Cited in Ann Morisy, *Beyond the Good Samaritan* (London: Mowbray, 1997), 73.

[406] Email communication from Tom Allen, Campaigns and Media Officer, British Overseas NGOs for Development (BOND), October 20, 2006.

[407] Ibid.

Fair or Free Trade

Two hundred years ago, this mixture of politics and faith was a success-ful one in tackling the slave trade (see the later chapter in this book):

> The Christian campaigners were not naive idealists and were not afraid to appeal to British interests – Clarkson wrote a major work on the "impolicy" of the trade, and the Evangelical James Stephen eventually persuaded Parliament that dismantling the Atlantic slave trade would undermine the colonial power of Britain's rivals, especially France.[408]

If this political action worked two hundred years ago (and tackling slav-ery was taken step by step: first the trade was abolished, and then the institution of slavery was dealt with over twenty years later), it could work now: you will do more and better trade with people who have money and resources and who know they are on a level playing field, than with people who are barely scraping a living, and who cannot trade anyway because Western trade rules are biased in favor of their own products.[409] And so, "[j]ust as eighteenth-century Britons learned that their consumption of sugar sustained the slave economy, so we need to see that our consumer choices can contribute to the exploitation of the world's poor,"[410] and take appropriate action: is what we buy fairly traded, do the farmers who grew the products in the Two-Thirds World get a fair price?

> After oil, what is the world's most traded and, therefore, valuable com-modity? The answer, coffee, surprises many people, not least the coffee farmers of Africa and Latin America who find themselves at the bottom of global systems heavily weighted in favour of the developed world and the trans-national companies who dominate its trade.
>
> José Juarez Varela is a member of a Mexican coffee farming co-opera-tive which supplies Cafédirect – the fairly traded coffee found in almost every UK supermarket. Ask him about the benefits of the fair trade

---

[408] John Coffey, "The Abolition of the Slave Trade: Christian Conscience and Political Action," *Cambridge Papers* 15.2 (June 2006), 2.

[409] When the European Union spends $2 per day on each cow, and yet expects to be allowed into (say) the Kenyan cattle market, when African countries can-not afford such largesse, then it is difficult to see such trade as fair, even when it is defined as "free." See "Why More Free Trade Won't Help Africa: EPAs Through The Lens Of Kenya": *Traidcraft*, 2005, www.traidcraft.co.uk

[410] Coffey, "The Abolition of the Slave Trade," 6.

approach and he answers without hesitation. "The guaranteed price we are paid goes directly into the hands of the producer and that money is used for the product, to improve the nutrition of children, to send them to school, to improve conditions in the community and, in general, to dignify their lives."[411]

Fairly traded goods, not just coffee, are now available at most supermarkets in the UK, and even when they are slightly more expensive than other goods, they are selling. It remains to be seen how far such "consumer pester power" will go in the USA. As John Coffey notes, the abolitionist "Clarkson and his allies succeeded because they produced compelling evidence of the cruelty of the trade, evidence presented to Parliament in a famous report and relayed to a wide audience in harrowing narratives of human suffering."[412]

Religion and Aid

Perhaps Easterly would not be so depressed if he was prepared to take account of the Christian basis of such movements as Make Poverty History, but the ignoring of such a basis could be symptomatic of "the sheer prejudice of many secular thinkers . . . [that] any reflection informed by religious claims cannot possibly be serious."[413] Unfortunately, secular thinkers are often given a lot of ammunition by the very people who are trying to "get results" by religious means. "When the U.S. Congress passed Bush's fifteen-billion-dollar AIDS program . . . in May 2003, it placed a restriction that no more than 20 percent of the funds be spent on [cheap] prevention, while 55 percent was allocated for [expensive] treatment." This was bad enough, in terms of helping people on the ground: prevention is always better than cure. Besides which, the treatments only extend life; they don't cure the disease. This is a brutal fact, but it is true, and in Africa it is often difficult to maintain the supply of the required drugs, and ensure that people take them. However, Congress went one better.

> In a fit of religious zealotry, Congress also required organisations receiving funds to publicly oppose prostitution. This eliminates effective organisations

---

[411] See Peter Collins "Correcting the balance," *Traidcraft*, February 2006, www.traidcraft.co.uk

[412] Coffey, "The Abolition of the Slave Trade," 2.

[413] Stanley Hauerwas, *Against the Nations* (Minneapolis: Winston Press, 1985), 26.

that take a pragmatic and compassionate approach to understanding the factors that drive women into prostitution. Programs that condemn prostitutes are unlikely to find a receptive audience when they try to persuade those prostitutes to avoid risky behaviour.[414]

With such examples of religious correctness, it is unsurprising that there are those who do not wish to accept that "any reflection informed by religious claims cannot possibly be serious." We also have many problems facing us in tackling poverty: big pushes, as I have noted, have been tried before. No "top-down" approach that does not take into account what Bonhoeffer called "the view from below" will work.[415] But never before has there been such a popular movement pushing Western leaders into action. There is more than "top-down" leader, or Western led aid. There is "bottom-up" activism as well, but this needs to address one issue in particular (and one that I have noted above).

Victim Mentality

It is, to use Freire's phrase, the "partial penetration" of the poor by the ideology of the "oppressors." Partial penetration of the poor occurs when the poor are so oppressed (or so used to the situation) in which they find themselves that they cannot conceive of any way of improving or changing their situation – they often feel that they "deserve" their poverty. This can be expressed in opposition by the poor to any attempts to conscientize, or help them to help themselves. An alternative way of looking at it is to say that the poor develop a "victim mentality" and think that only "the kindness of strangers" will help them: that the solution is not in their own hands.

Of course, many of the poor decide to accommodate themselves to the *status quo*. Liberation theologians, such as Gutiérrez, often seem to make the rich and poor "two antagonistic, irreconcilable social groups"[416] whereas the reality is more complex. There is often a

---

[414] Easterly, *White Man's Burden*, 225. However, British lawmakers can be equally obtuse. See the chapter on slavery.

[415] As I have noted in the chapter on Bonhoeffer, his approach was nearer noblesse oblige than "power to the people," but nonetheless, as I shall try to show in this chapter, no successful approach is entirely top-down, or bottom up. The Make Poverty History movement might be "people power" but to affect the Two-Thirds World it requires action on the part of Western leaders.

[416] Cadorette, *From the Heart*, 57.

"middle class" that mediates the dominant, capitalist structure to the poor.[417] And there are, of course, those few poor people who "make it" in the capitalist society, even if for most it is a struggle to survive. The ultimate paradox is that any struggle to overcome the system (in this case one that has left a few countries rich, and many poor – even while those rich countries still have poor people living within them) has to exist alongside the accommodations made by the very same poor people with that system as they seek to provide daily necessities for their families.

So it is this "partial penetration" that needs to be addressed. "It is getting increasingly clear that one of the root causes of Africa's problems is inside the minds of the African people," says Serah Wambua. Serah heads up CMS Africa's work with the Samaritan Strategy, which inspires African Christians to meet the needs of their communities with no need for outside help.[418] The church in Africa, according to the Hope for Africa program, "has largely failed to demonstrate the intentions and love of God outside church walls."[419] However, just as things are changing, led by inspired Christians in the West, things are also changing in Africa. "Seed Projects" are now being set up where churches use their own and the community's resources to show that love of God. "Even in the poorest countries, God has provided resources that can be discovered and used."[420]

> While serving as a church pastor, Luke [Jakoywa] got the challenge to pay attention to the social needs that were glaring in his face whenever he walked through the community. Many children roamed idly on the streets, men spent their time drinking, and women eked a livelihood out of making local brew.
>
> Luke decided he would do something to help the community.
>
> Shortly after that he attended Vision Conference 2002, organised by Samaritan Strategy and CMS. Luke was excited to discover that many other people shared his vision for holistic ministry.[421]

---

[417] Ibid., 57–8.

[418] Quoted in *Inspire* magazine, December 2006 (London: CPO Publishing), 21. www.inspiremagazine.org.uk Also see webarchive.cms-uk.org/news/2006/ hope_for_africa_131006.htm (accessed December 9, 2006).

[419] Quoted in *Inspire*, December 2006, 21. www.inspiremagazine.org.uk.

[420] Serah Wambua in ibid., 22.

[421] webarchive.cms-uk.org/eshorts/eshorts160905.html (accessed December 9, 2006).

So street children and AIDS orphans were offered a place, and an education, at the Sheepcare Community Centre in Nairobi which opened its doors in 2002. Luke says, "I realized that the children need love and understanding, not just schooling – they had been exposed to a lot of suffering."[422] Other projects in the slums of Africa "have consisted of collecting garbage and recycling it into compost, tiles, fuel briquettes and fence posts."[423]

Other new ways of helping people help themselves, different from old-fashioned handouts, include loans. These are not the bilateral (government to government) or multilateral (generally IMF or World Bank) loans that have caused so many problems for poor countries, but small loans to small businesses in developing countries where the whole enterprise is run by people on the ground, not far away in another country. One such organization, which raises funds in both the UK and the USA, is Five Talents. It gives loans of about £100/$150 to enable budding entrepreneurs to lift themselves and others out of poverty. According to its website:

> Microfinance initiatives support small businesses. Through training and small loans, Five Talents helps to establish and nurture small businesses. Training in business skills combines with loans – for stock, equipment, raw materials, land, premises etc. – to help establish grocers, hairdressers, bakers, brick-makers, shoe-repairers . . . This tackles poverty bottom up. Each business builds economic independence for the individual entrepreneur, their families and the families of those they employ. Employment and independence bring dignity. Five Talents creates jobs to fight poverty.
>
> Microenterprise development is an efficient and effective method for fighting poverty and raising entrepreneurs in developing countries. By contrast, top-down grant programmes often lead to dependency. Micro-loans programmes maintain ownership and responsibility with the entrepreneur – significantly enhancing the success rate. Since the loan capital is constantly revolving to other entrepreneurs, it is an extremely cost-effective method of micro-enterprise development.[424]

As an organization, still less than ten years old, "Five Talents International has provided funding for technical assistance and thousands of small loans to entrepreneurs in 12 countries in Africa, Central

---

[422] Ibid.

[423] Quoted in *Inspire*, December 2006, 22.

[424] www.fivetalents.org.uk/whatwedo.php

and South America, and Asia."[425] It is no free ride for the people it
seeks to help. Like the demands of accountability at government level
advocated by the Make Poverty History movement, microfinance initiatives insist on strict (often monthly) reports and will make on-site
visits to the enterprises it supports. This has in turn helped to ensure
that over 85 percent of its loans are repaid, so that more people can be
helped. People work in groups, so that a loan will go not to one individual, but to a group of people who wish to set up their own (different) projects.

> Local banks cannot afford to lend small sums of money to many entrepre-
> neurs who have little or no collateral. The risks are too high.
>
> But Group-lending is a proven methodology of micro-enterprise devel-
> opment. Groups are normally formed of 5–10 people who self-select each
> other. Each member of the group co-guarantees the loans of the others.
> This peer pressure ensures high repayment rates, averaging 85–100%. The
> group method also reduces the costs of loan administration, monitoring
> and follow-up.[426]

So, can it work? Let me quote one example from the work in the
Philippines:

> In the year 2000, Five Talents helped to establish a Micro-Enterprise
> Development programme in the community of Cainta in the slums of
> Manila. By the end of 2005 this programme had helped more than 1,500
> poor families begin to break the cycle of poverty! With a 99.4 percent
> repayment rate on four loan cycles, this has been a remarkable investment
> in the poor. In 2001, the programme expanded to incorporate the Taguig
> community and this has also helped hundreds of families to start and
> grow in business.[427]
>
> Reuben is a father of 5 children. He used his successive loans to buy the
> ownership of his motorbike rickshaw. He has enjoyed the business train-
> ing that accompanies the loan programme. He now sells registration per-
> mits to other taxi-drivers to supplement his family income.[428]

Of course, this method of aiding communities is slow. It relies on people
who are not sunk into the dependency or victim culture – in another

---

[425] Ibid.

[426] www.fivetalents.org.uk/whatwedo.php

[427] www.fivetalents.org.uk/programmesphillipines.php

[428] Ibid.

context, these people would be seen as the "organic intellectuals" who operated in the Base Ecclesial Communities – and it does not necessarily capture the headlines. Nor does it always work. If over 85 percent of the loans are repaid, this means that up to 15 percent of them are not. Whether a commercial bank would stand such losses in the Two-Thirds World from people who are at the bottom of the economic ladder is a moot point to say the least; so there are tensions inherent in such a process.

"There will be No One in Need Among You":[429] The Eschatological Tension

The liberation theologians (discussed above) have been accused of being too this worldly in their approach to eschatology. They have been overly wishful in their description of the new humanity that has overcome oppression. Perhaps a bit of Augustinian realism, or cynicism, might be appropriate in looking at the intractable nature of world poverty. But then a cynic, as Oscar Wilde noted, knows the price of everything and the value of nothing. Human life and well-being are always worth more than we are prepared to give; and Paulo Freire is nothing if not passionate as he proclaims his "utopian theology of hope":

> The utopian posture of the denouncing, announcing, historically committed Christians who are convinced that the historical vocation of humankind is not to adapt, not to bend to pressures, not to spend 90 percent of their time making concessions in order to salvage what we call the historical vocation of the church. We humans have an unbelievable historical vocation, and we cannot jeopardize it for any one fact, nor can we compromise it for any single, isolated problem, because the church has the whole world.[430]

In the same vein, Christians in the Make Poverty History movement will be all too aware that past promises have come to nothing. They will have noted that the former (unlamented) US ambassador to the UN, John Bolton, submitted 750 amendments to a UN summit to derail the commitment to the Millennium Development Goals to halve world poverty by 2015 – so what price the promises the USA made at the G8 summit in July 2005? However,

---

[429] Deut. 15:4
[430] Freire, "Conscientizing as a Way of Liberating," in Hennelly (ed.), *A Documentary History*, 8.

they will also have noted that the same John Bolton is no longer ambassador to the UN. There are always signs of hope: the "now" side of the eschatological tension; but there are always, also, those who gainsay, those who think it cannot, will not, be done. These serve as a reminder of the "not yet" side of that tension. We know that the Israelites were told, on their entry to the Promised Land, that there should be "no one in need among you," and yet the words of Jesus tell us that "you will always have the poor among you . . . "[431] This does not mean we do not serve the poor as our neighbors, our brothers and sisters in Christ; but we must remember that these are the people who "have a mysterious place in the purposes of God."[432]

If a Poor Person . . . Comes In:[433] The Ecclesiological Tension

But how are we to behave toward these people with this "mysterious place"? Make Poverty History, Trade Justice and other movements have made small but significant differences to the political agenda. But it remains to be seen how far middle-class, non-marginalized Christians are prepared to go in having their own "habitus . . . educational background . . . [and] possibly even one's acquired coherent and systematic view of the world"[434] disturbed by contact with the marginalized.

For Freire, the church stands as a witness in terms of how it educates its congregation to stand with the oppressed. This political stance will provoke a reaction, and is therefore a test for the church: will its leaders, its "committed intellectuals . . . retreat, keep quiet, [and] adjust to the situation," or will they "react by taking on new commitments?"[435] Freire expects many to belong to the former camp, but praises those in the latter.[436] These for Freire, are the committed, prophetic Christians, but let us not be naïve: when the church does act alongside the marginalized, then there will be opposition from those who do well out of the *status quo*. Gutiérrez, in response to this (and speaking from a situation where "opposition" goes up to and includes, martyrdom), refers to the Beatitudes, specifically Matthew 5:10–11 (and Lk. 6:22).

---

[431] Jn. 12:8

[432] Morisy, *Good Samaritan*, 34.

[433] Jas. 2:2.

[434] Peter Mayo, "Gramsci, Freire, and Radical Adult Education: A Few 'Blind Spots'," *Humanity and Society* 18 (1994) 90.

[435] Freire, *The Politics of Education*, 128. For this section , see my "Base Ecclesial Communities and Community Ministry," in *Political Theology* 5.4 (2004) 462.

[436] Freire, *The Politics of Education*, 128–9.

Matthew [therefore] prepares the way for the surprising identification in chapter 25 between love-inspired actions done for the poor and actions done for the son of man . . . To give one's life for the sake of justice is to give it for Christ himself.[437]

Here, of course, is the rub: not many people wish to be persecuted but, as noted above, the call of the church is still "to die shivering in the cold."[438] But if we are to die, what message will we have for those who watch, and those with whom we die?

"Mourning and Crying and Pain will be no More":[439] The Prophetic Tension

In *The Power of the Poor in History*, Gutiérrez points out that:

> The prophets proclaim a reign of peace. But peace presupposes the establishment of justice . . . The conquest of poverty and abolition of exploitation are signs of the Messiah's arrival and presence . . . To work for a just world where there is no servitude, oppression, or alienation is to work for the advent of the Messiah.[440]

This working for a just world has to be undertaken without demanding that God must act – or that he must act in a particular way. In an odd sort of way, despite the vivid word pictures of Revelation 21 and other passages, we proclaim a reign without knowing exactly what it will look like. Which is perhaps why this tension is so acute: what are the precise steps we should use to move the world toward the poverty-free goal? However, if the church becomes (or remains) fearful of the change that political action will bring, it "badly loses its way." As a consequence, "[i]t can no longer test itself, either through the denunciation of the unjust world, or the annunciation of a more just world to be built by the historical-social praxis of the oppressed."[441] We must note that not even Paulo Freire says this world will be just – but hopefully it will be more just than the one we leave behind.

---

[437] Gutiérrez, *The God of Life*, 128.

[438] Freire, "Conscientizing as a Way of Liberating," 13.

[439] Rev. 21:4.

[440] Gutiérrez, *The Power of the Poor*, 32.

[441] Freire, *The Politics of Education*, 127.

Conclusion

So, something must be done – without trying to make history come out right. It is our job to do what is right. What is right is to love our poor neighbor, and give them the best. As the Archbishop of Canterbury put it:

> "the poorest deserve the best": when you hear that, I wonder if you can take in just how revolutionary it is. They do not deserve what's left over when the more prosperous have had their fill, or what can be patched together on a minimal budget as some sort of damage limitation. And they don't "deserve" the best because they've worked for it and everyone agrees they've earned it. They deserve it simply because their need is what it is and because where human dignity is least obvious it's most important to make a fuss about it.[442]

---

[442] The Archbishop of Canterbury's Christmas Sermon, December 2006. See www.archbishopofcanterbury.org/sermons_speeches/061225.htm.

Seven

Slavery

Biblical "Acceptance" to Modern Anathema?

A Bicentenary

This year, 2007 is the bicentenary of the passing of William Wilberforce's Act abolishing the slave trade in the British Empire. Given Wilberforce's Christian commitment, this is an event that Christians, and others, are seeking to commemorate. However, there is a problem. Slavery isn't dead. One estimate puts the numbers of those held in slavery world-wide at 12 million:[443] whether this slavery is due to sex trafficking, or bonded labor, we still have a major lack of humanity to our fellow human beings when we allow one person to have ownership rights over another. As John Wesley put it:

> Give liberty to whom liberty is due, that is, to every child of man, to every partaker of human nature. Let none serve you but by his own act and deed, by his own voluntary action. Away with all whips, all chains, all compulsion! Be gentle toward men; and see that you invariably do with every one as you would he should do unto you.

Of course, if we look back at the arguments raging 200 years ago, we find that the Bible is not necessarily as helpful as we might have hoped.[444] Indeed, in certain quarters (and, up until the late 1700s, this

---

[443] See Set All Free and Anti-Slavery International, *Act to End Slavery Now* (London: Anti-Slavery International and Churches Together in England, 2006), 3.

[444] For the following analysis, I am indebted to Willard M. Swartley, *Slavery, Sabbath, War and Women: Case Issues in Biblical Interpretation* (Scottdale, PA: Herald Press, 1983), 31–46.

was the majority opinion); it was argued that the Bible said nothing to condemn slavery as sinful.

As far as this argument went, slavery was "divinely sanctioned among the patriarchs." Not only can we consider Noah's curse upon Canaan, there is the slave-owning Abraham, and the story of Joseph who, in the famine, and acting under God's command, reduced the Egyptians to slavery under Pharaoh. Slavery, it was noted, was "incorporated into Israel's national constitution."[445] The laws of Moses allow Israelites to own foreign slaves in perpetuity, and even fellow Hebrews can sell themselves into slavery.

Finally, it was argued, slavery was recognized and approved by Jesus Christ: given that Jesus lived and worked surrounded by a slave-owning culture, it is remarkable that he said nothing against the practice. Further, the pro-slavery lobby looked to the apostolic writings to support their case.

The case went as follows: firstly, while the apostles may have disapproved of the abuses of slavery, they did not condemn the practice of slavery itself. The apostolic writings make it clear that the church has no authority to interfere with slavery as a political system. Also, as both slave-owners and slaves are addressed in the apostolic letters, it is clear that distinctions between master and slave are not an impediment to faith. Also, it is quite clear (to look no further than Philemon), that slave-holders were accepted and affirmed both as church members and as leaders. Citing 1 Corinthians 7:20–24, the pro-slavery argument pointed out that Paul made it clear that slaves should remain in their existing state. Also, in 1 Timothy 6:1–6 Paul declares his doctrine of slavery is based on "the words of our Lord Jesus Christ himself."[446] Therefore Christ backs slavery (and was not silent on the issue, even if the gospels do not record the words). And finally, the letter to Philemon shows that Paul fully supports slavery, by the fact that he is sending the runaway slave back to his owner.

Biblical scholars may well now be questioning the way in which these people have used their Bible. In fact, if you haven't already, it might be worth just looking at these texts to see what is said, and to see how you might rebut the arguments.[447] However, the abolitionists were themselves God-fearing men and women. They read the same Bible. And, against the above arguments, they made their case:

---

[445] Swartley, 33.

[446] See Swartley, 36.

[447] I did this exercise at the Partners in World Mission Conference, Derby, UK (October 30 to November 2, 2006). It was interesting to see that, given twenty minutes (and some encouragement) people were able to come up with the main points of the abolitionist argument from scripture.

[The abolitionists] succeeded because they produced compelling evidence of the cruelty of the trade, evidence presented to [the UK] Parliament in a famous report and relayed to a wide audience in harrowing narratives of human suffering. But . . . [t]o say that "abolitionists placed their hope not in sacred texts, but in human empathy" . . . is to divorce two things that Christian abolitionists wedded together, and to ignore the evidence of antislavery texts. If religious argument did not stir people to action, why did abolitionists give it so much space? For in publication after publication, critics of the slave trade quoted Scripture and rooted their campaign in Christian values and ideals.[448]

A summary of the abolitionist argument would look something like this.[449] The so-called slavery of the Patriarchs in no way justifies the system of [Negro] slavery. Canaan's descendants do not include the African peoples, so this text cannot be applied to them. Also, the servitude under Abraham "was a condition of privilege, including circumcision and the benefits of community, both religious and social."[450]

Moving from Genesis to Exodus, it was clear to the abolitionists that God's deliverance of Israel from slavery in Egypt demonstrated his hatred and condemnation of slavery. Also, while there were many similarities between Hebrew slavery in Egypt and Negro slavery in trans-Atlantic trade, there were also differences: for example, the Hebrews had their own land, possessions, and community. These differences showed that Hebrew slavery in Egypt was less onerous than the Negro one, yet God still acted to bring the Israelites out.

In a summary of the Mosaic slave laws, the abolitionists pointed out that Hebrew servitude in the time of Moses was voluntary, merciful, and of benefit to the servant. The slave could be redeemed at any time by a kinsman-redeemer; and, in the seventh year (and in the jubilee year), all slaves were to be freed – and with enough resources to be able to make their way in society. The Mosaic law provided that any runaway slave should not be returned to his or her "owner" – in order to protect slaves from oppressive masters. These were all points at which Hebrew slavery differed substantially from Negro slavery as it was practiced in the eighteenth century.

The abolitionists used every part of the Old Testament in their assertion that God would have condemned slavery had it existed. The history of the kings of Israel and Judah showed no trade in slaves. Solomon

---

[448] Coffey, "The Abolition of the Slave Trade", 366.

[449] Again, I am indebted to Swartley, *Slavery, Sabbath, War and Women*, 31–46.

[450] Ibid., 40.

may have used forced labor for the building of the Temple, but this was temporary – and his son's suggestion that he would make the Israelites work harder was one reason for the collapse of the Davidic Empire into the two kingdoms of Israel and Judah. Jeremiah told the people that one reason for their exile was the failure to grant the required freedom to their servants. If there was servitude in Old Testament Israel, it could not be seen as the same as slavery as practiced in the States (and elsewhere) in the eighteenth century.

Moving to the New Testament, the abolitionists flatly contradicted the pro-slavery argument: neither Jesus nor the apostles approved of or condoned slavery. If we are to argue from silence that Jesus was in favor of slavery, then, we must suppose "that he was favorable to the sports of the amphitheatre at Rome, or to the orgies which were celebrated in honor of Bacchus, or to the claims to inspiration of the oracles of Dodona or Delphi."[451]

Rhetoric aside, it is clear that all appeals to scripture (and, note, its interpretation) were contested. And hermeneutics played a significant part in the debate, as the way in which texts were read often depended on which side of the debate you stood. However, if we return to scripture, and Paul's letter to the slave-owner Philemon, a detailed analysis would show that, given the strictures placed on a small new religious sect, Paul's position was at best equivocal on slavery.[452] There are considerable hints in the text that Paul expects Philemon to treat Onesimus with leniency in an age when a runaway slave could expect severe punishment or even death on their return to their master. Also the requirement to see Onesimus as a brother (v. 16) would, in itself, undermine the whole master-slave relationship. However, although Paul "seems to have had at least some awareness of the incongruity of Christian masters owning Christian slaves, he was unable to make a general recommendation for their *manumission* [setting free]."[453] Given the fact that Roman and Greek culture at the time depended on slave-ownership, it would be implausible – to put it mildly – to see how Paul could have done otherwise than he did; if for no other reason than the fact that the wealthier members of the church would be unable to retain their "social status or their houses without ownership of slaves; and he and his churches depended on

---

[451] Quoted in Swartley, *Slavery, Sabbath, War and Women*, 44.

[452] For this section, I am indebted to John Barclay, "Paul, Philemon and the Dilemma of Christian Slave-Ownership," in *New Testament Studies* 37 (1992), 161–86.

[453] Ibid., 184.

such people as financial supporters and hosts of the Christian movement."[454]

As I have intimated above, there is a difference between the slavery discussed in scripture, and the slavery that the abolitionists faced. In the Roman world many slaves lived well compared with the "free" poor. A slave was worth keeping fit, housed, and well-fed – a system of security that the free poor did not have. Further, although ownership gave a person complete rights over the owned, the Roman *paterfamilias* had "rights," even of life and death, over his whole household (including his family) that we would reject now; and, of course, the whole concept of manumission was alien to nineteenth-century slave-owning society. Manumission was the process whereby a slave could buy, or be given their freedom; while it may well be the case that owners often granted manumission to serve their own interests. The price exacted would more than compensate for the loss of the ex-slave's service and could easily buy a new, younger, fitter slave; also, a freed slave might well still continue to be obliged to their former owner. However, a freed slave could do well in Roman society (there would be no legal barrier to such success) – and, within a generation, blend seamlessly into that society. This is clearly not the case for the descendants of those enslaved in the trans-Atlantic trade, even 200 years later.[455] The current Archbishop of York, John Sentamu, tells tales, from when he was working in London, of being stopped, or "pulled over" by the police, simply because of the color of his skin.

The abolitionists won the day back then; what were the Christian ideas behind their arguments? First was their conviction that all people were equal before God, being made in his image. The famous "logo" of the abolitionist movement showed a slave on his knees asking his owner "Am I not a man and a brother?" (There was also a female version, where the question was "Am I not a woman and a sister?") This belief in human unity across the bounds of race clashed sharply with the fashionable views of the day:

> early antislavery writers like James Ramsay and Granville Sharp repeatedly identified the theory of racial inferiority with Hume, Voltaire and materialistic philosophy in general; they explicitly presented their attacks on slavery as a vindication of Christianity, moral accountability, and the unity of mankind.[456]

---

[454] Ibid.

[455] For these points, see *The Anchor Bible Dictionary* Volume 6, 69–71.

[456] D.B. Davis, *Slavery and Human Progress* (Oxford: Oxford University Press, 1984) 130–6, quoted in John Coffey, "The Abolition of the Slave Trade," 3.

Indeed the black converts to Christianity were eloquent in their views: Olaudah Equiano,[457] commenting on one book that argued for racial inferiority of the African, wrote: "Oh fool! See the 17th chapter of the Acts, verse 26: 'God hath made of one blood all nations of men, for to dwell on all the face of the earth.' "[458]

The right to liberty also has Christian, not just Enlightenment, roots. The abolitionists saw themselves in the tradition of Jesus, who, in Luke 4, set out his manifesto, his mission statement. This statement includes (in Lk. 4:18): "he has sent me to proclaim release to the captives . . . to let the oppressed go free." The abolitionists made much of both Britain's "boasted love of liberty" and the American Declaration of Independence – with its line that "all men are created equal" – and set this against both country's enslavement of others. "The emancipation of slaves," the abolitionists argued, "was on the agenda of Jesus, and an outworking of his Gospel of the Kingdom."[459]

Christians of all hues were aware, or were supposed to be aware, of the Golden Rule of Matthew 7:12, "In everything do to others as you would have them do to you; for this is the law and the prophets." It took the nineteenth-century abolitionists to apply this to slavery; though not all went as far as Benjamin Ley who "even kidnapped a child (temporarily) from its slave-owning parents to help them see the distress their practice caused!"[460] In other words, "do as you would be done by" was applicable to slaves too.

Also, and more controversially for us today, the abolitionists recalled that the Lord God insisted: "Vengeance is mine." They were not afraid to discuss the idea of judgment on unrepentant sinners. While today, sin is often explained away, it would perhaps do nobody any harm to be reminded that no one is perfect, "since all have sinned and fall short of the glory of God" (Rom. 3:23): and that national sins have national consequences. In the UK, the big slave ports of Bristol and Liverpool were compared with the biblical Tyre and Sidon, whom God destroyed for their sins, their growing rich by, among other things, trafficking in humanity.[461]

The profoundly Christian character of the abolitionist movement constitutes a serious stumbling block for secular commentators who rail

---

[457] A freed slave and abolitionist campaigner along with Wilberforce.

[458] Quoted in ibid.

[459] Ibid.

[460] Ibid., 4. Coffey does not record if the parents changed their view of slavery following this incident.

[461] For more on these Christian motivations, see Coffey, 3–4.

against the "mixing of religion and politics." Yet, as the abolitionist movement illustrates, public religion has proved a powerful force for reform in Western society. In the last half-century, Christian churches made a vital contribution to the American Civil Rights Movement, the overthrow of Communist regimes in Eastern Europe and the fall of apartheid in South Africa. And this shows us that, in continuing the fight against slavery and trafficking, it is not good to pander to those who would indeed separate religion from politics. In other words, we need, especially in this case, to learn the correct lessons from history. The year 1807 was a milestone, and no one can or should seek to take away anything from Wilberforce and his fellow abolitionists; but, as they knew, the story would not end with the abolition of the slave trade.

It was a long fight – the British Parliament did not abolish slavery itself until 1833, and, in the US, President Abraham Lincoln did not move against slavery until the Civil War had broken out – and then the "Emancipation Proclamation" held that all slaves held in rebelling territory (only) were to be free from January 1, 1863. The Thirteenth Amendment to the Constitution that abolished slavery throughout the US was not ratified until 1865.

And the Picture Today

I begin this section with four stories or reports. The first three are from Set All Free, a body set up by Churches Together in England to coordinate the commemoration of the 1807 Act of Parliament. Its agenda is to encourage everyone to *remember* the past, *reflect* on what it means for us today (whether we are descended from abolitionists, slaves, slave owners or merely from those who failed to act), and to *respond* to the current situation of worldwide slavery:

> There are estimates that world- wide over 500,000 people are traded across international borders for the purposes of sexual exploitation. There are trafficked people within the swelling numbers of those who migrate across international borders to seek legitimate work, opportunities, safety and education. Source countries include the countries of the Commonwealth of Independent States (the former Soviet Union), West African, North African and Central African countries, India, Nepal, Thailand, Vietnam, China, South American countries and the Balkans. It is now estimated that trafficking in persons in general revenues more for international crime than the drugs industry, and it is certainly perceived as an easier crime to evade detection and prosecution. As the internet,

mobile phones, the leisure pound, and sexual leisure industries of the West continue to expand so this abusive trade in flesh will continue to develop unless a concerted sense of community responsibility and criminal justice accountability kicks into play.

[R]esearch has found that trafficked women, from countries including Albania, Moldova, Romania, Thailand and Nigeria have been forced to work as prostitutes in every London borough [UK]. The forced sexual labour is typically carried out in massage parlours, brothels and in people's homes, organised by a network of semi-independent pimps and profiteers who can sell on their victims several times, to maximise profitability and deter escape attempts. This form of modern day slavery is in all probability taking place in a city near you. The difficulty is it is so subterranean, violent and protected, that little is known of the real extent of this scourge to politicians, police or indeed parish priests.[462]

The second report tells a tale from India:

Sonali stands in a doorway . . . waiting. Stolen from her village she was then dragged, wide-eyed and innocent, to the back streets of Calcutta where she was sold into prostitution by a stranger. The first customer drugged and then raped her. She was just thirteen.

There is nothing glamorous about this place. Sonali is among the six thousand women who work in Sonagacchi, the oldest and largest of Calcutta's many sex districts serving twenty thousand men every day. Some women are paid as little as US20 cents per customer – just enough to buy a simple meal. Indian society shuns these women. They are branded "outcasts" for life. They didn't choose prostitution – it chose them . . .

Talk prostitution and people usually think sex. They think exploitation. They think AIDS. But really prostitution is about money – it's about BUSINESS.[463]

The third story comes from Russia:

Sergey is 27 years old and is from Perm in Russia. In 2001, he saw an advert in a local newspaper for a job agency. They were looking for construction workers to work in Spain. The salary offered was US$1,200 per

---

[462] www.setallfree.net/sexual_exploitation.html (accessed November 17, 2006).

[463] www.setallfree.net/prostitution.html (accessed November 17, 2006).

month. This was much more than his monthly salary of just $200 and more than he could ever hope to earn in Perm. He applied to the agency who booked his plane ticket to Madrid. They said he would need to pay back the money for the ticket when he started work. When he arrived in Spain, Sergey was picked up by a person from the "agency" who took his passport. He was taken to Portugal and forced to work on a construction site without pay for several months. The site was surrounded by barbed wire.

Without his passport he was afraid that the Portuguese authorities would arrest him. One day Sergey managed to escape and begged his way to Germany. Because he did not have a passport the German authorities arrested him. He says that the police beat him and took away what little money he had. Then they sent him back to Russia.

Now back home, Sergey is very traumatised by his experience. He suffered psychological problems and for several months was unable to work. He received no counselling or support to help him overcome his ordeal. Meanwhile his traffickers remain unpunished.[464]

Finally, a story from America, where "[t]he U.S. Central Intelligence Agency estimates that 50,000 people are trafficked into or transited through the U.S.A. annually as sex slaves, domestics, garment, and agricultural slaves."[465] "According to the research and advocacy group Free the Slaves, forced labor is largely concentrated in illegal or minimally regulated industries: nearly half of trafficking cases involve forced prostitution, about 27 percent involve domestic service, and manufacturing and farm work collectively account for approximately 15 percent."[466] Our story comes from Free The Slaves:

> In July of 2001 police responded to a domestic dispute call in San Diego County. When the police arrived they found Reina, a teenage Mexican girl who had been beaten and abandoned . . .
>
> Reina recounted that a kind man named Arturo approached her in Tijuana, Mexico, just across the border from San Diego. He took a clear interest in her and told her many sweet things. Reina wanted a boyfriend

---

[464] From Anti-Slavery International, quoted on www.setallfree.net/trafficking.html (accessed November 17, 2006).

[465] www.gvnet.com/humantrafficking/USA.htm (assessed November 17, 2006).

[466] See ibid.

who could provide for her and her infant son. It was not long before Reina's new boyfriend proposed to marry her. They would have to go to San Diego, though, where Reina would work in the job which her boyfriend promised he would arrange for her. Arturo said she would have to leave her child behind but that she shouldn't worry since he would register himself as the father. She agreed, believing that his safety would be ensured while she was away. Once in San Diego, however, Arturo changed completely. He forced Reina to have sex with strangers. She was horrified; this was not the work she expected to do. What she expected did not make any difference to Arturo and for four months he forced Reina to service 25–30 men a day in the remote gullies behind the strawberry fields of San Diego County.[467]

Three stories from around the world: all going to show that slavery is far from dead. That there are people prepared to exploit others. Such a situation would come as no surprise to Augustine: his strictures against the *libido dominandi* (the lust for mastery over others)[468] are such that he was, to say the least, equivocal about the idea of improving society (as I have noted above).[469] People were to be loved, their good desired; they were not to be "used." This, of course, along with our examination of scripture, has to be seen alongside Augustine's toleration of slavery. "Like St. Paul and all the Fathers of the Church, St. Augustine was more concerned to ennoble the existing relation between master and slave than to reconstruct the social order . . . "[470] As I have noted, there is, therefore, no evidence of a call to liberate the slaves. The fact that slaves often wanted for nothing while the poor-but-free could be seen begging for bread, meant that the "more serious social problem for Augustine was massive poverty."[471]

For Augustine, yes; for us, there is a link between both problems: had Reina not been poor, would she have been so easily trapped into sexual

---

[467] freetheslaves.net/slavery/reports/austin-choifitzpatrick (accessed November 17, 2006).

[468] See *DCD* 14:28: "In the earthly city, princes are as much mastered by the lust for mastery as the nations which they subdue are by them."

[469] He did, however, make clear in *DCD* 19:15 (and other places) that humanity was created to "have lordship" over the rest of creation, not over other people.

[470] van der Meer, *Augustine the Bishop*, 135.

[471] Robert Dodaro, "Eloquent Lies, Just Wars and the Politics of Persuasion: Reading Augustine's City of God in a 'Postmodern' World," *Augustinian Studies* 25 (1994), 113.

slavery by Arturo? It may be that her story has a reasonably happy ending: the police involvement led to her release from Arturo's clutches, but what scars – both physical and psychological – will she have for the rest of her life?

But, on the other hand, if slavery was practiced in Paul's, Augustine's, or Wilberforce's time; if there was such a campaign 200 years ago to eradicate it, and yet millions are still enslaved, why should we carry on? Why should we seek to change the unchangeable: if humanity was in the grip of *libido dominandi* 1600 years ago, and it clearly is still today, what can we do to change things? The first is to accept that we will always live in tension between the reality of the "is" and the prophetic scope of the "ought." That what is true in the end (that in Christ there is no slave or free), may be striven for in the here and now, and that the church still has its role to play in proclaiming the truth, the freedom of Christ.

In Christ there is Neither Slave Nor Free:[472] The Eschatological Tension

"In the Jewish morning prayer, which Paul must all his pre-Christian life have used, the Jew thanks God that 'thou hast not made me a Gentile, a slave or a woman.'"[473] Yet the Christian Paul turns it completely upside-down in this verse: "in Christ there is no longer Jew or Greek, there is no longer slave or free, there is no longer male and female; for all of you are one in Christ Jesus." The old differences are done away with when someone joins Christ in baptism. He or she could not, or should not, behave in the same way. Philemon, as we have noted, is expected to treat Onesimus as a brother in Christ, not as a piece of property. And yet neither Paul nor Augustine took it upon themselves to tackle slavery as an institution. So, there are two ways to treat Galatians 3:28 in our context. It is only meant for the Christian churches: they are to act as if there is neither slave nor free in their congregations – no matter what the situation may be once they leave the church building? Or it is meant as a sort of spiritual, end-time aspiration? This verse will only apply when Christ comes in all his glory. Until then, unfortunately, we will have to put up with the fact that some will be obliged to serve others, and some (including some Christians) will have mastery over others.

---

[472] Gal. 3:28.

[473] William Barclay, *The Daily Study Bible (Revised Edition): The Letters to the Galatians and Ephesians* (Edinburgh: The Saint Andrew Press, 1976), 32.

There are obvious objections to both these options. In Paul's time, "churches" met in peoples' houses. Those houses, if they were of any size, had household slaves running them: this was inevitable given the slave economy of the time. So it would be very difficult indeed to step out of role in one's own house. Should the master, or mistress, of the house not act as such during the service, and resume her or his role once the church had dispersed? In what practical ways should a slave behave differently in the service? The difficulties become impossible – so maybe Paul is speaking eschatologically?

If Paul is speaking in a spiritual, end-time aspiration sort of way, then the whole passage must be taken similarly: the law must be the disciplinarian until Christ comes again (see v. 24). Except that Paul is clearly talking of Christ's first coming: we *have* faith, therefore we are children of God, we are baptized into Christ, and there is no longer slave nor free (vv. 26–28). Therefore in Christ we are somehow to behave as if those differences – and they are fundamental, touching on our race, culture, and sex – no longer matter because we owe everything to Christ and what he has done for us. So we have come full circle. We are dealing with a spiritual aspect that has, always has had, and will continue to have, practical implications.

So maybe Paul is speaking more deeply eschatologically: that is, he must be fully aware that there are differences between us, but he asserts that "the dividing wall of hostility" (Eph. 2:14)[474] has been torn down so that such differences do not matter for those in Christ. It may well be that the fullest completion of "in Christ there is no slave nor free" will not happen this side of the parousia, but Paul gives no indication, in his letter or elsewhere – including the letter to Philemon – that we should sit back and wait for that eventuality and do nothing to help make Paul's assertion a reality: Paul says "there *is* no," not "there *will be* no." It may well be that only when Christ comes again Galatians 3:28 (like much else of scripture) will be fulfilled in its entirety, but until then we have still to live as if the verse is true, and to work so the sentiment expressed in the verse will come about. So how does that affect church life?

"Welcome Him as You Would Welcome Me":[475] Philemon Again

In living out its alternative view of society, yet being fully part of that society, has always occasioned tensions in church life. None more so

---

[474] Here I am assuming that the letters traditionally ascribed to Paul are indeed Pauline; but the sense of the paragraph still follows from Galatians 3.

[475] Phil. 17.

than here. How is Philemon to cope with a runaway slave? If he treats him leniently, why should his other slaves not run away? If he treats Onesimus harshly, how is he to face Paul if and when Paul comes on his visit (v. 22)? If he sets Onesimus free – which would be extremely lenient treatment of a runaway slave! – how would the other slaves react, except by demanding their freedom? And if Philemon ends up with no slaves, how could he run his household, much less the church that meets there (v. 2)? We do not have Philemon's answer, we can but speculate. Perhaps Onesimus was sent back to Paul, but still as Philemon's slave, once Paul had paid what was owed. This might, given the culture of the time, have worked – if Philemon was able to stand up to his social equals in Roman society, and control his other slaves, perhaps Paul's offer to repay Onesimus' debts meant that those debts were remitted. Maybe. But we have speculated enough, I hope we can now see that Paul's letter to Philemon would have created, or reinforced the tension of *how* to "be in the world, but not of it."

One of the big differences between then and now, is the fact that Paul's radical proposal that in Christ there is neither slave nor free is broadened. The abolitionists insisted, as we have seen above, that the whole of humanity was made in God's image (Paul's message to the Galatians was, if we wish to be pedantic, to the church – not to all and sundry), and therefore none could own another. The image of Christ exists in the slave just as much as in you or me. This isn't always easy to see:

In West Africa, child slavery is commonplace, and indeed across much of Africa, girl slaves as young as 7 or 8 are to be found as domestic servants in many houses, especially of working middle class families. When I was teaching in Africa, I knew of such a child in Malawi – she "worked" for one of my colleagues. In other words, although my colleague was a teacher and, supposedly believed in education, this child was not even in compulsory free primary education. I regret enormously that I did nothing even to get her into school. Such slavery is justified locally because a girl from a poor family who cannot afford to keep her is fed by the owner, so keeping her alive at no expense to the family, while her sale will have contributed a little to the family's funds. But with no pay, and no education, what is her future?

Many slaves are in the sex trade in one form or another. The woman I freed in Central Africa was the domestic and probable sexual slave of a male teacher. Perhaps she had been a child domestic slave and had no other means of survival. But she had obviously got to the end of her tether. She was going to burn her master's papers – papers that allowed him to have the coveted teaching post. I don't know how she got hold of these papers, but her frantic master had begged me to leave my evening's marking and help. When I arrived, she was holding the certificates over an open fire, and threatening to let them drop into it, holding her master at bay with a large kitchen knife. By guaranteeing her the fare to town and offering that she could come with me that night – she could sleep in my spare bed – I was able to persuade her to part with the precious documents. She accompanied me back to my home, but next morning she had disappeared. Yes, she was free, but again, I had to ask what prospects she had. My colleague continued teaching at the school.[476]

This took place ten years ago, not 200 years ago. Twenty years ago, I taught in another area of Africa, and again thought nothing of the women "employed" by staff. If it was part of their culture, who was I to interfere, or ask questions? Perhaps some "holy boldness" might have been in order; but we all benefit from hindsight.

We have seen above that slavery is still a worldwide problem, and neither the US nor the UK are immune. Maybe some stories come from faraway places, but the issue of human trafficking goes on in a town or city near you and me. Many thousands and millions of men, women, and children are in slavery because we want our goods on the cheap. Or we are prepared to look the other way while men "take their pleasure" on the body of some young girl who was promised a better life in another country.

But this doesn't go on in church – we know better, don't we? But before we contemplate doing nothing, let us return to Gutiérrez's *Theology of Liberation*. Gutiérrez tells us that:

> Those who reduce the work of salvation are indeed those who limit it to the strictly "religious" sphere . . . It is those who in order to protect salvation (or to protect their interests) lift salvation from the midst of history, where individuals and social classes struggle to liberate themselves from the slavery and oppression to which other individuals and social classes have subjected them. It is those who refuse to see that the salvation of Christ is a radical liberation from all misery, all despoliation, all alienation. It is those who by trying to "save" the work of Christ will "lose" it.[477]

---

[476] Charis Scott; World Development Adviser to Newcastle Diocese (UK): this is an edited version of the story she told at my workshop on "Modern Slavery" at the Partners in World Mission Conference, October 31, 2006.

[477] Gutiérrez, *Theology of Liberation*, 104.

Gutiérrez reiterates the point a few pages later. As far as he is concerned, if we refuse to get involved with the poor, with the oppressed, if we refuse make these our neighbor, then we have abstained from serving, and this "is to refuse to love: to fail to act for another is as culpable as expressly refusing to do it."[478] It is all a part of the idea that by not acting, by refusing to act, we are supporting the *status quo*. The *status quo* here is one that, if it doesn't allow trafficking, at least is yet to be seen to be doing enough to stop trafficking.

The problem with "getting involved" is that we enter morally murky waters. If we want to stop the trafficking in women for sexual purposes, how do we find out whether the prostitutes on our streets and in our brothels are trafficked – are being coerced into offering sex with strangers? We can, presumably, ask the men to help the authorities. However, a British Government report notes the following:

> While sexual intercourse without consent is clearly an offence, we consider that men who have used the services of trafficked prostitutes should not be discouraged from reporting to the authorities their suspicions that the women concerned may have been trafficked. While we note and welcome Mr. Coaker's [a minister at the Home office] view that those who genuinely come forward to identify trafficking victims would not be prosecuted for rape, it is clearly inconsistent for the authorities to suggest that men who use the services of a prostitute who has been trafficked will be prosecuted for rape . . . and at the same time urge such men to report such activity to the authorities or a helpline.[479]

Unsurprisingly, the report goes on to say that the threat of rape charges has "been counter-productive" in the fight against trafficking. However, this point illustrates the difficulties of political engagement. With members of the UK parliament "on all sides of the house" (that is, whether in the governing or one of the other political parties) calling for those who have sex with trafficked women to be charged with rape, asking the men to come forward so that the women can be identified and, ostensibly, helped, will not work. On the other hand, if the men are not to be charged, to be granted immunity from prosecution, does this not say that having sex with a prostitute is acceptable?

At what point do we, in Bonhoefferian terms, "sin boldly?" At what point do we regard a politically expedient action as a mere

---

[478] Ibid., 113.

[479] House of Lords, House of Commons Joint Committee on Human Rights, *Human Trafficking: Twenty-Sixth Report of Session 2005–06* (London: The Stationary Office Limited, 2006), 50 (para. 148).

incremental step on the way to changing today's realistic "is" to tomorrow's "ought?"

He Will Wipe Every Tear from Their Eyes:[480] Today's "Is" and Tomorrow's "Ought"

Stolen Smiles, a report from the London School of Hygiene and Tropical Medicine,[481] paints a disturbing picture of the reality of trafficking:

> I was locked in the basement with my friend. We were only free to work, and when the boss was drunk he would rape me.
>   They told me they would cut me into pieces and send me back like that. Every single day I heard the threat 'I'll kill you bitch.'

Ninety-five percent of the women (12 percent of whom were adolescents aged between fifteen and seventeen), experienced some form of physical or sexual violence while being trafficked. Apart from their physical symptoms, it is unsurprising that these women also exhibit psychological trauma. This includes depression, anxiety attacks and "significantly impaired cognitive functioning." Unsurprising, but it seems that the authorities need to be made aware of this as the women try to seek assistance from them, including asylum. Also, an astonishing one in five of the women reported "that a relative knew their trafficker." Also "36% of the women reported threats to children and other close relatives." This fact alone would make it unsafe for the women to be transported back home, but Amnesty International reports that "the law often treats these women as simply illegal immigrants"[482] to be deported as quickly as possible, without the help and support they need after such a traumatic experience.

The "ought," of course, is that no one is trafficked, that if they are trafficked, they are rescued and cared for properly, and only returned to their country of origin (or their home – trafficking occurs within countries, not just between them) if they so wish, and if it is safe for them there: that they will receive the care and protection they will need.

However, in order to get from the "is" to the "ought" there is a painful road. Governments need to sign up to the international agreements

---

[480] Rev. 21:4.

[481] www.lshtm.ac.uk/hpu/docs/StolenSmiles.pdf (accessed November 17, 2006).

[482] *Amnesty* magazine, September/October 2006, 9. (See also www.amnesty.org.uk).

already in existence, and keep to them. Among the recommendations (there are more than I quote here) in the London School of Hygiene and Tropical Medicine report, are the following:

> 1. States should approve national legislation that requires provision of healthcare for women who have been trafficked.
> 2. Implement a recovery and reflection period of a minimum of 90 days to ensure that women's cognitive functioning has improved to a level at which they are able to make informed and thoughtful decisions about their safety and wellbeing, and provide more reliable information about trafficking-related events.[483]
>
> . . .
>
> 8. Working with international organizations (e.g., WHO, IOM, Unicef), develop and make available health promotion booklets designed for distribution to women at risk of trafficking or women in situations of exploitation. Booklets should include, at a minimum:
>
> - A clear definition of trafficking and its estimated magnitude;
>
> - An overview of the health complications commonly experienced by trafficked women, including descriptions of signs and symptoms of illness and options for treatment; and
>
> - A summary of the rights to health services of non-residents in known countries of destination, and the rights of women who have been trafficked to health services in receiving and/or countries of origin.[484]

This is not to say that the UK and the USA, for example, are not working with other organizations, or have no legislation in place, but as part of the remit of "speaking truth to power," we must be prepared to tell governments where they are failing the weakest in our communities; and to suggest ways of doing better. One way of doing this is to look for "best practice" elsewhere in the international community. Care, a Christian organization based in London, responded to a government consultation paper by, among other things, pointing to the shift in Sweden's legislation. Their law now links prostitution and trafficking and it is now "an offence to pay for sex with a woman."

> This new approach means that the trafficker, pimp and user are criminalised but the prostitute is decriminalised allowing for greater

---

[483] See ibid., 3.
[484] Ibid.

cooperation between prostitutes and the police to tackle organised crime.[485]

> There has also been a 75% drop in the number of men buying sex as the criminal emphasis has shifted to them. Men are far more reluctant to risk their freedom for cheap sex. Another result of this legislation change has been to dramatically reduce the number of women trafficked into prostitution because there is no longer the demand and the risks for the traffickers are too great.[486]

However, this legislation is seen as controversial, and is certainly radical. But, it appears to work. If men are reluctant to use prostitutes for fear of criminalization, then this means fewer opportunities for traffickers to make money from their "slaves."

There are practical suggestions: get involved with Stop the Traffik – this is "a global initiative for organizations, schools, charities, clubs, churches, businesses . . . who are concerned about the issues of people trafficking."[487] Its own stories of trafficking are harrowing and heartbreaking, but it does not stop the work; the ideal is still to eradicate the modern slave trade 200 years after William Wilberforce successfully piloted his bill through the UK Houses of Parliament to outlaw the slave trade in the British Empire. Let us hope and act so that indeed every tear will be wiped from their eyes.

---

[485] Care, *Human Trafficking Briefing Pack: The Modern Slave Trade* (London: Care, 2006), 8. This is also available from www.care.org.uk

[486] Ibid., Care, *Briefing on Human Trafficking*, 4.

[487] See www.stopthetraffik.org

Eight

Love, Marriage, and the Church

"Do you take this man for an idiot?"[488] Thus the headline of a *The Times* (London) article about marriage. Unusually, this article made a defense of marriage as an institution: despite the 40 percent divorce rate, despite noting university research purporting to show that "as soon as a woman gets her man her libido drops dramatically" (and the writer notes: "men aren't going to stick around if overnight their sexy bride becomes a frigid trout who sighs 'Pull my nightie down when you've finished', are they?"), Carol Midgley is still determined to say her vows a few weeks after penning her article.

But why? What is it about this institution that causes men and women, with so much awareness – often from their own experience – of the downside, determined to attach themselves "for better or for worse" to one person of the opposite sex?[489] Is it really the notion of "sex on tap" that causes this rush into holy matrimony? I suggest not. The problem for many people, especially single people – of whatever sexual orientation, of whatever character, background, or genetic make-up – is loneliness. It was Mother Theresa who pointed out that loneliness was the worst form of poverty in the world, and therefore her Missionaries of Charity could and should operate in places like London and New York. And yet. And yet marriage does not solve this problem: there are few lonelier places than a marriage bed when communication has broken down, and there are very few places where it is so impossible to escape the latest argument or irritation outside the cauldron that is "marriage."

In other words, if you do get married, you marry the wrong person.

> Like any good law it is, of course reversible. You also always marry the
> right person. My law was . . . to help them [my students] see that the

---

488 *The Times*, Saturday, August 19, 2006, 20.
489 The issue of homosexuality will occur later in this chapter.

church rightly understands that we no more know the person we marry than we know ourselves.[490]

But this law is as contrary to the "love and marriage" ideal that it is possible to get. Surely no one would be walking up the aisle (assuming we get that far: that we are beyond, or not entertaining "living together," or some civil ceremony) without thinking that they had met and "fallen in love with" the right person. This one person is the one with whom I can fulfill my (romantic) visions and dreams; with this one person, I can face the world. We can be a unit, a piece, a "family." But, inevitably, it doesn't work out like that. We know we said "for richer, for poorer, for better, for worse; in sickness and in health" – but we said nothing about his moodiness, her inability to sleep without tossing and turning all night, or that he can't see dust until it's an inch thick (and then he doesn't do a thing about it).

Indeed, to be personal for a moment, my wife is not the person I married: she is now a full-time family doctor, and mother of two. She's changed. So have I. She married a "Mr" who's now a "Dr" (PhD variety), she married a bachelor, who's now a father. Many times during those years the romantic has disappeared completely: it is very difficult to regard a woman's body in quite the same way after you've watched her screaming as she tries to push your son into the world! On the other hand, of course, you can find time, once the kids are in bed to indulge in time together with the TV *off*, whether or not this leads to sex . . . But over time, as both bodies sag, get less fit and firm, bulge in all the wrong places, the romantic ideal thrust on us by the media fades to dust. As it must, and as the Christian church would expect it too – because the romantic ideal is all about fulfilling *my* wants, *my* dreams. It is about "intensity, not continuity" and Christian marriage, if it is to be about anything, must be about continuity – fidelity.

According to Hauerwas (and I agree), marriage for Christians is "heroic," not "romantic." The heroic qualities are those that enable people to stick it out together "not stopping . . . to wonder if they are fulfilled"[491] – whatever that last word means. But a heroic marriage is able to contain (in both senses of the word) the romantic, but not the romantic "ideal" within it. There will be moments – some longer, some shorter – of romance: these will not be the same as the moments of newly weds, but will build on the fidelity that has sustained and continues to sustain the marriage, because the romantic self-giving (rather than the

---

[490] Stanley Hauerwas, *The Hauerwas Reader*, 513.
[491] Haughton, quoted in *Hauerwas Reader*, 500.

using of the other to fulfill my romantic notions) is all the more profound and deep because of the knowledge that the other will still be
there when I don't "feel romantic."[492]

And if we go even further back, to Augustine, we find him regarding
the "goods" of marriage as: unity and mutual society; procreation; remedy for sin (see 1 Cor. 7:2, but also see v. 28); and a school for charity. This
doesn't sound very romantic, but more like hard work.

We also have to counter the romantic myth that there is that one person
who can totally fulfill all my needs, who can totally complement me for life:

> It is impractical to hope that one person can be completed by another, or that
> one's spouse would be able to receive the "total" personality and texture of
> the other. We should hope that friends and co-workers will tease out and cul-
> tivate personal qualities and make demands that our husbands and wives
> cannot. Even if marriage is a primary source of one's identity, it is quite a dif-
> ferent matter to assume that we can exhaust one another's "total" self.[493]

So if the church seems uncompromising to those approaching it from
outside, over what it understands about marriage, it is because it understands marriage in a different way. It understands marriage, family, and
singleness in the context of hope. Hauerwas again,

> we must remember that the "sacrifice" made by the single is not that of
> "giving up sex," but the much more significant sacrifice of giving up heirs.
> There can be no more radical act than this, as it is the clearest institutional
> expression that one's future is not guaranteed by the family, but by the
> church. The church, the harbinger of the Kingdom of God, is now the
> source of our primary loyalty.[494]

So if singleness is so good, what did those long ago make of "marriage?"

Augustine, prior to his conversion lived with a concubine for some
years, and by whom he had a son Adeodatus (gift of God), only to put
her off when he contracted a marriage with a nobly born, but young,
lady. The marriage never went ahead as Augustine was converted back
to Christianity – but he notes that, after he had put off his concubine, and
sent her back to Africa (her vowing to live a chaste life henceforth), he
was unable of himself to be chaste until marriage, but took other women

---

[492] A deep irony! See David Matzko McCarthy, *Sex and Love in the Home*
(London: SCM, 2004), 163–4.

[493] Ibid., 123.

[494] Hauerwas, *Hauerwas Reader*, 498.

to his bed. On conversion, he lived as a monk in community – and relied on those communities for all the companionship he felt he needed. In the late Roman period, the classical ideal was still followed that companionship, and friendship, could only really be found among free men of the leisured classes. That there could be friendship between men and women (whether or not this was part of a marriage relationship) was not something Augustine thought to address within his defense of marriage.

So, from the church's point of view, what is so wrong with marriage? Andrew Goddard puts it this way:

> both the New Testament (for example 1 Cor 7) and the early church (and much in later Christian tradition), clearly recognised that the supremacy of the call of God on each person's life renders even marriage to some degree an ethically complicated . . . state. This is partly because, unlike singleness and natural family relationships, it represents a willing undertaking of a lifelong bond to another person and this commitment limits a person's freedom to respond wholeheartedly to the demands of serving God and his kingdom in the church and the world.[495]

This wholehearted response to the demands of serving God is not, however, to be seen as a lonely quest. A careful reading of the Pauline epistles will show that Paul did not work alone (see Col. 4:10–12), and when he was alone he felt lonely and wanted his companions to be with him (see 2 Tim. 4:9–12). In later centuries, Augustine, the austere monk, always lived in community. In other words, we need friends, we need companionship. We all need – like Bonhoeffer – to be intimate.

> Edwin Robertson reports that when *Letters and Papers from Prison* was published in 1953 it was not known that Bethge was the friend who received the letters. Nor was it known who was the subject of the poem, "The Friend." However in 1957 Bethge was speaking at a student conference in New Hampshire where one of the participants asked him who the recipient of letters and poem might be because "it must be a homosexual partnership." Bethge replied immediately, "No, we were fairly normal!" and he went on to show that there was no such sexual relationship.[496]

---

[495] Andrew Goddard, *Friends, Partners or Spouses? The Civil Partnership Act and Christian Witness* (Cambridge: Grove Books Ltd, 2006), 25.

[496] Stanley Hauerwas, "Friendship and Freedom: Reflections on Bonhoeffer's 'the Friend,'" a paper given at the Bonhoeffer Conference, Oxford, January 6, 2006. Internal quotes from Edwin Robertson (ed. and trans.), *Dietrich Bonhoeffer's Prison Poems* (Grand Rapids: Zondervan, 2005), 89–90.

However, the intimacy of lines like:

> Beside the staff of life,
> taken and fashioned from the heavy earth,
> beside our marriage, work and war,
> the free man, too, will live and grow toward the sun.
> Not the ripe fruit alone –
> blossom is lovely too . . .
> Finest and rarest blossom, at a happy moment springing
> from the freedom of a lightsome, daring, trusting spirit,
> is a friend to a friend.[497]

must lead us to a lack of surprise that "an American assumed a poem as intense and intimate as 'the Friend' must indicate a sexual relation." Such an assumption would probably be made (in ignorance) anywhere in the Anglo-Saxon world; but intimacy is not the same as sex. Conversely, it's also a tragedy of our fallen existence that so much sex is divorced from intimacy; we must indeed "be persuaded, with Augustine, that there is some deep disorder in the sexual instinct, as it exists at present in the great majority of the human race."[498] Indeed, at the moment, this chapter seems to have sex, marriage, intimacy, and friendship all muddled together as discussion has swung from one to another to another.

So let us try to look at them a bit more clearly. Traditionally, the church has recognized two conditions: marriage and celibacy. People are either married or single, and those who are single but who hope to be married must, nonetheless, lead a celibate life until the happy moment when they marry. Despite attacks on this position (even if it is not often stated as starkly as I have just put it), the Archbishops' Council (of the Church of England) stated that the church's teaching on sexual activity was that "sexual activity outside marriage, whether heterosexual or homosexual . . . [is still regarded] as falling short of God's purpose for human beings."[499] In other words, the church teaches that it is possible to survive without sex, but we cannot survive without relationships, without intimacy. But our culture is afraid of intimacy.

---

[497] Bonhoeffer, *LPP*, 388.

[498] Gerald Bonner, *God's Decree and Man's Destiny* (London: Variorum, 1987), 311.

[499] www.cofe.anglican.org/info/socialpublic/civil_partnership_response_from_the_archbishops_council (Cf. Goddard, *Friends, Partners or Spouses?*), 11. This is despite the continuing debate within the church about "committed homosexual relationships" – a topic to which I shall return later in the chapter.

I experienced this fear in a most dramatic way when I started teaching: "Do not touch the children," I was told, "if you touch them you will either be delivering physical abuse [presumably if they were hurt], or sexual abuse [if it didn't hurt]." This advice appertained whether I was in school, or out of school: there was no way in which any contact could or would be interpreted in a positive manner. You could not comfort an upset child by giving them a hug: touch from an adult was wrong in all circumstances.

Years later, I was crossing a school playground when I heard a shout, "Mr Oakley!" I turned and there was Megan, running toward me, arms outstretched, for a hug. What was I supposed to do? The rules said I could not touch her, but if I stepped aside, she'd certainly fall. I gave her the hug. As her mother taught in the school, and the "incident" took place outside the staffroom window, I was (relatively) safe. But what a comment on our society that I should have to be worried about giving a hug to an eight-year-old girl in a school playground.

Mike Pilavachi founder of the Soul Survivor youth organization, tells a similar story of a clergyman friend who won't let his twelve-year-old daughter sit on his lap any more "in case anyone gets the wrong idea." Mike continues: "I wanted to shake him and say, 'Don't you dare! Don't you dare give in to the prejudices of society. She is your kid, she is your daughter: Not sit on your lap? If you take all of that away, where is she going to look for intimacy?' "[500]

Mike also points out that "[m]uch of the promiscuity of teenagers is not simply because they want sex, but because they want intimacy and there is no other way of getting to that place."[501]

The sort of intimacy that is needed is when you can turn up at 11:15 at night, and Mike's friends "know exactly why I had turned up at 11:15 at night" but they did not ask. They chatted together, drank hot chocolate together, and acted what they were: friends.[502] Or: the kids are giving me a hard time, my wife has (another) meeting, so I pack them in the car and drive to Sue and Lee's. They do not need to know why I am there – they have kids too! But we sit, we chat, the kids all play together – suddenly my kids are behaving much better, isn't that the way of it? And I go home, hours later, feeling better, more relaxed.

Friendship, to be friendship, must include intimacy – to be sure that intimacy must have boundaries, but what relationship does not? After

---

[500] "Mike Pilavachi speaks frankly about Sex," in *UK Focus* (London: Holy Trinity Brompton, August 2006), 2.

[501] Ibid.

[502] See ibid., 3.

all, isn't part of marriage negotiating not to have sex, not to talk about work all the time, not to assume that this one person will answer all my needs – but that intimacy need not (as it did not for Bonhoeffer and Bethge) include sex. Also, the intimacy of friendship is not exclusive – you have more than one friend, and the best of best friends realize this. Bonhoeffer himself had to realize that Bethge had, and would continue to maintain friendship with other friends. On one occasion Bonhoeffer wrote to apologize to Bethge's cousin for behaving in such a way on a trip that the cousin – Gerhard Vibrans – felt an outsider. "I spoke to Eberhard [Bethge] about what you said to me. He thought you were right."[503] It appears that both Bethge and Vibrans had stood up to Bonhoeffer: and Bonhoeffer had accepted this. (Vibrans replied to Bonhoeffer's letter in which he acknowledged "his own fault in the matter").[504] Bonhoeffer and Bethge were "best friends" if we can put it that way, but this was not to exclude others. Indeed, when Vibrans was killed in the Second World War, Bethge preached at his memorial service, and, after the war, Vibrans' widow married Bethge's younger brother.[505]

So we have an intimacy that allows for correction and rebuke, but not for exclusivity. David Matzko McCarthy puts it like this in *Sex and Love in the Home*:

> Friendship is founded on likeness and agreement, accompanied by mutual regard and affection. Friends will be able to see themselves more clearly and truly through the eyes of a good friend . . . Friendship is good will toward one another and willing good for one another . . . Friends avoid pretense and useless flattery. They correct one another in cases of wrong-doing, and they suffer each other's troubles . . . [G]ood friendships are open to risk, growth, and the goodness of other friends.[506]

McCarthy here follows Augustine, whose "notion of friendship begins with an intimate circle and widens to characterize the unity and charity of the church."[507]

Of course, somewhat unlike Augustine, who, although he accepted that "the rationale for entering marriage (and justifying sexual

---

[503] Quoted in John W. de Gruchy, *Daring, Trusting Spirit: Bonhoeffer's Friend Eberhard Bethge* (London: SCM Press, 2005), 31. Cf. Hauerwas, "Friendship and Freedom."

[504] Ibid., 32.

[505] Ibid.

[506] McCarthy, *Sex and Love in the Home*, 167–8.

[507] Ibid., 169.

intercourse) does not provide a full account of all that marriage is," tended to look not to marriage but to the company of friends "for examples of love, union, and common life."[508] McCarthy, looks for friendship also within marriage and family, but again, "[f]rom a theological angle . . . good friendships and loving marriages are always incomplete, and are dependent on a wider circle of friends."[509]

However, marriage is an exclusive relationship. It is a "willing undertaking of a lifelong bond to another person" that "limits a person's freedom to respond wholeheartedly to the demands of serving God" – this is why it was seen as "ethically complicated." However, this "limitation is acceptable in relation to marriage because it is a divinely ordained created institution to which God continues to call people in Christ."[510] The question remains as to "[w]hether it is right to make a similar life-long commitment in other circumstances requires serious discussion in relation to . . . any form of acceptable same-sex covenantal relationship."[511] It is my contention that our failure to counter the romantic myth, and our fear of (non-sexual) intimacy, leads us into more, rather than fewer, problems in this area.

A Same-Sex Partner?

In the London *Times* on January 25, 2006, "Gemma" writes to Bel Mooney, the agony aunt.[512] She is, she says, happily married but – but she's "violently attracted" to this other mother at the school gates. She's had "a couple of sexual encounters with women in my early twenties" but "made a decision to pursue a 'normal' heterosexual life." So what should she do? Her husband is "(uncomfortably) accepting" of her past but is "prone to sexual jealousy."

Mooney points out that her desire for the woman is "set against your love for your husband and children," her feelings can be described as a variety of "the grass is always greener [on the other side of the fence]" – "which has been a potent cause of human misery since Eve gave way to the serpent's blandishments . . . The forfeit may be greater than the gain."

However, the principal objection to Gemma indulging her fantasy is the "subtle loss . . . of concentration on your partner." And this is adultery and, "the effect of adultery (even if it takes place in the mind)

---

[508] Ibid, 176–8.

[509] Ibid., 172.

[510] Goddard, *Friends, Partners or Spouses?* 25.

[511] Ibid.

[512] *The Times*, January 25, 2006.

usually mirrors the chemical process: to adulterate is to make something weaker by adding another substance." This still leaves the question of what to do: make friends with the woman is the suggestion, and see if reality abates the fantasy. "If not . . . well, there's always the girlie package trip to New York, to see what happens." "Which might be . . . nothing."

Apart from wondering what a perceptive husband who knows about Gemma's past would make of such a trip – would it not be too much to expect that Gemma would go on such a trip hoping that nothing would happen? – it is intriguing to note that we live in such a sexually free society that an "agony aunt" who issues all sorts of warnings against heterosexual affairs (and has issued warnings here) cannot bring herself – despite her apt definition of adultery – to say an emphatic "No" to this potential relationship. Fantasies may not go away (or they may on better knowledge of the real mother at the gates, not just Gemma's image of her); but is it ever worth risking a marriage for a fling? What would Gemma gain, and what would she lose?

The homosexuality issue has become, for many, *the* divisive issue within the Christian church – on both sides of the debate. The current situation within the Anglican Church (my own denomination) looks untenable, and a split has yet to be avoided. It is also an issue that many of us would rather not talk about: not just because it's embarrassing, but because sexuality has become such a core aspect of "who we are," that a different sexuality questions our very identity. If I am friendly with my homosexual neighbor, what does that say about me (and my sexuality)? Our reactions are often deeply felt; so deeply that we may not wish to articulate them to others, or even ourselves.

But this is not the whole story, many people are genuinely torn. On the one hand, we find ourselves

> Fundamentally suspicious of arguments based on "personal experience," I am unable (and unwilling) to disregard what the Church has taught about the authority of the Scripture and about marriage . . . being the appropriate context for the expression of sexually explicit love . . . Yet my life has been graced repeatedly by the presence of faithful gay and lesbian Christians.[513]

So we either stay silent, or react, and risk getting the issue out of perspective. Again, on the one hand, we can belittle the subject, by saying "only 1 percent are gay." But Jesus talks of the shepherd who left the ninety-nine in

---

[513] Joel James Shuman, "Eating Together: Friendship and Homosexuality," in Hauerwas and Wells, *The Blackwell Companion to Christian Ethics* (Malden, MA: Blackwell, 2004), 402.

the sheepfold to search for the one who was lost. (The question here for much of today's church would be whether it would leave the ninety-nine "straight" to search and befriend the one "gay"?) Or, on the other hand, we can inflate the issue so that a worldwide church seems to talk about nothing else. This has been the danger in my own (Anglican/Episcopal) tradition. But, much as some advocates on either side might be tempted to disagree, the issues and arguments over one aspect of sexuality are still less important than global poverty: once every three seconds, a child dies from a preventable disease caused, or exacerbated, by poverty.

Perhaps the best way to examine the debate is to read a quote from an anonymous, homosexual Christian:

> Over the years I've continued to struggle with emotional attractions and attachments to other men that have torn away at my insides and eroded my confidence in myself and in God. I continue to struggle from time to time with thoughts that my wife and sons would be better off if they didn't have to deal with such a moody husband and father . . .
>
> My position on homosexuality – while it may be realistic and grounded in true experience – seems to offend many and please almost no one. My fervent belief that God intends us to live in heterosexual and monogamous fidelity offends the liberals who think I should accept and live out my supposedly God-given sexual nature. At the same time, my experience that grace may abound but that it doesn't necessarily "fix" me or make it easy for me to live the "straight" life offends the conservatives.[514]

So, what is the consensus of the Anglican Church on this issue? Its recent publication "Some Issues on Human Sexuality" says that,

> In relation to homosexual conduct it is therefore clear that "the various suggestions for revising the traditional view of biblical material have not succeeded in changing the consensus of scholarly opinion . . . At the moment [2003], the traditional understanding of these passages remains the most convincing one in the minds of most biblical scholars.[515]

However, I am not going to rehearse the arguments over the texts: I will just briefly consider three of the key issues that come up in the debate,

---

[514] "No Easy Victory," *Christianity Today*, March 11, 2002, 52.

[515] Quoted in Goddard, *Homosexuality and the Church of England: The Position Following "Some Issues in Human Sexuality"* (Cambridge: Grove Books, 2004), 16.

and try to see where some Christian ethical considerations (backed by reference to scripture) may lead us. The issues I have chosen are:

- What cultural attitudes about sex must be rejected in a Christian context?

- Do we need to open the church to lesbians and gay men as the early Church was opened to the Gentiles?

- How should we respond pastorally to lesbian and gay Christians?

The first issue: What cultural attitudes about sex must be rejected in a Christian context?

> It is widely assumed and argued today that to explore, express and enhance one's sexuality through "sex" (where "sex" is narrowed to "sexual intercourse") is indispensable to one's growth and development and happiness as a human being; not to do so is to be repressed, deprived and oppressed. This is a modern "myth," in the sense of a basic world-view through which life is approached and experienced, a view which remains largely impervious to evidence to the contrary (i.e. failure to develop one's true self through sexual encounters means that one needs other, better sexual experiences; such failure does not call in question the role of sexual encounter in human growth and development). Thus there is a sense of genuine moral outrage in the response of many people (of whatever sexual orientation) towards most reaffirmations of some kind of traditional Christian biblical morality, on the grounds that people are being denied something essential to their human well-being and prospects of happiness.
>
> [. . . However] sex is not a necessity, nor even a priority. What matters most in human life can be achieved without it, and missed with it (consider 1 Cor. 13, Gal. 5.22, and famous Old Testament summary statements such as Deut. 10.12–22; Mic. 6.8). A distinctive and recurrent form of Christian witness to this has been the monastic life – the vows of poverty, chastity and obedience embody the claim that neither money, nor sex, nor power is indispensable to the living of life to the full; for Jesus lived life fully without them. It is a hard witness, to which in its full form only some Christians are called, but one which captures something central to Scripture.[516]

This is not the whole answer. If we are sexual beings, we are going to have sexual feelings, so why should we say to the homosexual man that

---

[516] Walter Moberly, "The Use of Scripture in Contemporary Debate about Homosexuality," in *Theology* 103/814 (July/August 2000), 253–4.

he should not kiss his boyfriend, or to the lesbian that she should not kiss her girlfriend? After all, are there not passionate friendships in the Bible: David and Jonathan, Ruth and Naomi, Jesus and the beloved disciple (a *self*-designated term) – "which is not in any sense to claim these characters as gay or lesbian,"[517] but any sympathetic reading of Scripture shows that there was a passion, a *sensuality* about their friendship that present-day culture confines to the sexual. How do we, in the heterosexual majority, recognize homosexual people *as people* with hopes and fears? How are they to express love and affection? How are they to know when physical touch (which we all need) becomes sexual – assuming that we are saying sexual contact is only to be allowed within heterosexual marriage? Again, perhaps part of the answer lies, as I have discussed above, in a rediscovery of intimacy, of friendship, of real acceptance that goes with intimacy and friendship.

Do we need to open the church to lesbians and gay men as the early church was opened to the Gentiles?[518] This question opens up a hermeneutic and a pastoral concern. However, I shall focus on the hermeneutics here, and leave the pastoral concerns until we discuss the third question. The early church had a problem in Acts 10: Gentiles were clearly being blessed, so Peter got on with baptizing them! What is going on here? Has God suddenly changed his mind about the Gentiles? Well, no, as Acts 15 tells us, God has always intended that, through Abraham, all nations/peoples would be blessed. In other words, the early church did not reject the teaching of scripture as a distortion of the truth;[519] it established that a greater truth of God's blessing of all nations was there in scripture, before and during his particular blessing of the Jewish nation. Unfortunately, as I have intimated above, a similar approach to homosexual practice has not yet succeeded in appealing to the wider church. Which brings us to the third point, how, then, shall we respond pastorally to our homosexual brothers and sisters?

Michael Vasey made the point well, as an evangelical, but homosexual Christian; he felt that the church was a place, not of comfort and care, but of danger.[520] If this is so, and it is for a lot of homosexual Christians, then

---

[517] Elizabeth Stuart, "Dancing in the Spirit," in Timothy Bradshaw (ed.), *The Way Forward?* (2nd edn.; London: SCM Press, 1997), 83.

[518] The debate usually centers on homosexual *practice* as distinct from orientation. A non-practicing homosexually orientated person should be as welcome as anyone else in a church congregation, however "conservative".

[519] Cf. Goddard, *Homosexuality and the Church of England*, 16.

[520] Ibid., 31.

are those of us unwilling to abandon traditional teaching on abstinence for all those not in a married relationship (straight or gay), prepared to make the costly choices about our common life and enable and assist those who bear the cross of "singleness" in our sex-obsessed society? Will we create Christian communities where church teaching is not harsh law, but a gospel of grace[521] – can we let our gay neighbor meet Jesus and meet us as well? And can we be consistent in our life and work? Back to our anonymous friend:

> To be honest, I myself sometimes have a hard time loving the sinner while hating the sin . . . I struggle with hating promiscuous heterosexual men, because they seem so self-justifying and because some people – even some Christians – seem so accommodating of that sin while so condemning of mine. Just last week I was talking with a Christian friend about concerns I had for members of our youth group. His response was something like, "Well, you know, with all those hormones . . ." I don't get it. Do young male heterosexuals benefit from some sort of special dispensation? Why is their giving in to their urges so understandable while my giving in to mine would be such an abomination?[522]

We do need to be consistent: "Use of Scripture with regard to the homosexual must not be different from that with regard to the heterosexual: one cannot concede to inflated heterosexual claims about the significance of 'sex' and then deny parallel homosexual claims."[523]

"Like Angels in Heaven": The Eschatological Tension

Enough has now been said to show that the whole area of sexuality is fraught with tension in our era. Perhaps we need to draw back a bit and examine this area through the lens I sketched out in the first half of the book. Eschatologically, certainly looking at the issue from an "end-time" perspective, Jesus tells us that "when they rise from the dead, they neither marry nor are given in marriage, but are like angels in heaven."[524] So, in the end, marriage doesn't matter? Not quite. Jesus never suggests this – even if he does (controversially for his time) allow for singleness for the sake of the gospel. Marriage, as the New Testament scholar

---

[521] For the above para, see ibid., 30–1.
[522] "No Easy Victory," 52.
[523] Moberly, "Use of Scripture," 255.
[524] Mk. 12:25.

Richard Hays puts it, is "the way of suffering service" – enough has been said above to indicate that marriage need not be "a bed of roses" (or, more prosaically, the bed of roses also has plenty of thorns!), but marriage "is also a sign of the eschatological redemption of all things." Hays continues: "It figuratively foreshadows, even in the ambiguities of the present time, God's unbreakable covenant faithfulness which will finally bring healing to the world."[525] Hays' comments come in his discussion of divorce, which I have not mentioned before in this book. So, let me (all too briefly) mention divorce, or, more accurately, the Christian prohibition of divorce.

Divorce and eschatology are not usually considered bedfellows, but let us follow Hays again. As we have already noted, Hays regards marriage in such a way that:

> It figuratively foreshadows, even in the ambiguities of the present time, God's unbreakable covenant faithfulness which will finally bring healing to the world. Thus, the community's renunciation of divorce is a signal, an outward and visible sign of the eschatological salvation of God. Mark [10:2–12], by pointing back behind the Mosaic Law to God's original design, dares to suggest that through unwavering faithfulness to the one-flesh union of marriage, Jesus' disciples embody *new creation*, manifesting what was meant to be "from the beginning of creation." Likewise, Matthew [5:31–32] . . . makes the point with unmistakable clarity: the *polis* on the hill is a sign of hope for the world . . . Matthew's exception clause, however, is a clear concession to the "not yet": until the kingdom arrives in its fullness, human unfaithfulness will necessitate realistic measures to cope with pastoral problems. Paul [in 1 Cor. 7] emphasises even more clearly the "not yet" side of the eschatological dialectic . . . Even . . . in view of the urgency of God's coming kingdom, marriages remain valid – even marriages to unbelievers.[526]

However, Paul also says that "if the unbelieving partner separates [from the marriage], let it be so; in such a case the brother or sister is not bound [to the marriage]. It is to peace that God has called you" (1 Cor. 7:15). It is, as Hays notes, the case that "[h]ope and common sense are kept in delicate balance." Even as the permanence of the "one-flesh union" is seen as an eschatological sign, the church itself has to live with both the "not yet" and the "already here," especially in an age where so many marriages, so many relationships, fail.

---

[525] Richard B. Hays, *The Moral Vision of the New Testament: A Contemporary Introduction to New Testament Ethics* (Edinburgh: T&T Clark, 1996), 366.

[526] Ibid. 366.

"Be Renewed in the Spirit of Your Minds":[527] In, But Not Of the World, The Ecclesiological Tension

So many relationships fail. So many Christian relationships fail. So many wish to revise, or disregard, scripture with regard to homosexual unions, so how is the church to "proclaim Christ until he comes"?

> On a typical wedding day, a glowing bride and groom will be embraced and congratulated on the auspicious beginning of their new family. Invariably, they will greet this new beginning and its well-wishers with joy, even though they and everyone gathered understands that this starry-eyed couple, if they are in fact starting a new family, is being left alone on hard and unforgiving terrain. Only the strong or lucky will survive.[528]

This might be true for many, but it should not be true for Christians. While it might be true for many that their relationship, their marriage, is founded on "nothing but interpersonal intimacy" and they are shocked when their pastor is not about "to negotiate terms," shocked that the marital commitment is not "a form of market exchange," but "taking on a way of life in the community of faith."[529] Interpersonal intimacy, as the sole foundation of any relationship, goes back to the myth of romanticism and, as I have noted above, marriage is not like that: "heroic," not "romantic."

The way of life in the community of faith is one that is begun at baptism (if infant baptism is practiced) or earlier (if it is not). Children are to be welcomed into the worshiping community: we need look no further than Mark 9 and 10 for confirmation of this: whoever welcomes a little child in Jesus' name welcomes him, and if we do not receive the kingdom of God as a little child, we cannot enter it. These are stark words, but key to understanding the topsy-turvy world that is the Christian community.

> [T]he point is not so much that [children] are innocent, but that their frankness and spontaneity – their simple willingness to be embraced by Jesus – offers a kind of parable of life with God . . . The claim is that God [blesses the church] in part by giving adults children, and children adults, within a larger economy of blessing.[530]

---

[527] Eph. 4:23.

[528] David Matzko McCarthy, "Becoming One Flesh: Marriage, Remarriage, and Sex," in *The Blackwell Companion to Christian Ethics*, 276.

[529] See ibid., 278–9.

[530] Joseph L. Mangina, "Bearing Fruit: Conception, Children, and the Family," in *The Blackwell Companion to Christian Ethics*, 473–4.

And within the larger family of the church. It is not just within the "nuclear family" that children learn about God as the one who is talked to, who is supremely (and mysteriously) in control, but it is "in worship where we learn the gestures of God's love and are called to God's way of reconciliation and peace in a world of violence and estrangement." Therefore we can see that for married, and family, life "[t]he symmetry of Ephesians 5 is not interpersonal love, but a mutual subordination for the purpose of fostering holiness, which in turn serves as a witness to Christ (cf. 1 Peter 3:1–7)."[531]

Christian relationships, therefore, stand as a witness to another way, a better way, of doing "relationships." The church stands as a community against individualistic romantic "interpersonal intimacy." Against a throwaway culture, the church witnesses to the long haul: the recognition that "marriages are in good working order when they are cultivated within and also foster and enhance an expanding circle of friends."[532] Against this, it has been shown that "[t]hose who live together 'are as likely to return to singleness as to enter marriage,' and . . . [t]hose who cohabit while raising children are more likely to separate."[533]

Other statistics make for grim reading: "Cohabiting partners suffer higher levels of conflict, domestic violence, abuse, and infidelity than married partners do." Further, "[r]elationships between live-ins and the children of their partners are less stable and satisfying, and far more prone to sexual and physical abuse (including assault and murder), than in families where the adults are married to each other."[534] Against this background, a firm and public witness is more than ever necessary.

"It Is Actually Reported . . .":[535] "Is" and "Ought" in Marriage

It seems that the early church did not always get it right. Without going into the whys and wherefores of how the Corinthian church came to tolerate such sexual immorality that "is not found even among the pagans," it is clear that the whole area of sex, relationships, singleness and all the other variations we have looked at in this chapter are nothing new. Paul, of course, had his

---

[531] McCarthy, "Marriage, Remarriage and Sex," 281.

[532] Ibid., 286.

[533] Cited in ibid.

[534] David P. Gushee, "A Crumbling Institution: How Social Revolutions Cracked the Pillars of Marriage," in *Christianity Today* (September 2004), 44.

[535] 1 Cor. 5:1.

answer, "you are to hand this man over to Satan,"[536] and "drive out the wicked person from among you."[537] If only life were so simple! This chapter has dealt with beliefs about marriage, and homosexuality. En route, it has touched on singleness, and having children, and it has discussed friendship in terms of intimacy and familiarity. We know, at least in the Anglican/ Episcopalian Church (though these questions are there in other churches too), that questions of sexuality, and how to deal with such drives, will not disappear in the foreseeable future. So I want to end with three questions.

The first is to those who might wish to revise, or ignore, the teachings of both scripture and the historic church about the exclusive sexual nature of marriage and about homosexuality: "Why must sanctifying friendships be sexually explicit;" can there not be other satisfying ways of sharing life together "without the stimulation of genitalia?"[538] The second question is for those who cannot, or will not, accept such revisionist proposals: how do we accept and live with difference within the body of Christ? How can we meet, love and share – how can we be hospitable with – our brothers and sisters with whom we do not agree?

And thirdly, how far are we in the church willing to tackle society and its fear of intimacy allied to its glorification of overt sexuality, to show that there is another way – that "the long haul" may not appear as glamorous, but involves more romance, more joy and more life in the end? After all, the effect on others is profound:

> if by 16 you are living with only one of your biological parents, you are more likely to suffer from multiple disadvantages, compared with other children. You are 70% more likely to have a criminal conviction by the age of 15; you are twice as likely to leave school with no diploma . . . you are no better off if your mother remarries or if your grandmother moves in. As adults, people from single-parent families are more likely to die young and to get divorced themselves.[539]

In asking these questions, I suspect readers will realize that I do not have the answers. I can only hope that thinking about these questions will be a start to enable the church to engage. How we live our lives – our sexual, sensual lives – might be a personal area, but I trust enough has been said to show that it is not a private one.

---

[536] 1 Cor. 5:5.

[537] 1 Cor. 5:13.

[538] See Joel Shuman, "Friendship and Homosexuality," in *The Blackwell Companion to Christian Ethics*, 412.

[539] Quoted in Spencer, "Doing God," 54.

Nine

War and Peace in the Twenty-first Century

The cry "where is God?" echoed through the last century, from the trenches of the first world war to the carpet bombing of the second, through the Gulag and Auschwitz, through the killing fields of Cambodia and Rwanda and in a million smaller disasters which show, if any demonstration were needed, that the much-vaunted European Enlightenment of two centuries ago is still a long way from producing liberty, equality and fraternity. Now, with our present century only a few years old, we've already amassed a similar tally, with a similar question. Where was God on September 11th 2001? . . . Where was God in Beslan . . .? Where was God in Lebanon a few months ago, and where is God today in the Gaza strip?[540]

It is perhaps because the First World War shattered so many liberal hopes of humanity's progress toward eternal peace that such a question was asked in such a heartfelt way. It seemed that the God who had blessed the Enlightenment project had all too quickly withdrawn his support. Some answered the "where is God" question with a defiant "nowhere, because he doesn't exist." Others still insist that God exists, but the trouble is *which* God was being asked to show a presence?

Most people in our culture still assume that the word "God" is more or less   univocal, referring to a being located at some distance from our space-time universe, and that the options are *either* that this God keeps his distance and doesn't "intervene" within the world *or* that this God does sometimes reach in to the world from the outside and do things which can be called "intervention."[541]

[540] "Where is God in the War on Terror," a public lecture by N.T. Wright, Bishop of Durham in Durham Cathedral, November 9, 2006. See www.ntwright-page.com/Wright_War_On_Terror.htm (accessed November 27, 2006).
[541] Ibid.

Whereas the God who ought to be asked to show a presence is already here: for Christians, Jesus – both fully human and fully divine – is

> the one who completed and fulfilled a long and winding story, of how the creator God had decided to heal his wounded creation, to rescue his rebel subjects, not by simply acting upon it and them from the outside, nor by hoping the world would sort itself out without his help, but by acting *from within the world* to put the world to rights at the last . . .[542]

But whereas that might leave us with a suffering God (as Bonhoeffer would put it), does it leave us with anything, or anyone, who can show us any good? Wright continues:

> The presence of God within the world at a time of war must be calibrated according to what Paul says in Romans 8, that the Spirit groans within God's people as they groan with the pain of the world . . .
>
> But, though that is the first word in answer to tonight's question, it is not the last. *If* my analysis is anything like correct, we should also see God in the calling to account of those who abuse power, in the reminding of the rulers and authorities that they have a task of justice and mercy, anticipating God's eventual rule and implementing the achievement of Jesus.[543]

If is a loaded term, and Wright's analysis has been sharply attacked. Gilbert Meilaender, for one, has taken issue with any suggestion that the war on terror might also be an abuse of power: "responsible government officials must also use and be prepared to use force against those whose willingness to commit inhumane acts is announced and well known."[544] However, Meilaender needs to note Hauerwas' assertion that "[i]f this is war, then Bin Laden has won" because "[h]e thinks he is a warrior not a murderer."[545] If, on the other hand, Bin Laden is a murderer then surely the reation ought to be to arrest him in order to put him on trial? This option does not require war, or even vengeance, it requires justice and perhaps even an understanding of the murderer. Hauerwas again:

---

[542] Ibid.

[543] Ibid., emphasis added.

[544] www.firstthings.com/article.php3?id_article=5412&var_recherche= meilaender+war+on+terror.

[545] Hauerwas, *Dissent from the Homeland*, 184.

> We know it is possible to love our enemies . . . if we do not think it possible to love our enemies then we should plainly say Jesus is not the messiah. But Jesus is the messiah, not dead but alive . . .[546]

In other words, God, in the war on terror, is both "grieving and groaning within the pain and horror of his battered but still beautiful world."[547]

We cannot avoid the tensions that have been discussed in this book: Wright's words point us to an eschatology that we hope to be more realized than it appears to be at present: proclaiming peace in the midst of a war, especially when that proclaimed peace does not involve the destruction of the enemy, is not usually considered "the done thing." Stanley Hauerwas has, post 9/11, been attacked for daring to suppose that a Christian pacifist position has any right to a public voice. On the other hand, some of those theologians who rushed to bless George W. Bush's war on terror, may well now be wishing that they had shown more restraint before enlisting God on the side of the American angels. Not that Bush, or his British allies, are about to abort their campaign, however flawed and failing it may be. Despite setbacks in the mid-term elections of November 2006, it seems that the war goes on. So what should we do in the face of such seeming deafness on the part of our rulers? Sometimes, it is just a case of silence and prayer; but sometimes it is right to look again at Christian tradition, so that we might better know how we are to speak truth to power.

Just War and How We Got There

As we have seen in the case of slavery, the Bible does not speak with one voice on the question of war. "Thou shalt not kill" is there along with the rest of the Ten Commandments, and is clearly foundational to the Jewish, Christian, and Islamic faiths. And yet, any close reading of the Old Testament will reveal a God who commands the military conquest of Canaan by the Israelites and clearly fights for (and then against as the Old Testament story approaches the Exile) Israel. Therefore, most commentators assume that the commandment against killing is more properly read as a commandment against murder: it is private vengeance that is forbidden, rather than the public policy of killing in war.

By the time we come to the New Testament, the social context has changed: Israel is no longer an independent state, but a province – or

---

[546] Ibid., 191–2.
[547] Wright, "War on Terror."

indeed provinces – under the superpower of the time. It is, however, clear that Jesus chooses not to side with the Zealots in their campaign of seeking the violent overthrow of Roman rule. We have the clear instruction of the Sermon on the Mount, where Jesus calls the peacemakers blessed. Bonhoeffer is equally clear that not only are his followers "to have peace, but they are to make peace":

> To do this they renounce violence and strife. Those things never help the cause of Christ. Christ's kingdom is a realm of peace, and those in Christ's community greet each other with a greeting of peace. Jesus' disciples maintain peace by choosing to suffer instead of causing others to suffer. They preserve community when others destroy it. They renounce self-assertion and are silent in the face of hatred and injustice. That is how they overcome evil with good. That is how they are makers of divine peace in a world of hatred and war.[548]

There is no talk here of differentiating private vengeance and statecraft, of public and private. Christians are called to be peacemakers in all aspects of life. The question, of course, is how that is to be done. Bonhoeffer himself, for all his talk of a "peace that must be dared" in the 1930s, became an anti-Hitler conspirator, and so can be seen as a sign of contradiction. On the one hand, peace; on the other, he was involved in plotting violence against the leader of the Nazi system.

But the New Testament itself contains its own contradictions: Jesus chided a disciple for using force to defend him ("all who take the sword will perish by the sword," Mt. 26:52) and chose not to make use of his Father's twelve legions of angels, but faced death by crucifixion instead. On the other hand, Luke records Jesus saying, before he went to the Mount of Olives to meet his accusers, "the one who has no sword must sell his cloak to buy one" (Lk. 22:36). Also, John the Baptist did not tell soldiers to leave the army ("be satisfied with your wages," Lk. 3:14). And Romans 13 shows that Paul believed that "the governing authorities" had the right to use force.

Force for the authorities, yes: but not for the emerging church. Although there is no evidence either way that Christians either participated in, or abstained from, military service in the first 150 years or so of its history, a noted pagan commentator, Celsus, criticized Christians in the second century for not participating in military service. As time went on, many churches made soldiers reject military service before baptism; and there are third-century church orders in existence which suggest

---

[548] Bonhoeffer, *Discipleship*, 108.

that Christians who refused to leave the army were excommunicated.

This, of course, was the situation before Constantine: the church was,
broadly, pacific in tone and outlook, but we must view such pacifism
with a degree of caution as "the question of military service was not dis-
entangled from the general question of involvement with a hostile
pagan government."[549] Not only must we remember that, throughout the
first to fourth centuries, the church was subject to persecutions, of varying intensity, and with varying official sanction; but also we must note
that soldiers (who could well be charged with hunting down these
Christians) were required to make sacrifice to the gods – often including
the Roman emperor himself. However, we know that Emperor
Constantine was converted to Christianity in AD 313, and by the end of
that century, Christianity was the only official religion of the Empire.
Now, in a reversal of the policy mentioned above, soldiers who left the
army were excommunicated, and by AD 416 non-Christians were forbidden to serve in the army.

Therefore, the church suddenly had to wrestle with public policy
issues it had never had to face before, and whether this endorsement
by the Roman Imperium was the church's downfall or its coming of
age is still debated. But, at the time, it is difficult to see what else the
church could have, or should have, done. Should it really have said to
Constantine: "No, we don't recognize your conversion; we don't want
to be part of the official Roman apparatus, nor do we want to have any
influence over the state. Instead we prefer to go back to the days of
your predecessor, Diocletian, and be persecuted to our deaths." As
Gustavo Gutiérrez points out, wishing for one's death is a sin, not just
because life is precious in itself, but also it involves wishing that
someone else sins (by killing you and thus breaking the commandment).[550]

However all empires have engaged in war. All states use coercion to
bend both its subjects and other states to its will. Sometimes this coercion involves war, war itself being "nothing but the continuation of policy by other means."[551] Be that as it may, the church had to come up with
a new way of approaching the problem of war as part of statecraft. As I
have noted Augustine was one of the first Christian thinkers who wrestled with the concept of the just war:

---

[549] O'Donovan, *The Just War Revisited* (Cambridge: Cambridge University Press,
2003), 11.

[550] Gutiérrez, *We Drink From Our Own Wells*, 117 and 167 n. 8.

[551] Carl von Clausewitz, quoted in O'Donovan, *The Just War Revisited*, 95.

> But the wise man, they say, will wage just wars. Surely, however, if he remembers that he is a human being, he will be much readier to deplore the fact that he is under the necessity of waging even just wars . . . Let everyone, therefore, who reflects with pain upon such great evils, upon such horror and cruelty, acknowledge that this is misery. And if anyone either endures them or thinks of them without anguish of soul, his condition is still more miserable: for he thinks himself happy only because he has lost all human feeling.[552]

In other words, war must be carried out by proper authority, have just cause, and right intention; but it must be remembered that war is an evil, however much it is a necessary evil, and soldiers must do penance after involvement in war. This tradition survived into medieval times: the Norman soldiers after the battle of Hastings in 1066 did penance for the shedding of blood – even though the Pope had blessed their cause.

Also, the wise man wages war "for it is the iniquity of the opposing side that imposes upon the wise man the duty of waging wars." In other words, the wise man goes to war to avenge wrongs or injustices committed by another state (or its subjects), or to restore what has been seized unjustly: under these circumstances, war can be seen as charity to a third party. As a further consideration: "Be a peacemaker, therefore, even in war, so that by conquering them you bring the benefit of peace even to those you defeat."[553] Therefore, war must be fought to preserve order and achieve peace; and use of force must be limited: Augustine urges the Roman general, to "use mercy towards the defeated or the captive."[554]

As with all doctrines, the concept of the just war has evolved over time, until there is now a broad consensus that there are two basic conditions for a just war: *jus ad bellum*, and *jus in bello*. These are not meant to be "tick boxes" so that you know you have a just war once you have got the conditions right, not least because throughout history there has always been a presumption against war, simply because war, as we have noted, is so evil. However, for the record, the *jus ad bellum* are the conditions examined prior to going to war, and *jus in bello* are those conditions required in addition once war has commenced. These two parts of the just war tradition are usually set out as follows:

---

[552] Augustine, *DCD* XIX. 8.

[553] *Letter* 189 to Count Boniface, a Roman general, *Augustine: Political Writings* (trans. E.M. Atkins and R.J. Dodaro; Cambridge: Cambridge University Press, 2001), 217.

[554] Ibid.

Modern Just War Theory – *jus ad bellum*

1. Just cause: we must be confronting a real and certain danger; for example, a just cause would be the protection of innocent life and securing basic human rights.

2. Competent authority: war can only be declared by those responsible for public order, not private groups or individuals.

3. Comparative justice: this condition requires us to look into which side has comparative right on its side and ensure the values that are at stake are critical enough to override the presumption against war.

4. Right intention: we cannot use just war theory as an excuse for fighting wars intended on other grounds. (That is, we cannot decide we are going to fight a war, and then try to make the theory "fit").

5. Last resort: all peaceful alternatives must have been exhausted.

6. Probability of success: if fighting is likely to be futile, the war should not be fought.

7. Proportionality: the damage inflicted and the costs incurred by the war must not outweigh the good expected by engaging in conflict.

Modern Just War Theory – *jus in bello*

1. Proportionality: the military means used must be in proportion to the expected result.

2. Discrimination: military action must not be directed against non-combatants.

Of course, it is relatively easy to see from these conditions that there has never been a "just war" – but this is not the point. The just war "theory" is not a theory, "but a proposal of practical reason; and it is not, in the second place, about 'just wars,' but about how we may enact just judgment even in the theatre of war."[555] It is often seen as profoundly

---

[555] O'Donovan, *The Just War Revisited*, 12–3.

unsatisfactory against the moral certainty of pacifism (discussed below), but the church has to work out how it is to live in these "in-between" times: where Christ has come, but has yet to return. For this period, it seems that the Old Testament sensibility about the commandment "thou shalt not kill" may yet have some time to run. But before we hang onto this conclusion too tightly, let us turn to the alternative view, that of pacifism.

Pacifism and the End of Violence

Pacifists are called to live out the nonviolent possibilities granted by God's Spirit in all of life: this means that they belong to "a church constituted by people who would rather die than kill."[556] Therefore the pacifist response to the attack on the twin towers, to the call to Americans to continue to shop, to the declaration of an open-ended, indeed never-ending "war on terrorism" is to "go on 'as though nothing has happened;'" accepting that God has "given us all the time we need to respond to September 11 with 'small acts of beauty and tenderness,' which . . . if done with humility and confidence 'will bring unity to the world and break the chain of violence.'"[557]

This will not satisfy those who want "to kill the bastards" who perpetrated the events of September 11, 2001, but it is not meant to: both sides in the just war/pacifism debate have a presumption against violence. However, for the noted pacifist Stanley Hauerwas, the church's story is about a God who, through Jesus, "has judged between the peoples, God has beat the swords of the nations into plowshares. God has abolished war. We need no longer to learn of war."[558]

In the light of what I said above, we should note the tense, and set this against Isaiah 2:4 and Micah 4:3, where the prophecy is set in the future. Of course, we may say that Jesus himself is the fulfillment of the (Old Testament) Law and prophets, but this prophecy in Isaiah is about Judah and Jerusalem – which has yet to see much peace. And neither do we yet have the situation where, to continue Isaiah 2:4, "nation shall not lift up sword

---

[556] Stanley Hauerwas, "September 11, 2001: A Pacifist Response," in Stanley Hauerwas and Frank Lentricchia (eds.), *Dissent From The Homeland: Essays After September 11* (Duke University Press: Durham, NC & London, 2003), 186.

[557] Ibid., 189; internal quotes from Jean Vanier, founder of the L'Arche movement.

[558] Ibid., 191.

against nation, neither shall they learn war any more." This, of course, does not answer how the church is to live, nor does it necessarily address how the church is to speak peace to the non-believing, war-mongering world. Does a church which takes a pacifist position have nothing to say?

Saying nothing

Of course, post-9/11, Hauerwas has famously said that he has nothing to say (but spends a whole essay saying it!). That "nothing" is to continue living in a manner that shows the change in the world occurred at the first Eastertide, not at 9/11.[559] It means living in a manner that makes the trivial important, and relativizes the important (at least, the important in worldly terms). This nonviolent nothing does, however, become confrontational over this very issue of the trivial – because if the trivial, like getting married, having children, watching baseball, are important; then the important, like what gets decided in the Oval Office, must be trivial in the sense that, however important the world thinks such decisions may be, they are relativized by God's peaceful presence in the world. If God has decreed that life must go on, that creation, despite all we have done to it and with it, is still good and still to be enjoyed: then the trivial things do matter.

Punishment

But if pacifists cannot condone war – and argue for "peaceableness" in all circumstances – what should they do about the trivial matter of punishment? John Milbank, a commentator on Augustine's theology, reduces punishment to "the self-punishment inherent in sin."[560] However, he does not say how he proposes to raise a person's conscience, or install self-discipline, without external discipline being imposed first (even Pinocchio needed his Jiminy Cricket). However, as Milbank notes, in all punishment, or coercion, "however mild and benignly motivated, there is still present a moment of 'pure' violence, externally and arbitrarily related to the end one has in mind."[561]

For Augustine, it is a matter of regret that our authority structures require "reinforcement by mechanisms of compulsion"[562] but this is due to our fallen state. However, he is also aware that there is no guarantee that punishment would work: "I don't know whether more

---

[559] See ibid., 188, quoted above, page 66.

[560] Milbank, *Theology and Social Theory*, 421. Incidentally, Milbank is not a pacifist, perhaps Hauerwas is right, and he ought to be one.

[561] Ibid., 421.

[562] Williams, "Politics and the Soul," 63. Cf. Deane, *Political and Social Ideas of St. Augustine*, 189.

people are reformed than slip into worse ways through fear of impending punishment."[563] Augustine is caught in the dilemma that punishment could lead to a person's destruction, but that leaving that person unpunished could "lead to someone else being destroyed."[564] Therefore, we can see that while Augustine is clear in his "unambiguous approval of the official use of force . . . there are times when he makes no secret of his misgivings."[565] Rowan Williams points out that the power of coercion that "so readily converts itself into a tool for selfish interest, a means of exercising the *libido dominandi*, is a sign of how far fallen we are."[566]

Stanley Hauerwas has noted, correctly, that "[o]f course Christians know the world does not share our faith, that the world cannot be expected to live as Christians should live, but that does not mean there is some line drawn in the sand that determines what Christians cannot ask of societies in which we find ourselves."[567] There is no reason, therefore, not to challenge the world "to move up one [more] notch in approximation of the righteousness of love."[568]

Hauerwas accepts that there is a distinction "between the police function and the war function." Of course, in the time of the early church both functions were carried out by the military; this is usually not the case in domestic policies.[569] Indeed, while in conversation with Milbank, Hauerwas expressed the hope that "it might be possible to train police in a way that they do not have to carry guns to do their job well within our communities."[570] These police could then "be trained to intervene in violence." Milbank's response is to point out that "[t]here is a funny little island [that is, Britain] that has been doing that for a long time." In

---

[563] *Letter* 95. 3.

[564] Ibid.

[565] John M. Rist, *Augustine: Ancient Thought Baptized* (Cambridge: Cambridge University Press, 1994), 226.

[566] Williams, "Politics and the Soul," 63.

[567] Stanley Hauerwas, *Performing the Faith: Bonhoeffer and the Practice of Nonviolence* (London: SPCK, 2004), 196.

[568] Ibid., 197, quoting John Howard Yoder.

[569] I am, for the sake of this argument, excluding the calling in of the National Guard *in extremis* (for example in the case of the breeching of the levees in New Orleans in 2005), and the idea that our military may be sent to places to carry out peacemaking tasks akin to police actions.

[570] Stanley Hauerwas and John Milbank, "Christian Peace," in Kenneth R. Chase and Alan Jacobs (eds.) *Must Christianity Be Violent? Reflections on History, Practice, and Theology* (Grand Rapids: Brazos Press, 2003), 221.

other words, despite the rise in violent crime, and increased security in the war on terror, it is still true that "most policemen on the beat [in the UK] don't have guns."[571]

For Christians, the purpose of punishment is restoration, reconciliation, not just with God, but also with our brothers and sisters in "the community of forgiven sinners called church."[572] This, in and of itself, does not answer the question of how this is to be relayed to "the world." Hauerwas' aim, in the article I have quoted, is to justify his argument against capital punishment; but his ideas do give us a clue as to how we are to behave. We are a community called to peace (and we know that there will be no real peace without justice); how we punish and what we punish, must also be indicative of that calling to peace. We must be able to name sin – and crime – and deal with it. We must accept that, at our best, we are but forgiven sinners. But how this is to avoid the "moment of 'pure' violence," he does not say.

Peacemakers

But it is to be more than restoration. Jesus did not say blessed are those who keep the peace; blessed are those who do nothing to promote war; but blessed are the peacemakers (see Mt. 5:9).

> Peacemaking is not magic . . . it is a great costly positive principle. Peacemakers must move back across the divide of hostility. "Love your enemies and pray for those who persecute you," commands Jesus ([Matthew] 5:44). The Son of God requires us to go through barriers that have hitherto led to war, and to be for the enemy, for their good . . . This approach is costly, as the Gospels show. It leads to persecution and insults, but it breaks the causal law of evil with the power of the love of God.[573]

Bonhoeffer's message in *Discipleship* (quoted above) echoed the call he had made at the Fanö conference in 1934:

> For the members of the ecumenical church, in so far as they hold to Christ, his word, his commandment of peace is more holy, more inviolable than the most revered words and works of the natural world . . . These brothers in Christ obey his word; they do not doubt or question, but keep his

---

[571] Ibid.

[572] Ibid., 199.

[573] Alan Storkey, *Jesus and Politics: Confronting the Powers* (Grand Rapids, MI: Baker Academic, 2005), 141.

commandment of peace . . . They cannot take up arms against Christ himself – yet this is what they do if they take up arms against one another![574]

Here, of course, is a possible answer to those who insist that, even if the
Second World War was fought unjustly, the scourge of Hitler, or, more
generally fascism, had to be fought: what if Christians had refused to
fight neither for Hitler or against him because in doing so they would
have been taking up arms against their fellow human beings – their fellow Christians?[575] And what did the Second World War lead to, but the
Cold War, which has led in turn (with a very short historical gap) to the
unwinnable, and unconcludable war on terror?

But this begs the question: "Who will call us to peace so that the
world will hear, will have to hear?" Once again, Bonhoeffer makes a suggestion:

> The individual Christian cannot do it . . . he can indeed raise his voice and
> bear witness, but the powers of this world stride over him without a word.
> The individual church, too, can witness and suffer – oh, if it only would!
> – but it also is suffocated by the power of hate. Only the one great
> Ecumenical Council of the holy church of Christ over all the world can
> speak out so that the world, though it gnash its teeth, will have to hear, so
> that the peoples will rejoice because the church of Christ in the name of
> Christ has taken the weapons from the hands of their sons, forbidden war,
> proclaimed the peace of Christ against the raging world.[576]

In other words if only the churches would act together and proclaim the
peace of Christ, the world would be forced to hear. There is no promise
that the world would act (except against the church). However, as it is,
with so many in the church allowing for and even advocating war,
Christ's voice of peace, remains lost in the quiet of the dead and dying –
lost under the bombs of our aircraft and the shells of our guns.

Of course, there is the example of those who have stood for peace.
Whether we talk of a St. Francis, or of Martin Luther King, or of Oscar
Romero, it is clear that these people have "punched above their weight."
But they have also paid a high price. To die in a hail of bullets is not what
we want: the blessing for being a peacemaker comes from God, not
worldly humanity. This, we must be prepared for (to quote Bonhoeffer
again):

---

[574] Bonhoeffer, *No Rusty Swords*, 290.
[575] See Hays, *Moral Vision*, 342 for a similar point.
[576] Bonhoeffer, *No Rusty Swords*, 291.

While Jesus calls, "blessed, blessed," the world shrieks, "Away, away with them!" Yes, away! But where will they go? Into the kingdom of heaven . . . Wounded and martyred bodies shall be transformed, and instead of the clothing of sin and penitence, they shall wear the white robe of eternal righteousness. From that eternal joy there comes a call to the community of disciples here under the cross, the call of Jesus, "blessed, blessed."[577]

We may not be called to suffer martyrdom, but there is no getting away from the fact that we are called to travel the hard road of peace.

The Church's Calling

"The church is born to die shivering with the cold." So said Paulo Freire. The church is repeatedly told that it must get out there and "be with" the poor, the marginalized, the destitute, and the oppressed. It may be that we have to deal with living in tension here: being called to peace, yet trying to discern how "we may enact just judgment even in the theatre of war." Is the choice as stark as this? Either we allow for war, and try to exercise just judgment given this fact, or we insist that all war is, and has to be, wrong?

One of my students, who was not a pacifist, put it this way:

I fully accept that active non-violence and passive resistance, for example, Gandhi and Martin Luther King and others have shown another way of combating unjust regimes from within. But how long should active non-violence and passive resistance continue in societies where the government has no compunction in using lethal force against those who disagree with them.

A pacifist response could go something like this:

Whether something "works", of course, is not the basic criterion of Christian action. A Christian's first concern must be to be obedient to the

---

[577] Bonhoeffer, *Discipleship*, 110. Before any dualism is suggested by my readers, I shall point out that Bonhoeffer then goes on to talk of the people of God, who could be seen as "people unworthy of living" as being salt, "the most indispensable commodity on earth," and light, "the visible community of faith." Ibid., 110–14.

Lord, even if this leads to suffering, death and apparent failure. However, an assertive non-violent stand was often effective, even in the face of scheme's as satanic as Hitler's.

In Bulgaria in the early 1940s . . . Thousands of Jews and non-Jews resisted all collaboration with Nazi decrees. They marched in mass street demonstrations and sent floods of letters and telegrams to authorities protesting all anti-Jewish measures. Bulgarian clergy hid Jews and accepted a large number of Jewish "converts" . . . These and other non-military measures saved all of Bulgaria's Jewish citizens from the Nazi death camps . . .

Although always a minority movement, similar non-violent resistance to Hitler took place in many parts of Europe, with Christians often being key actors. Danes . . . saved 93 per cent of their Jewish population in a dramatic non-violent rescue action . . .

In France, Pastor André Trocmé, a strong pacifist, made his whole town of Le Chambon a center for hiding Jews and smuggling them to Switzerland . . .

Most non-Jews in Europe failed to speak or act against Hitler's genocide. Those who did resist paid a heavy price in imprisonment, torture and death. Yet their actions saved tens of thousands of Jewish lives. They did not submit to Nazi rule, yet they fought non-violently. They refute the notion that only military means are effective in defending people and their values against the very worst form of tyranny.[578]

Well, maybe. All these actions took place after the military defeat of their country – so other means of resistance had to be tried if there was to be any resistance at all. We do not know how long this nonviolent resistance could have held out against the Hitler machine if most of its resources were not engaged in the military struggle against the Allies. The nonviolent resistance was time limited in any case, as, by mid-1945, the Nazi menace had been destroyed (by military might). So, yes, nonviolence worked, and many brave people suffered for standing up for what was right. But to take these stories and argue, for example, that we should not have fought the Second World War is, in my opinion, going a step too far.

This is not to decry the work of those who resisted, but the nonviolent resistance "worked" alongside the military resistance going on elsewhere. Let me say that while the nonviolent response appeals, and clearly in the situations outlined above, worked (Finland saved all but

---

[578] Sojourners *Christians and Nonviolence*, 15 (see www.sojo.net "Sojourners on the issues").

four of its Jews),[579] I remain unconvinced that we can ask and expect states, with all their ambiguous duties and concerns, not to go to war in this or a similar situation. We could say that this war has no justification, or that war is impolitic; and we can insist on nonviolent protest if we ever are in a similar situation to occupied Europe in the Second World War. But we need, in my opinion, something like a just war theory, if we are to seek to engage with states who will go to war.

"And the Lion Shall Lie Down with the Lamb":[580] The Eschatological Tension

As we have just noted,

> Christians live in a meantime . . . [with] God having *already* made the reign of God present in Jesus Christ, and God not yet having brought the fullness of the reign at the culmination of history . . . Christians impressed by the "not-yet" tug of this eschatological tension are more likely to argue that they have a responsibility to live out their Christian faith amid the constraints and complexities of the world as it is, which is what seems to require a reluctant use of violence. Christians impressed by the "already" tug of this eschatological tension are more likely to argue that "the world as it is" is one in which God's Spirit is always offering new possibilities, and empowering people of faith to live now according to the future.[581]

It is this eschatological tension which can be seen as the nub of the tension between pacifists and those advocating the just war theory. Of course, there is also the problem of what is meant by the eschatological peace we are supposedly striving for. Are we searching for the peace of God, or "world peace"? World peace, in worldly terms, tends to mean an absence of war. God's peace may be that, but it encompasses so much more: it comes with justice for all, for a start. So, as I noted at the start of this chapter, theological conceptions of peace are not necessarily the same as the "post-Enlightenment notions of moral progress and post-Industrial and Information Age technological

---

[579] Ibid.
[580] Is. 11:6.
[581] Gerald W. Schlabach, "Breaking Bread: Peace and War," in Stanley Hauerwas and Samuel Wells (eds.), *The Blackwell Companion to Christian Ethics* (Blackwell: Malden, MA & Oxford, 2004), 367, emphasis original.

progress . . ."[582] The "already" and "not yet" tension of the eschaton is perhaps solved best, if we follow the Roman Catholic bishops in their *The Challenge of Peace*:

> Individuals may opt for a non-violent "witness," but governments may not. The bishops commend Francis of Assisi, Dorothy Day and Martin Luther King, Jr., for choosing the first option as a way of embracing the "already" of the kingdom. But as the "already" is joined to a "not yet," the first option cannot stand alone as the Christian response to injustice. The "already" of non-violent witness must be balanced by the "not yet" of governmental responsibility for repelling evil and overcoming injustice.[583]

Of course, this juxtaposes individuals and governments. How are churches to behave?

"Wars and Rumors of Wars:"[584] The Ecclesiological Tension

In their October 2002 submission to the House of Commons Foreign Affairs Select Committee (which was discussing the then prospect of war against Iraq), the Anglican bishops described their task, on the part of the national church, as raising "those moral and ethical questions, which the government needs to address before there is any recourse to war."[585] The submission clearly relies on just war thinking, and makes the excellent point that a just peace needs to be sought as the result of any war; the removal of Saddam Hussein is not to be seen as an end in itself. However, the submission also says that "[i]t is the privilege of individual Christians to campaign one way or another for or against military action."[586] The bishops thereby gave individual Christians the responsibility to think through

---

[582] Joseph E. Capizzi, "On Behalf of the Neighbour: A Rejection of the Complementarity of Just-War Theory and Pacifism," in *Studies in Christian Ethics* 14:2 (2001), 96.

[583] Ibid., 103.

[584] Mt. 24:6.

[585] "Evaluating the Threat of Military Action Against Iraq: A submission by the House of Bishops to the House of Commons Foreign Affairs Select Committee's ongoing inquiry into the War on Terrorism," www.cofe.anglican.org/papers/Bishopssubmission.doc (January 16, 2003), para. 70.

[586] Ibid,. 63. The bishops do not view the United States as having a good record in helping to build alternate regimes in those countries where it has recently intervened militarily.

the issues involved with war, without giving them the means so to do. I, for one, have not, even yet, heard a single sermon about the rights and wrongs of going to war with Iraq or any other state.

Perhaps clerics may argue that sermonizing is not the way forward on such an issue. But it seemed that the church was engaging the powerful on this issue, without engaging the people who went to church. While there were many opponents to the war in October 2002, the *Daily Telegraph* in London reported, in a clear difference from the bishops' line in their submission, that 57 per cent of Church of England clergy would support a war against Iraq.[587]

What are we to teach in our churches? How are we to be "in the world but not of it" when we know that there will always be "wars and rumors of wars"? Should we not be teaching peaceableness within our churches that in itself forms an "ethic of resistance" against state injustice? Even though Bonhoeffer knew that his own Confessing Church had failed to hold the Nazi government to account, he clearly felt that the church still had responsibilities toward the state. These responsibilities were laid on the church in order to answer "the claim of government on the church."[588] These responsibilities consisted mainly of "call[ing] sin by its name and. . . warn[ing] men against sin. . ."[589] These warnings, however, must go in two directions: to government, and to the peoples. The Confessing Church failed due to a lack of teaching about the "costly" grace that following a Jesus Christ of the Beatitudes entailed: that making peace can, and often does, provoke a violent reaction from the world. Are we now guilty of making the same mistake and letting people off with a "cheap grace" where

> I can thus remain as before in my bourgeois-secular existence . . . The conflict between a Christian and a bourgeois-secular vocation is resolved. Christian life consists of my living in the world and like the world, my not being any different from it . . .[590]

But this leads to the question: what is that difference?

---

[587] www.telegraph.co.uk/news/main.jhtml?xml=/news/2002/10/06/nbish06.xml (January 16, 2003).

[588] Bonhoeffer, *Ethics*, 345. The government's claim on the church consists in keeping and, if called upon, to restore, "the rightful order within which the spiritual office can be rightfully discharged and both government and Church can perform their own several tasks" (ibid., 344).

[589] Ibid., 345.

[590] Bonhoeffer, *Discipleship*, 50–1.

"My Peace I Give You, Not as the World Gives It":[591] The Prophetic Tension

This is the tension most exercised by the just war versus pacifism debate. Pacifism clearly looks to realize the peaceableness of the kingdom of God in the here and now. The just war side seeks to recognize that, however terrible the idea of war may be, there will be times when states resort to such an extreme measure, and if we are to be engaged with the world, Christians must find some way of engaging which says more than "this is how it ought to be."

One hundred and fifty years ago, lines could be written as follows:

> Their's not to make reply,
> Their's not to reason why,
> Their's but to do and die.[592]

Augustine would no doubt have agreed with the soldiers' approach in Tennyson's poem. But do we really live in a world now where such assumptions can be made – either about ordinary soldiers or ordinary Christians "in the pews?" Can our leaders and bishops really try to talk with governments on issues like the Iraq war without engaging their congregations in their churches?[593] If bishops find it difficult and/or cumbersome to call emergency synods (or whatever means is used to discuss the issues of the day), surely an emergency such as "our country is going to war, we don't think this is a good idea and here is why" ought to be a good reason for calling such a meeting – or a series of meetings.

Of course, "the priority must be to indicate the moral posture of those who recognize their responsibilities for Iraq [or anywhere else] in Christ Jesus."[594] Yes, we want to see a world where the lion lies down with the lamb, where swords are beaten into plowshares, but in order to get there we need to accept two things. One is that states can and will go to war. The second is that we must recognize that killing, even in war, is sinful. We do wrong when we kill, even when we justify and allow for killing. The Christian tradition (of just war) allows that there may be other considerations, other evils or injustices that will require – or at least allow – states to engage in war. The corollary therefore is that we need

---

[591] Jn. 14:2.

[592] Alfred, Lord Tennyson, "The Charge of the Light Brigade" (1854).

[593] See the discussion in O'Donovan, *The Just War Revisited*, 129.

[594] Ibid., emphasis original.

to accept, with Bonhoeffer, the need to sin boldly and throw ourselves on the mercy of God – and constantly seek ways of trying to engage in policy that pursues war by other means.

Ten

A Wonderful World?
The Environment

It is mid-December and the roses still bloom in my garden. Durham (UK) is in the north of England, and although this country is warmed by the ocean currents from the Gulf of Mexico, it seems that winter has yet to arrive only two weeks before the shortest day of the year (we are already being told that 2006 is the warmest on record). The shops are playing their seasonal fare: "Let it Snow," and "I'm Dreaming of a White Christmas" will remain dreams this year, unless we get a dramatic change in the weather. The climate is changing. Temperatures are increasing. Skiers in the Alps are enjoying their sport this year on imported snow. On the other hand, wine is being made from grapes grown in southern England. So what's to do? The climate is always changing: if we are only, on a global average, 5°C warmer than the last ice age, then we can cope with a little more heat – can't we? It isn't all bad,[595] and anyway, what we do now will not have any effect for fifty years or so.[596]

Sir John Houghton, who was co-chairman of the Scientific Assessment for the International panel on Climate Change from 1998 to 2002, points out that,

> [t]he human activities of an increasing world population together with the accompanying rapid industrial development, are leading to degra-dation of the environment on a very large scale. Notwithstanding,

---

[595] "Climate change may initially have small positive effects for a few developed countries . . . " and "In higher latitudes, cold-related deaths will decrease": two highly selective quotes from the *Stern Review*.

[596] See the *Stern Review*, i, www.hm-treasury.gov.uk/media/8AC/F7/Executive_Summary.pdf (accessed December 11, 2006).

some deny that degradation is happening; others that degradation matters.[597]

Despite the success of Al Gore's "An Inconvenient Truth", it still appears that ecology is irrelevant for some Christians. For them, sustainability campaigns are irrelevant because God will destroy the world anyway. And if God will destroy the world anyway, why should we even try to do anything to preserve it? It is unsurprising that the USA refused to sign up to the Kyoto Protocols. After all, it was doing America no harm – until hurricane Katrina breached the levees in New Orleans. But global warming is no big deal, and even if it is, surely the jury is still out on whether it is our fault, and even if it is our fault, do we really think that changing the American way of life will solve the problems (even if we could find a way of that not being political suicide)?

But the American, the Western, way of life, with its commerce, consumerism, and "nothing is ever quite enough" attitude (so go and buy the next "must have" item), simply by supporting and encouraging the industrial, fossil-fuel based, conglomeration, has done its share in increasing greenhouse gases. "The current level or stock of greenhouse gases in the atmosphere is equivalent to around 430 parts per million (ppm) CO_2 compared with only 280ppm before the Industrial Revolution."[598]

By employing a dodgy eschatology, the Christian Right has simply bought into a legitimation of the American dream, and a social Darwinian "survival of the fittest" world-view. But "the American way of life and national security serve to legitimate the escalation of global warming through withdrawing from the Kyoto Accord, and isn't this an act of anti-creational and unneighborly violence?"[599] However, the attitude from the Christian Right might explain why it has taken so long for environmental concerns to resonate with Christians. After all, climate change and global warming are still contentious issues – at least in those countries of the world that are some of the world's most powerful polluters (like the UK and the USA).

So if dodgy eschatology leads us to dismiss ecology, what is the "right" eschatology here? Right eschatology looks at the whole overarching story of the Bible, from creation to re-creation: "I saw new heaven and new

---

[597] Sir John Houghton, "Global Warming, Climate Change and Sustainability: Challenge to Scientists, Policy Makers and Christians," *The John Ray Initiative Briefing Paper 14, 2007* (JRI, University of Gloucestershire, www.jri.org.uk) 2–3.

[598] *Stern Review*, iii.

[599] Walsh and Keesmaat, *Colossians Remixed*, 165.

earth." The old, fallen world will be restored: but is it an act of God solely, to be undertaken at the end of time, at the last judgment? Or are there undercurrents, smaller stories within this overarching narrative that encompasses Genesis to Revelation?

Of course, there are. God's plan for salvation begins at Genesis 12 with the call of Abram. And it climaxes with Christ Jesus; whose resurrection (if nothing else) shows us that heaven and earth (or, if you will, the kingdoms of heaven and earth) overlap: they are not separate space/time entities. We are not therefore about to be rescued out of the one and plonked into the other. When Christ shall come with his angels and we are "caught up with him in the air;" we shall become part of the escort to bring him to his kingdom on earth. This is the correct imagery – we are emphatically not "caught up" as a means of escape from this evil world: as our discussion of Bonhoeffer's theology has shown, God may say "No" to the world, but he says "Yes" as well. We will be seen as we are already seen, as his stewards and servants – or else why do we pray that his "kingdom will come on earth as it is in heaven?" And, of course, we too shall be judged for our actions:

> For no one can lay any foundation other than the one that has been laid; that foundation is Jesus Christ. Now if anyone builds on the foundation with gold, silver, precious stones, wood, hay straw – the work of each builder will become visible, for the Day will disclose it, because it will be revealed with fire, and the fire will test what sort of work each has done. If what has been built on the foundation survives, the builder will receive a reward. If the work is burned, the builder will suffer loss; the builder will be saved, but only as through fire. (1 Cor. 3:11–15)

Further, what does Christ's resurrection show, if not that God's kingdom has begun on earth? That God continues in his "yes" to the world, as well as his "no." So what are we to do? Are we to continue in our "dominion" of the earth as its domination? Or to regard our "stewardship," surely a much better translation of Genesis 1:26, over the rest of worldly creation as having responsibilities before God – as well as our brothers and sisters in the rest of humanity – to care and manage for the benefit of all (and not just for all humanity)?

The Beginning of Things

We have, I think, approached a point where we have to look not at the end of things, but the beginning of things: when God created man and woman and gave them "dominion over the fish of the sea and over the birds of the air and over every living thing that moves upon the earth."[600] After all, if God has given us this dominion, then surely we can do whatever we like? No.

> Because man [sic] is created in God's image, he is king over nature. He rules the world on God's behalf. This is of course no license for the unbridled exploitation and subjugation of nature. Ancient oriental kings were expected to be devoted to the welfare of their subjects, especially the poorest and weakest members of society (Ps 72:12–14). By upholding divine principles of law and justice, rulers promoted peace and prosperity for all their subjects. Similarly, mankind is here commissioned to rule nature as a benevolent king, acting as God's representative over them and therefore treating them in the same way as God who created them.[601]

This is all very well, but what does this "treating them in the same way" mean? How are we to exercise dominion? I shall now look at how Bonhoeffer has treated this subject.[602]

Bonhoeffer's comments were made in his lecture series "Creation and Sin" given in the winter of 1932–3, and which were later published as *Creation and Fall*. During this time of confusion, when the Weimar Republic would give way to the rise of the Third Reich, "Bonhoeffer called his students to focus their attention on the word of God as the word of truth in a time of turmoil."[603] However, the lectures' "essential topical relevance" became "evident in the face of the revolutionary changes then brewing in the political, ecclesiastical, and social spheres, even though the lectures kept a steady focus on the text of Genesis."[604] Bonhoeffer's discussion follows directly on from his thoughts on humanity being created in the "image that is like God." In other words,

---

[600] Gen. 1:28.

[601] Gordon J. Wenham, *Genesis 1–15* (Word Biblical Commentary; Nelson Reference and Electronic: 1987), 33.

[602] Lack of space means that I am leaving out Augustine's allegorical treatment of Genesis at the end of *Confessions* and his return to the topic in *The City of God*, and elsewhere. I have noted in the chapter on slavery that he believed humanity was placed in authority over animals and not other people, but his concerns were often elsewhere than how we should have authority over and in creation.

[603] John W. de Gruchy, "Editor's Introduction to the English Edition," in Bonhoeffer, *Creation and Fall*, 1.

[604] Ibid., 2–3.

he discusses humanity's rule over creation before he quotes Genesis 1:28. In his lecture, Bonhoeffer defines the "image that is like God" as a relational image. Further, "it is a given relation, a relation in which human beings are set, a *justitia passiva!*"[605]

> And it is in this relation in which they are set that freedom is given. From this it follows, secondly, that this analogia [analogy] must not be understood as though humankind somehow had this likeness in its possession or at its disposal. Instead the analogia or likeness must be understood very strictly in the sense that what is like derives its likeness only from the prototype, so that it always points us only to the prototype itself and is "like" it only in pointing to it in this way . . . The relation of creature with creature is a relation established by God, because it consists of freedom and freedom comes from God.[606]

Therefore Bonhoeffer sees not a "blood and soil"[607] relationship with the ground and other aspects of creation, but it is a ruling relationship that ties us to the ruled. "[T]he ground and the animals over which I am lord constitute the world in which I live, *without which I cease to be*."[608] This is part of what has been forgotten: we cannot keep using and abusing the world in which we live without it, in the end, affecting us: affecting humanity, and even the Western, developed world.

The *Stern Review*, commissioned by the British government, and which reported in late 2006, tells us that "[o]n current trends, average global temperatures will rise by 2–3°C within the next fifty years or so." Of course, if emissions continue to grow, then there will be even more warming. There will be several results of this – here I will just quote one:

> Rising sea levels will result in tens to hundreds of millions more people flooded each year with warming of 3 or 4°C. There will be serious risks and increasing pressures for coastal protection in South East Asia . . . small islands in the Caribbean and the Pacific, and large coastal cities, such as Tokyo, New York, Cairo and London . . . [609]

Our world domination, mediated through our technological revolution, along with our attempts to forget the tutelage of God, is, therefore, an

---

[605] Bonhoeffer, *Creation and Fall*, 65.

[606] Ibid., 65–6.

[607] "Blood and Soil" was a slogan of Hitler's Nazi Party. See Bonhoeffer, *Creation and Fall*, 67, note 30.

[608] Bonhoeffer, *Creation and Fall*, 66, emphasis added.

[609] *Stern Review*, vi.

illusion. In an ironic reversal of what we think is going on, "[t]ech-
nology is the power with which the earth seizes hold of humankind and
masters it."[610] We no longer think we can cope without technology, but
its effects are what is causing the earth to warm up with the potential
disasters predicted by Stern and others. We wind up, to follow
Bonhoeffer, being ruled by what we think we rule.

> And because we no longer rule, we lose the ground [soil] so that the earth
> no longer remains our earth . . . The reason why we fail to rule, however,
> is because we do not know the world as God's creation and do not accept
> the dominion we have as God-given but seize hold of it for ourselves.
> There is no "being-free-from" without a "being-free-for". There is no
> dominion without serving God; in losing the one humankind necessarily
> loses the other.[611]

Of course, in serving God, we need to serve each other, and that inevitably
includes – indeed it must include – the poorer brothers and sisters who are
already losing homes and livelihoods due to global warming. And, equally,
of course, the evidence for global warming is overwhelming. The
Intergovernmental Panel on Climate Change (IPCC) "has documented the
steady rise in global temperatures over the last fifty years, [and] projects
that the average global temperature will continue to rise in the coming
decades, and attributes 'most of the warming' to human activities."[612]

What Can Be Done?

The *Stern Review* seeks to put the problem within the orbit of economics:
yes, it will cost to reduce emissions, but

> the world does not need to choose between averting climate change and
> promoting growth and development. Changes in energy technologies and
> the structure of economies have reduced the responsiveness of emissions
> to income growth, particularly in some of the richest countries. With
> strong, deliberate policy choices, it is possible to "decarbonise" both

---

[610] Bonhoeffer, *Creation and Fall*, 67.

[611] Ibid., 67.

[612] Quoted in *Climate Change: An Evangelical call to Action*, Evangelical Climate
Initiative, January 2006, Claim 1, 4, see www.christiansandclimate.org The
same document describes the IPCC as "the world's most authoritative body
of scientists and policy experts on the issue of global warming."

developed and developing economies on the scale required for climate stabilisation, while maintaining economic growth in both.[613]

Stern gives four ways of cutting greenhouse gas emissions:

- Reducing demand for emissions-intensive goods and services.

- Increased efficiency, which can save both money and emissions.

- Action on non-energy emissions, such as avoiding deforestation.

- Switching to lower-carbon technologies for power, heat and transport.[614]

This is not the place to go into all the economic arguments Stern advances, but basically the long-term costs of doing nothing, what he calls "business as usual (BAU)," will outweigh any costs of cutting greenhouse gases to sustainable levels, and the latter will also, according to Stern, allow for economic growth in both developed and developing worlds. So we can appeal to self-interest. Others appeal to "rights": a right to clean air, to a non-polluted world, and so on. But I wish to argue, along with Stanley Hauerwas, that we need to engage this topic (as we need to engage with all other topics) as Christians. Our starting point must be with God and his creation of the world.[615] The present ecological crisis, while it is, as I have noted, mainly down to human activities, has a spiritual dimension. If we read Genesis 1:31 by itself ("God saw everything that he had made, and indeed, it was very good"), we will have missed the point. We "must read this passage in conjunction with Romans 8:19–21 and Isaiah 11, where the original creation is understood in relation to the present bondage of creation, and the dawning eschatology of the new creation."[616] There is a difference between "creation" as described in Genesis 1:31, and "nature":

---

[613] *Stern Review*, xi.

[614] Ibid., xii.

[615] For what follows, I am indebted to Hauerwas' essay, co-written with John Berkman, "A Trinitarian Theology of the Chief End of All Flesh," in Stanley Hauerwas, *In Good Company: The Church as Polis* (Notre Dame: Notre Dame Press, 1995), 185–97. This essay looks at the world of animals and juxtaposes it with the world of humans; I am expanding the theme, I hope justifiably, to include all of the created world.

[616] Ibid., 193.

Too often the story of God's creation of humans in God's image has been read falsely as licensing humankind to dominate the animal world. Thus, the language of 'domination' in Genesis 1:28 is used to justify human manipulation of the rest of God's creation for humanity's own ends, thereby underwriting the presumption that all the world is created for the flourishing of humankind.[617]

This is not the case – at least it should not be the case for Christians. Animals and the rest of creation "exist not to serve us, but rather for God's good pleasure."[618] Of course, with creation, too, "groaning in labor pains"[619] we have to see creation as "a Christological and eschatological affirmation": this is to say that "the universe is part of the drama that is not of its own making."

Therefore, for Hauerwas, "the original creation was aimed at a new creation," and "the church is faithful when it lives out the fact that 'nature' has a sacred element, not because Christians wish to uphold or preserve 'nature' for its own sake, but because 'nature' is creation in travail and as such has its own end to glorify God rather than to serve humans."[620] However, and here I wish to nuance Hauerwas' stance, we must not assume that the glorification of God and the service of humanity is always incompatible. Genesis 1:28 still exists in the canon of scripture, and so we must take account of it, even if we no longer can accept the old meaning of domination: any "stewardship" over creation mandated to humanity must, as Hauerwas notes, imitate God's rule over us. However, we still are deputized "rulers" we still have the responsibility of care and of use. Just because some plant or animal is not immediately of use to us, does not mean that it is "useless," but, on the other hand, a plant or animal that is useful to us, is still useful. And by this, I (against Hauerwas) will include the responsible eating of meat.

I have no time for cruelty, or wanton destruction of animals, but while it is still easier (especially in the developing world with its problems of malnutrition) to obtain a balanced diet by including meat-eating, then I find the case for "Christian vegetarianism" has yet to be made while we still are living in the in-between times – that is between Christ's first and second coming. In other words, here I follow Karl Barth, who "knew that the killing of animals was not part of God's vision of peaceableness"

---

[617] Ibid.

[618] Ibid.

[619] Rom. 8:22.

[620] Hauerwas, "A Trinitarian Theology of the Chief End of All Flesh," in *In Good Company*, 196.

but who thought that to stop eating animals entirely "would be 'wanton anticipation' of the kingdom of God."[621] Having said that, we must also note Hauerwas' observation that meat-eating for Christians

> must be understood as animals making a sacrifice for us that we might live, analogous to the way soldiers are seen to be making a sacrifice of their lives for their nation-state, empire or tribe. This is but a reminder that as Christians we cannot understand the story of our lives apart from the importance of sacrifice, because God sacrificed his son Jesus that we might live.[622]

Yes, absolutely – and just as (in the chapter on just war and pacifism) we must accept both that the shedding of blood is wrong, and that wars will be fought until Jesus comes again, then we must accept this idea of sacrifice. Indeed, if we did this, not only would meat-eating become a more thoughtful exercise, but if we applied the idea further to the rest of creation (not just the sentient creatures) then, just as aboriginals talk to the trees from which they remove the sap – telling the tree to what use its sacrificed fluid would be put – we would remember the sacrifice of so much of our natural environment for our mere comfort, and in so doing we might remember that:

> It is my world, my earth, over which I rule. I am not free from it in any sense of my essential being, my spirit, having no need of nature, as though nature were something alien to the spirit. On the contrary, in my whole being, in my creatureliness, I belong wholly to this world; it bears me, nurtures me, holds me . . . What so particularly binds human beings to, and sets them over against, the other creatures is the authority conferred on humankind by nothing else than God's word.[623]

Climate Change – Why Bother?

This means, of course, that it is as Christians that we are to address the problems of climate change. If "the earth is the Lord's and all that is in it"[624] then "any damage we do to God's world is an offense against God himself.[625] And we must be aware that the covenant with Noah does not preclude

---

[621] Quoted in ibid., 197.

[622] Ibid.

[623] Bonhoeffer, *Creation and Fall*, 66.

[624] Ps. 24:1.

[625] See *Climate Change: An Evangelical call to Action*, Evangelical Climate Initiative, January 2006, Claim 3, 7, see www.christiansandclimate.org

punishment on humanity for sin against nature. God promises that "the waters shall never again become a flood to destroy all flesh." However,

> this is [not] a guarantee against human disruption; in fact the greenhouse effect, resulting from humanity's failure to respect the internal order of the creation, now threatens to unravel exactly this dependability of the creation provided by God. Rather the insights from the Bible's Wisdom literature invite humanity to discover the harmony, wisdom, and grace given by God within the creation, and then to live accordingly.[626]

If we look at the sweep of scripture, we can see that "human rebellion and sin result in the land mourning." The curses promised to the Israelites if they fail to obey "his commandments and decrees" include "the fruit of your ground." God promises "fiery heat and drought": "the sky over your head will be bronze and the earth under you iron."[627]

I have, in this chapter, pursued a more consciously theological tone than I have in dealing with other issues. And I have done this deliberately. Although the *Stern Review*, the IPCC (quoted by the Evangelical leaders in the USA), and others have concluded that global warming is largely due to human activity, there are those who choose to contest such claims. And without going into the rights and wrongs of Exxon's expenditure of millions of dollars in trying to cast doubt on the scientific consensus,[628] it is perhaps enough to know that it is in certain people's and certain companies' interest to carry on as if nothing has gone wrong. Christians cannot react the same way. I wish to point toward another way of thinking: one which requires action even if humanity's direct role is contestable. It may be the case that we could argue about how much global warming is down to us, and how much "would have happened anyway," but this actually avoids the issue. Global warming is happening. Apart from the cities listed above that would be at risk from an increased average temperature over the next fifty years,

- Melting glaciers will initially increase flood risk and then strongly reduce water supplies, eventually threatening one-sixth of the world's

---

[626] Sojourners on the issues, *Christians and the Environment* (Washington, DC: Sojourners, 2006), 6.

[627] Ibid. See Deut. 28:15ff. Note I am *not* saying that those facing the worst excesses of climate change are worse sinners than the rest of us, merely that disobedience to God has an environmental fall-out.

[628] See "Exxon spends millions to cast doubt on global warming," in the *Independent* (London) Thursday, December 7, 2006, 33.

population, predominantly in the Indian sub-continent, parts of China, and the Andes in South America.

- Declining crop yields, especially in Africa, could leave hundreds of millions without the ability to produce or purchase sufficient food. At mid to high latitudes, crop yields may increase for moderate temperature rises (2–3°C), but then decline with greater amounts of warming. At 4°C and above, global food production is likely to be seriously affected.

- In higher latitudes, cold-related deaths will decrease. But climate change will increase worldwide deaths from malnutrition and heat stress. Vector-borne diseases such as malaria and dengue fever could become more widespread if effective control measures are not in place.

- Rising sea levels will result in tens to hundreds of millions more people flooded each year with warming of 3 or 4°C. There will be serious risks and increasing pressures for coastal protection in South East Asia (Bangladesh and Vietnam), small islands in the Caribbean and the Pacific, and large coastal cities, such as Tokyo, New York, Cairo, and London. According to one estimate, by the middle of the century, 200 million people may become permanently displaced due to rising sea levels, heavier floods, and more intense droughts.

- Ecosystems will be particularly vulnerable to climate change, with around 15–40 percent of species potentially facing extinction after only 2°C of warming. And ocean acidification, a direct result of rising carbon dioxide levels, will have major effects on marine ecosystems, with possible adverse consequences on fish stocks.[629]

Stern goes on to list other probable outcomes of global warming:

- Warming may induce sudden shifts in regional weather patterns such as the monsoon rains in South Asia or the El Niño phenomenon – changes that would have severe consequences for water availability and flooding in tropical regions and threaten the livelihoods of millions of people.

- A number of studies suggest that the Amazon rainforest could be vulnerable to climate change, with models projecting significant drying

---

[629] *Stern Review*, vi.

in this region. One model, for example, finds that the Amazon rainforest could be significantly, and possibly irrevocably, damaged by a warming of 2–3°C.

- The melting or collapse of ice sheets would eventually threaten land which today is home to 1 in every 20 people.[630]

It is not a pretty picture; especially for the world's poor. Christians have a responsibility to love their neighbor. This chapter contends that this responsibility extends to caring for the environment, in which we expect those neighbors to live, work, and raise their families.

What's to Do?

There is little point in preaching, on any subject, if our actions do not match our words. On the issue of the environment, it is all very well to march, to write letters, and seek to influence government – definitely we must continue with these actions, but there are things we can do in our local communities, in our own homes.

Tearfund, a Christian Organization based in the UK, published a booklet *For Tomorrow Too: Living Responsibly in a World of Climate Change* in 2005, by the second half of 2006, it was on its third edition. The booklet runs through the theology, the big issues of climate change, the effect climate change is having on the poor (did you know that the rainy season in Ethiopia used to last for eight months from February, but now often starts as late as May?), but it then moves to some practical things we can all do. These are:

- Don't fill the kettle full unless you need to. If everyone boiled just enough water for their cup of tea or coffee, the energy saved [in the UK alone] could power over three-quarters of the UK's street lights.

- Stay cozy: drawing the curtains at dusk keeps the cold out and heat in.

- Turn off the lights when you leave a room.

- Turn down your central heating thermostat: lowering the temperature by just a degree (Celsius) can cut 10 per cent off energy bills.

---

[630] Ibid., vii.

- Put lids on pans when cooking to conserve heat and cook food faster.

- Wash-up by hand rather than using the dishwasher.

- Close the fridge door: for every minute left open it takes three times as long to cool down

- Defrost your fridge and freezer regularly to maintain efficiency. Allowing space for air to circulate will also help them to run more efficiently.

- Unplug mobile [cell] phone chargers when not in use – 95 percent of the energy they use is when the phone isn't plugged in.

- Turn electrical appliances off at the mains rather than leaving them on standby. Eight percent of electricity consumed at home is from appliances that we aren't even using.

- Wash your clothes at lower temperatures (40°C or below), and always ensure you have a full load.

- Use hot water sparingly: take a shower rather than a bath.[631]

There are other things that can be done: for example, ensure that your taps are not dripping water; getting a washer replaced is usually easy, and will mean that you are not throwing away a bathload of water every day! There are also energy efficient light bulbs that use less power than ordinary bulbs.

Of course, these are things that we all need to do; if just one or two of us did these things, then we would merely appear strange or eccentric, but if we all did them, then we would make a substantial change to our energy use (as well as reducing our fuel bills), and we would have a much better moral base to engage with our governing authorities and asking them what they are doing in terms of tackling carbon emissions. The UK government has faced continual internal pressure with a "Stop Climate Chaos" rally in central London on November 4, 2006. In the USA, despite the continuing unwillingness by the White House to sign up to the Kyoto Accord, individual states have begun to set emissions targets, and city mayors are pledging their cities to abide by Kyoto. Progress is being made.

---

[631] Tearfund , *For Tomorrow Too*, 14. see also www.tearfund.org

It is being made in other areas too:

> The value of UK ethical consumerism last year exceeded the sales of "over-the-counter" beer and cigarettes, according to the Co-operative Bank's annual Ethical Consumerism Report published today [27 November 2006].
>
> The Report, which acts as a barometer of ethical spending in the UK, shows that in 2005 UK ethical consumerism was worth £29.3 billion, for the first time overtaking the retail market for tobacco and alcohol which stood at £28.0 billion.[632]

Of course, we must be cautiously welcoming of this news: just because "ethical consumerism" has done so well, on the Co-operative Bank website, Craig Shannon, Executive Director of Business Management, notes:

> the fact that the value of ethical consumerism is now higher than the retail figures for cigarettes and beers is a milestone. However, total ethical spending is spread over a wide range of products and services, and in very few markets has it become the market norm. Overall, spend on ethical foods still only accounts for 5% of the typical shopping basket.
>
> Where the ethical or eco-choice has become the market leader, for example in sales of A-rated energy fridges (which account for some 60 per cent of the market), this has been underpinned by an EU labelling scheme, inefficient products being removed from sale and the support of well targeted subsidies.
>
> If, as many scientists are saying, we have ten years to make a dent in climate change, it is this type of radical overhaul of the choices made available to people that is going to deliver the rapid market changes required.
>
> The efforts of far-sighted, highly motivated consumers need to be leveraged and supported with business innovation and government intervention.[633]

In other words, what is needed across the developed world is both a top-down and a bottom-up approach. If markets can be leveraged when it comes to fridges, it can be leveraged on other issues, sometimes following consumer power. If you now go into one of the biggest chain of

---

[632] www.co-operativebank.co.uk/servlet/Satellite?c=Page&cid=1077610044424 &pagename=CoopBank%2FPage%2FtplPageStandard (accessed December 12, 2006).

[633] Ibid.

supermarkets in the UK, you cannot but buy fairly traded bananas; there is no other option on the shelf.

Then I Saw a New Heaven and a New Earth: The Eschatological Tension

We return to where we began this chapter: eschatology. We have already glimpsed at how a faulty eschatology can damage and dampen environmental concerns. Yet that eschatology, which states that God is going to destroy the earth, is challenged by the verse at the start of Revelation 21. God will indeed recreate the earth, but it will still be recognizably the earth. God will "make all things new," but it is not the case that it will all end with "saved souls" snatched away to a distant heaven, leaving the unsaved and sinful bodies down here on earth, but with God dwelling "among mortals."

> "Resurrection" does not mean "going to heaven when you die" . . . [When y]ou die; you go to be with Christ . . . What is promised after that interim period is a new bodily life within God's new world . . .[634]

This world and God's new world are connected. It is this world that will be made new, and this "resurrected" world, I suggest, will show the scars of the old.

> Although the doors were shut, Jesus came and stood among them and said, "Peace be with you." Then he said to Thomas, "Put your finger here and see my hands. Reach out your hand and put it in my side. Do not doubt but believe." Thomas answered him, "My Lord and my God!"[635]

Just as the resurrected Jesus still had his scars – indeed this was the indisputable feature of his resurrected body that meant the disciples recognized their teacher – then the world, made new as it will be, will show how we have treated it.[636] As we live in the "not yet" of anticipation, we

---

[634] Tom Wright, *Simply Christian* (London: SPCK, 2006), 186.

[635] Jn. 20:26–28.

[636] I am here expanding N.T. Wright's point in *The Resurrection of the Son of God* (London: SPCK, 2003), 289, "what is done with the present body matters precisely because it is to be raised." By analogy, therefore, what is done with the present world matters precisely because it is to be made new – it is not going to be re-created *ex nihilo*.

must look toward the completedness of the times ahead. This means look-ing after this world, the one God has created for us; the world he says "Yes" to. Yes, it is good, but it is now flawed: somehow the whole of cre-ation fell, was subjected to "a bondage of decay"[637] and is waiting for the "freedom of the glory of the children of God."

It is, therefore the case that we are living more in the "not yet" side of the eschatological tension when it comes to climate change; both in the fact that most of the change has yet to happen – though the projections are dire: one estimate states that by 2050 climate change is likely to cause an additional thirty million people to go hungry – and the fact that even those countries who have signed up to the Kyoto Accord have yet to deliver on their promises: the British government "will not meet its own domestic target of reducing carbon emissions by 20 per cent by 2010 . . . [Currently] emission levels are on the rise again."[638]

If we are to live as Christians in these "in between" times, "we should celebrate the goodness of creation, ponder its present brokenness and, insofar as we can, celebrate in advance the healing of the world, the new creation itself."[639] We now move on to the question of how we do that.

The Earth is the Lord's:[640] The Ecclesiological Tension

How are we to be in the world, but not of it? How are we to react to reports like the *Stern Review* that seek to appeal to economic self-interest? "Markets for low-carbon energy products are likely to be worth at least $500bn per year by 2050, and perhaps much more. Individual companies and countries should position themselves to take advantage of these opportunities."[641] Not, I suggest, by ignoring such facts and opinions: not least because there may well be a role for Christian busi-ness people to take a lead in these areas. The US Evangelical leaders are right to commend

> the steps taken by such companies as BP, Shell, General Electric, Cinergy, Duke Energy, and DuPont, all of which have moved ahead of the pace of

---

[637] Rom. 8:21.
[638] Tearfund's magazine *Global Action* Autumn 2006, 5. Also see www.tear-fund.org/campaigning
[639] Tom Wright, *Simply Christian*, 201.
[640] Ps. 24:1.
[641] *Stern Review*, xvi.

government action through innovative measures implemented within their companies in the U.S. and around the world. In so doing they have offered timely leadership.[642]

However, Christian engagement with the world on this issue must be based on the considerations outlined above. The earth is the Lord's; therefore we must take care of it. All peoples, especially the poor, are our neighbors, and we are commanded to love our neighbor. We do not love our neighbor by causing global warming that causes the loss of his or her livelihood by floods, famine or drought. We do not love our neighbors of the future by visiting on them the results of the carbon and other emissions we still pump into the atmosphere.

So, we commend the actions of government and business that seek to tackle global warming. And we are motivated by biblical imperatives contained in our discussion of Genesis 1:28, Psalm 24:1, and the command to love our neighbor as we love ourselves and God. These two aspects do not have to be incompatible. For us as Christians, and citizens, as for any responsible business or government, we need to seek climate stability, so that we can all flourish, both those who are presently poor, and those who are presently rich.

It may be that our actions, some of which I have outlined above, may be similar to many people of goodwill who are also concerned, but as it is only God who sees into the heart of any one of us, maybe we should not be too quick to judge any apparent self-interest in anyone's actions in reducing the effects of climate change. And, of course, it may still be that all our actions will be in vain.

Yet Not One of Them Will Fall:[643] The Prophetic Tension

I have called this chapter "A Wonderful World? The Environment," and yet I have concentrated solely on climate change or global warming. Other things have happened that cannot be laid at the door of human-ity's willful misuse of the created world: the Boxing Day tsunami in 2004, earthquakes in Pakistan and Kashmir and, although people may argue about the cause of the severity of Katrina, hurricanes struck the American and other coasts before global warming became a factor in our calculations. These events have been news because of their effect

---

[642] *Climate Change: An Evangelical call to Action*, Evangelical Climate Initiative, January 2006, Claim 4, 9.
[643] Mt. 10:29.

on humanity, but they have all affected other aspects of creation. I mention these not to start a further discussion in the closing paragraphs of this chapter, but to point out that if our aim is to see the new earth that I have talked about above, then it will not all be down to us.[644]

To be even more gloomy, there is, of course, no guarantee that completing all the remedial actions on climate change will have the desired effect; but we are aware of what the best scientific models will predict. So part of our strategy must be to

> reduce our global warming pollution to help mitigate the impacts of climate change, as a society and as individuals we must also help the poor adapt to the significant harm that global warming will cause.[645]

In other words, our prophetic vision, which we must proclaim, of a new heaven and a new earth, will only come about when *God* does a new thing. It is our role to examine what we can do in the meantime to challenge the injustices caused by the Western world,[646] in particular, using fossil fuels and other products in such a wanton manner that the whole world – starting with the poorest parts of it – will suffer and continue to suffer if nothing is done. There are the individual actions outlined above, there is lobbying of our legislators for more effective action. After all, if even big business has started to wake up to this problem, it is about time our governments got on board, and did more than just talk about the problem.

We cannot say what the future will bring, except that business as usual, pumping yet more carbon into the atmosphere is not the way forward. Ethical shopping has taken off in the UK – concern for the other is beginning to show fruit (if I can put it that way). And as one

---

[644] If you wish to read further about the problems of evil raised by Katrina and other events, then try N.T. Wright, *Evil and the Justice of God* (London: SPCK, 2006).

[645] *Climate Change: An Evangelical call to Action*, Evangelical Climate Initiative, January 2006, Claim 4, 9.

[646] Other countries, such as China and India are catching up, but they can hardly be expected to cap carbon emissions if we, who have benefited considerably from not so doing, refuse to do so even now. On the other hand, it may be that if we can lead by example, internal political pressure may force these countries to consider the problems caused by climate change in their regions as well.

commentator has put it, "[i]t's harder for a wasteful consumer to get into heaven than an SUV to pass through the eye of a needle."[647]

---

[647] Sojourners on the issues, *Christians and the Environment* (Washington, DC: Sojourners, 2006), 26. (See www.sojo.net/index.cfm?action=resources.discussion_guides).

Eleven

By Way of a Conclusion

What I have hoped to emphasize in this book is that non-involvement with the world is a non-option for Christians. Whether you take the view of a Gutiérrez that any pretense at non-involvement is an involvement on the side of the *status quo*, or of a Hauerwas who says that the church is there to show the world how to be the world, or of an Augustine who – despite all his "realism" – still insists (as I have noted) that,

> our soul yields works of mercy "according to its kind" (Gen. 1: 12), loving our neighbour in the relief of physical necessities . . . This means such kindness as rescuing a person suffering injustice from the hand of the powerful and providing the shelter of protection by the mighty force of just judgement.[648]

So our action in the public sphere is motivated, at bottom, by the command to love our neighbor. Bonhoeffer also puts it clearly: "the church is the church only when it exists for others." In his "Outline for a Book," he continues:

> The church must share in the secular problems of ordinary human life, not dominating, but helping and serving. It must tell men of every calling what it means to live in Christ, to exist for others . . . It must not under-estimate the importance of human example . . . it is not abstract argument, but example, that gives its word emphasis and power.[649]

It is clear from this that Bonhoeffer has not become blind to the world's failings, but just very aware of how Christians are to live in the world, even if they are not to be of it. This inevitably involves tension. Change

---

[648] *Conf.* XIII. xvii (21).
[649] Bonhoeffer, *LPP*, 382–3.

has to be fought for. This fighting is "peaceable": we do not find a Christ of the New Testament advocating military or terrorist violence (whatever our "states" might wish).

> The equation "non-violent = apolitical" is of course absurd, as we who know about Gandhi [or Martin Luther King Jr] must realize; but it is frequently made none the less. To a nation bent on violence, anyone who claims to be speaking for God's kingdom and who advocates non-violent means as the way to it is making a very deep and dangerous political statement. He is likely to be caught in crossfire.[650]

Also, as the second half of the book has made clear, there are many issues of injustice that need to be tackled (for example, I have not dealt directly with how women are still oppressed in many parts of the world).[651] However, with so much poverty and oppression in the world, it must be opposed, and a better way exemplified.

That such points need to be made (and this book needs to be written) is indicative of how the post-Constantinian church has remained a friend of the powerful, or at best, an uncritical silent witness to the actions and attitudes of the powerful. Of course, there have been outstanding Christian counter-examples: we may only guess what the situation on racism might have been in the United States without the work of Martin Luther King.[652] However, the point has to be made that Christians still need to "witness" in the political realm, and not just on "issues of an individual nature."[653]

What you have got, given that you have read thus far with me, is a framework – no more than that – within which Christians need to work given that we must witness to the world a better way of being. There is

---

[650] N.T. Wright, "The New Testament and the 'State,'" in *Themelios* 16:1 (1990), 13.

[651] As one example of this see Linda Woodhead, "Can Women love Stanley Hauerwas? Pursuing an Embodied Theology," in *Faithfulness and Fortitude: In Conversations with Stanley Hauerwas* (Edinburgh: T&T Clark, 2000), 161–88, especially 171–6.

[652] Though he too faced criticism: his *Letter from Birmingham City Jail* was written to Christian pastors who had publicly rebuked him for his stand.

[653] Nigel Wright, *Radical Evangelical*, 107. Wright is discussing the resurgence of the "Religious Right" in the USA, which concentrates on "[o]pposition to abortion and euthanasia . . . yet they are accompanied . . . by devotion to the 'gun culture' which makes America one of the most violent countries in the world" (ibid.).

not a ten point plan on every issue given to frame your action. I cannot tell you (nor would I if I could) how, where, or what issues to get involved in. I cannot even tell you whether you will engage with one issue or many. I have covered all the ground I can in one book, except for one issue, deliberately kept until last.

That issue is prayer. Even where there is cooperation with other people, other organizations, this is a distinguishing mark of Christian engagement. It is by prayer, both personal and corporate; that we seek to discern God's will for us. It is by prayer that we can stay the course.

In *Faithfulness and Fortitude*, Samuel Wells describes his ministry at St. Elizabeth's, Norwich, UK. St. Elizabeth's was a church in a poor, deprived part of East Anglia. As such, it became part of a renewal grant sponsored by the British government entitled "New Deal for Communities." "Overnight," Wells says, he went from "being the priest of a deprived, neglected estate in a backwater of Britain . . . [to being] at the heart of the political agenda." There were many struggles and difficulties in dealing with the New Deal, but one of the differences was prayer as "part of the practices developed by the worshipping church":

> For church regulars saying a prayer at the start of a meeting may have become a habit given scant consideration. But a New Deal meeting, sensing something curiously missing which one has elsewhere taken for granted, one becomes slowly aware that this gathering is taking upon itself an enormous task – and is seeking to perform it in its own strength alone. How awesome is the sight! The spectacles that discern this are those given by the habit of corporate prayer.[654]

Prayer did not – and Wells would not wish it to – make it possible for his church to take over the New Deal, but it did give the church the patience, the fortitude, to keep going with the work: to discern that its place at the table was as a fellow traveler seeking what was lost. While we might be aware, as Christians, of the injustices that exist in the world, we must also be aware that we do not necessarily have the answers: all our "answers" must be made with fear and trembling, conscious that we live in the time between the arrival of the kingdom of God on earth and its completion; that the church must always struggle with finding out

---

[654] Sam Wells, "No Abiding Inner City: A New Deal for the Church," in *Faithfulness and Fortitude*, 136–7. Hauerwas also quotes this passage in his essay "The State of the Secular: Theology, Prayer and the University."

how it is to be in the world, but not of it, and how it is going to seek to move from today's "is" to tomorrow's "ought."

"But what can I do?" That is so often the cry and the excuse for doing nothing, and, no, we will not all be William Wilberforce – who campaigned against slavery for most of his life – or Martin Luther King Jr. But (as the Bishop of Durham put it in his Christmas midnight sermon, December 2006):

> we can pray, we can watch, and we can listen. We can, in fact, inhabit Luke's story of Jesus' birth right where we are. We can pray in love and devotion before the Christ-child, trusting that his new kingdom of peace and justice will come to birth within us and through us. But then we can watch for the empires of the world, the Augustus Caesars of our day: we can keep our eyes open for where the powers that run the world are crushing the little people who live on our street, in our town, in our local hospitals or prisons. And we can listen for the song of the angels. It will come in surprising ways, as it always does. God doesn't call everybody in the same way. But if you are learning to love the Christ-child you will find your eyes gradually being opened to what the powers of the world are up to and your ears gradually becoming tuned to the particular song that God's angels are trying to sing to you, and, more dangerously perhaps, *through* you. You will discover, in fact, the thing we call vocation: which may be as simple as volunteering to work a couple of evenings in a soup kitchen, or helping run a *Traidcraft*[655] stall, or writing letters to opinion-formers, or organising prayer vigils and chains, or running a website to raise awareness of key issues – the sorts of things, in fact, granted some different technology, that William Wilberforce and his friends got up to. Every great work begins with little steps; usually it continues with little steps too.[656]

However, "the one who began a good work among you will bring it to completion by the day of Jesus Christ" (Phil. 1:6).

---

[655] Traidcraft is a Christian organization that seeks to trade fairly by giving Third World producers a fair price for their product (even if that price is over the "market rate").

[656] "Emperors and Angels" *Isaiah 9.2–7; Luke 2.1–20* a sermon at the Midnight Eucharist, Durham Cathedral, Christmas Eve 2006 by the Bishop of Durham, Rt Rev Dr N.T. Wright.

Select Bibliography

Atkins, E.M. and Dodaro R.J. (eds. and trans.), *Augustine: Political Writings* (Cambridge: Cambridge University Press, 2001).

Barclay, John, "Paul, Philemon and the Dilemma of Christian Slave-Ownership" in *New Testament Studies,* 37, 1992. 161–86.

Barclay, William, *The Daily Study Bible* (rev. ed.): *The Letters to the Galatians and Ephesians* (Edinburgh: The Saint Andrew Press, 1976).

Berkman, John and Cartwright, Michael (eds.), *The Hauerwas Reader* (Durham, NC: Duke University Press, 2001).

Bethge, Eberhard, *Dietrich Bonhoeffer: A Biography*, rev. ed., trans. Eric Mosbacher et al (Minneapolis: Augsburg Fortress, 2000).

Bishops, House of, "Evaluating the Threat of Military Action Against Iraq: A submission by the House of Bishops to the House of Commons Foreign Affairs Select Committee's ongoing inquiry into the War on Terrorism" www.cofe.anglican.org/papers/Bishopssubmission.doc (January 16, 2003).

Boff, Leonardo, "Theological Characteristics of a Grassroots Church" in Sergio Torres and John Eagleson (eds.), *The Challenge of Basic Christian Communities* (Maryknoll, NY: Orbis Books, 1981), 124–44.

Bonhoeffer, Dietrich, *Creation and Fall*, trans. Douglas Stephen Bax (Minneapolis: Augsburg Fortress, 1997).

Bonhoeffer, Dietrich, *Discipleship*, trans. Barbara Green and Reinhard Krauss (Minneapolis: Augsburg Fortress, 2001).

Bonhoeffer, Dietrich, *Ethics*, trans. Neville Horton Smith (New York: Touchstone/Simon and Schuster, 1995).

Bonhoeffer, Dietrich, *Letters and Papers from Prison*, trans. John Bowden, Reginald Fuller et al (London: SCM Press, enlarged ed. 1971).

Bonhoeffer, Dietrich, *Life Together / Prayerbook of the Bible*, trans. Daniel W. Bloesch and James H. Burtness (Minneapolis: Augsburg Fortress Press, 1996).

Bonhoeffer, Dietrich, *No Rusty Swords*, trans. Edwin H. Robertson and John Bowden (London: Collins, 1965).

Bonner, Gerald, *God's Decree and Man's Destiny* (London: Variorum, 1987).

Bonner, Gerald, *St Augustine of Hippo: Life and Controversies* (Norwich: The Canterbury Press, 1986).

Bradshaw, Timothy (ed.), *The Way Forward?* (2nd ed. London: SCM Press, 1997).

Brown, Peter, *Augustine of Hippo* (London: Faber and Faber, 1967).

Cadorette, Curt, *From the Heart of the People: the Theology of Gustavo Gutiérrez* (Oak Park, IL, USA: Meyer-Stone Books, 1988).

Cadorette, Curt, et al. (eds), *Liberation Theology: An Introductory Reader* (Maryknoll, NY: Orbis Books, 1992).

Capizzi, Joseph E., "On Behalf of the Neighbour: A Rejection of the Complementarity of Just-War Theory and Pacifism," in *Studies in Christian Ethics*, 14:2.

Care, *Human Trafficking Briefing Pack: The Modern Slave Trade* (London: Care, 2006), www.care.org.uk.

Cargill Thompson, W.D.J., *The Political Thought of Martin Luther* (Sussex: The Harvester Press, 1984).

Chadwick Henry (trans.) *Saint Augustine: Confessions* (Oxford: Oxford University Press, 1991).

Chapman, G. Clark Jr., "Bonhoeffer: Resource for Liberation Theology," *Union Seminary Quarterly Review*, 36 (1981), 225–42.

Chase, Kenneth R. and Jacobs, Alan, *Must Christianity Be Violent? Reflections on History, Practice, and Theology* (Grand Rapids, MI: Brazos Press, 2003),

Coffey, John, "The Abolition of the Slave Trade: Christian Conscience and Political Action," *Cambridge Papers*, 15:2, June 2006.

Davie, Grace, *Religion in Britain since 1945* (Oxford: Blackwell, 1994).

de Gruchy, John W., *Bonhoeffer and South Africa* (Grand Rapids, MI.: Eerdmans, 1984).

de Gruchy, John W. (ed.), *Bonhoeffer for a New Day* (Grand Rapids, MI.: Eerdmans, 1997).

de Gruchy, John W., *Daring, Trusting Spirit: Bonhoeffer's Friend Eberhard Bethge* (London: SCM Press, 2005).

de Gruchy, John W. (ed.), *The Cambridge Companion to Dietrich Bonhoeffer* (Cambridge: Cambridge University Press, 1999).

de Lange, Frits, *Waiting for the Word* (Grand Rapids, MI: Eerdmans, 2000).

Dodaro, Robert, "Eloquent Lies, Just Wars and the Politics of Persuasion: Reading Augustine's City of God in a 'Postmodern' World," *Augustinian Studies*, 25 (1994), 77–137.

Doyle, Robert C., *Eschatology and the Shape of Christian Belief* (Carlisle: Paternoster Press, 1999).

Dyson, R.W. (ed. and trans.), *The City of God against the Pagans* (Cambridge: Cambridge University Press, 1998).

Easterly, William, *The White Man's Burden: Why the West's Efforts to Aid the Rest Have Done So Much Ill and So Little Good* (Oxford: Oxford University Press, 2006).

Elias, John L., *Paulo Freire: Pedagogue of Liberation* (Malabar, FL: Krieger, 1994).

Evangelical Climate Initiative, *Climate Change: An Evangelical call to Action*, January 2006, see www.christiansandclimate.org

Feil, Ernst, *The Theology of Dietrich Bonhoeffer* (Minneapolis: Fortress Press, 1985).

Freire, Paulo, *Cultural Action for Freedom* (Harmondsworth: Penguin Books, 1972).

Freire, Paulo, *Education: The Practice of Freedom* (London: Writers and Readers Publishing Cooperative, 1974).

Freire, Paulo, et al. (eds.), *Mentoring the Mentor* (New York: Peter Lang, 1997).

Freire, Paulo, *Pedagogy in Process: The Letters to Guinea-Bissau* (New York: Continuum, 1983).

Freire, Paulo, *Pedagogy of the Heart* (New York: Continuum, 2000).

Freire, Paulo, *Pedagogy of the Oppressed* (Harmondsworth: Penguin Books, 1972).

Freire, Paulo, *Pedagogy of Freedom: Ethics, Democracy, and Civic Courage* (Lanham, MD: Rowman and Littlefield, 1998).

Freire, Paulo, *Teachers as Cultural Workers: Letters to Those Who Dare Teach* (Oxford: Westview Press, 1988).

Freire, Paulo, *The Politics of Education* (Basingstoke: Macmillan, 1985).

Freire, Paulo and Faundez, Antonio, *Learning to Question: A Pedagogy of Liberation* (Geneva: WCC Publications, 1989).

Giroux, Henry A. and McLaren, Peter L. (eds.), *Critical Pedagogy, The State, and Cultural Struggle* (Albany, NY: State University of New York Press, 1989).

Goddard, Andrew, *Friends, Partners or Spouses? The Civil Partnership Act and Christian Witness* (Cambridge: Grove Books Ltd, 2006).

Green, Clifford J., *Bonhoeffer: A Theology of Sociality, rev. ed.* (Grand Rapids, MI: Eerdmans, 1999).

Gremmels, Christian, "Bonhoeffer, The Churches, and Jewish-Christian Relations," in Wayne Whitson Floyd and Charles Marsh (eds.), *Theology and the Practice of Responsibility* (Valley Forge, PA: Trinity Press International, 1994), 295–305.

Gushee, David P., "A Crumbling Institution: How Social Revolutions Cracked the Pillars of Marriage," *Christianty Today* (September 2004).

Gutiérrez, Gustavo, *A Theology of Liberation: History, Politics and Salvation* (London: SCM Press, rev. ed. 1988).

Gutiérrez, Gustavo, *The God of Life* (Maryknoll, NY: Orbis Books, 1991).

Gutiérrez, Gustavo, *The Truth Shall Make You Free: Confrontations* (Maryknoll, NY: Orbis Books, 1990).

Gutiérrez, Gustavo, *The Power of the Poor in History* (London: SCM Press, 1983).

Gutiérrez, Gustavo, *The God of Life* (Maryknoll, NY: Orbis Books, 1991).

Gutiérrez, Gustavo, *We Drink from Our Own Wells* (Maryknoll, NY: Orbis Books, 1984).

Harvard, Joseph S., "The Continuing Cost of Discipleship," in *Journal for Preachers*, 7:4 (1984), 2–7.

Hauerwas, Stanley, *A Better Hope: Resources for a Church Confronting Capitalism, Democracy, and Postmodernity* (Grand Rapids, MI: Brazos Press, 2000).

Hauerwas, Stanley, *After Christendom* (Nashville: Abingdon Press, 1999).

Hauerwas, Stanley, *Against the Nations: War and Survival in A Liberal Society* (Notre Dame, IN.: University of Notre Dame, 1992).

Hauerwas, Stanley, *Christian Existence Today: Essays on Church, World and Living in Between* (Grand Rapids, MI: Brazo Press, 1988 [reprint 2001]).

Hauerwas, Stanley, "Friendship and Freedom: Reflections on Bonhoeffer's 'The Frien,'" a paper given at the Bonhoeffer Conference, Oxford, January 6, 2006.

Hauerwas, Stanley, *In Good Company: The Church as Polis* (Notre Dame: Notre Dame Press, 1995).

Hauerwas, Stanley, "On Developing Hopeful Virtues," *Christian Scholars Review* 18/2 (1988).

Hauerwas, Stanley, *Performing the Faith: Bonhoeffer and the Practice of Nonviolence* (London: SPCK, 2004).

Hauerwas, Stanley, "Will the Real Sectarian Stand Up?" *Theology Today*, 44, 87–94.

Hauerwas, Stanley, *With the Grain of the Universe* (London: SCM Press, 2002).

Hauerwas, Stanley and Lentricchia, Frank, *Dissent from the Homeland: Essays after September 11* (Durham, NC: Duke University Press, 2003).

Hauerwas, Stanley and Wells, Samuel (eds.), *The Blackwell Companion to Christian Ethics* (Malden, MA/Oxford: Blackwell, 2004).

Hauerwas, Stanley and Willimon, William H., *Resident Aliens* (Nashville, TN: Abingdon Press, 1989).

Hauerwas, Stanley and Willimon,William H., *Where Resident Aliens Live* (Nashville, TN: Abingdon Press, 1996).

Hays, Richard B., *The Moral Vision of the New Testament: A Contemporary Introduction to New Testament Ethics* (Edinburgh: T&T Clark, 1996).

Hebblethwaite, Margaret, *Base Communities: An Introduction* (London: Geoffrey Chapman, 1993).

Hennelly, Alfred T., *Liberation Theology: A Documentary History* (Maryknoll, NY: Orbis Books, 1990).

Hennelly, Alfred T., *Theology for a Liberating Church The New Praxis of Freedom* (Washington, DC: Georgetown University Press, 1989).

Henry, Steve, *Change the World 9 to 5: 50 Actions to Change the World at Work* (London: Short Books Ltd., 2006).

Höpfl, Harro, *Luther and Calvin: On Secular Authority* (Cambridge: Cambridge University Press, 1991).

Horton, Miles and Freire, Paulo, *We Make the Road by Walking* (Philadelphia: Temple University Press, 1990).

House of Lords, House of Commons Joint Committee on Human Rights, *Human Trafficking: Twenty-Sixth Report of Session 2005–06* (London: The Stationary Office Limited, 2006).

Jones, Gareth Steadman, *An End to Poverty? A Historical Debate* (London: Profile Books, 2004).

Lash, Nicholas, "Considering the Trinity," *Modern Theology*, 2 (1986), 183–96.

Local Government Association, *Faith and Community: a good practice guide for local authorities* (London: LGA Publications, February 2002).

McCarthy, David Matzko, *Sex and Love in the Home*, new Ed (London: SCM Press, 2004).

McFadyen, A.I., "The Call to Discipleship," *Scottish Journal of Theology*, 43 (1990), 461–83.

Mayo, Peter, "Gramsci, Freire, and Radical Adult Education: A Few 'Blind Spots,'" *Humanity and Society*, 18 (1994), 82–98.

Medhurst, Kenneth N. and Moyser, George H., *Church and Politics in a Secular Age* (Oxford: Clarendon Press, 1988).

Milbank, John, *Theology and Social Theory* (Oxford: Blackwell, 1993).

Moberly, Walter, "The Use of Scripture in Contemporary Debate about Homosexuality" in *Theology*, 103/814 (July/August 2000), 251–8.

Moltmann, Jürgen, *Theology of Hope* (London: SCM Press, 1967).

Morisy, Ann, *Beyond the Good Samaritan* (London: Mowbray, 1997).

Nation, Mark Thiessen and Wells, Samuel, *Faithfulness and Fortitude: In Conversation with the Theological Ethics of Stanley Hauerwas* (Edinburgh: T&T Clark, 2000).

Oakley, Nigel W., "A Summary Grammar for Christian Prepolitical Education," *Journal for Education and Christian Belief*, 7:2 (October 2003), 143–155.

Oakley, Nigel W., "Base Ecclesial Communities and Community Ministry: Some Freirean Points of Comparison and Difference" in *Political Theology*, 5.4 (October 2004), 447–65.

O'Donovan, Oliver, "Augustine's *City of God* XIX and Western Political Thought," in Dorothy F. Donnelly (ed.), *The City of God: A Collection of Critical Essays* (New York: Peter Lang, 1995), 135–49.

O'Donovan, Oliver, *The Just War Revisited* (Cambridge: Cambridge University Press, 2003).

Rasmussen, Larry, *Dietrich Bonhoeffer – His Significance for North Americans* (Minneapolis: Fortress Press, 1990).

Rawls, John, *Political Liberalism* (New York: Columbia University Press, 1993).

Rist, John M., *Augustine: Ancient Thought Baptized* (Cambridge: Cambridge University Press, 1994).

Rochelle, Jay C., "Bonhoeffer: Community, Authority and Spirituality", *Journal of Current Theology and Mission*, 21 (1994), 117–22.

Scott, Peter and Cavanaugh, William T. (eds.), *The Blackwell Companion to Political Theology* (Malden, MA/Oxford: Blackwell, 2004).

Set all free and Anti-Slavery International, *Act to End Slavery Now* (London: Anti-Slavery International and Churches Together in England, 2006).

Shor, Ira, "Education is Politics: Paulo Freire's Critical Pedagogy," in Peter McLaren and Peter Leonard (eds.), *Paulo Freire: A Critical Encounter* (London: Routledge, 1993), 25–35.

Shor, Ira and Freire, Paulo, *A Pedagogy for Liberation: Dialogues on Transforming Education* (Massachusetts: Bergin and Garvey, 1987).

Sider, Ronald J., "Is God Really On the Side of the Poor?" in *Sojourners on the Issues: Christians and Poverty* (Washington DC: Sojourners, 2006), 24 (see also, www.sojo.net).

Spencer, Nick, *"Doing God": A Future for Faith in the Public Square* (London: Theos, 2006), www.theosthinktank.co.uk

Stern, Nicholas, *Stern Review*, iii www.hm-treasury.gov.uk/media/ 8AC/ F7/Executive_Summary.pdf (accessed December 11, 2006).

Storkey, Alan, *Jesus and Politics: Confronting the Powers* (Grand Rapids, MI: Baker Academic, 2005).

Swartley, Willard M., *Slavery, Sabbath, War and Women: Case Issues in Biblical Interpretation* (Scottdale, PA: Herald Press, 1983).

TeSelle, Eugene, *Living in Two Cities: Augustinian Trajectories in Political Thought* (New York: University of Scranton Press, 1998).

Thomson, John B., *The Ecclesiology of Stanley Hauerwas: A Christian Theology of Liberation* (Aldershot, UK: Ashgate, 2003).

van der Meer, F., *Augustine the Bishop*, trans. Brian Battershaw and G.R. Lamb (London: Sheed and Ward, 1961).

Walsh, Brian J. and Keesmaat, Sylvia C., *Colossians Remixed: Subverting the Empire* (Milton Keynes: Paternoster Press, 2005).

Wells, Samuel, *Community-Led Regeneration and the Local Church* (Cambridge: Grove Books Ltd, 2003).

Wells, Samuel, *Transforming Fate into Destiny: The Theological Ethics of Stanley Hauerwas* (Carlisle: Paternoster Press, 1998).

Wenham, Gordon J., Word Biblical Commentary, *Genesis 1–15* (Nelson Reference and Electronic: 1987).

Westmorland-White, Michael, et al., "Disciples of the Incarnation", *Sojourners*, 23 (1994), 26-30.

William Temple Foundation, first year synopsis of *Regenerating Communities – A Theological and Strategic Critique*, see www.wtm.org.uk

Williams, Rowan, "Politics and the Soul: A Reading of the *City of God*," *Milltown Studies*, 19/20 (1987), 55–72.

Wright, Nigel, *The Radical Evangelical* (London: SPCK, 1996).

Wright, N.T., *Evil and the Justice of God* (London: SPCK, 2006).

Wright, N.T., "The New Testament and the 'State'" in *Themelios*, 16:1 (1990).

Wright, N.T., *The Resurrection of the Son of God* (London: SPCK, 2003).

Wright, N.T., "Where is God in the War on Terror," a public lecture in Durham Cathedral, November 9 , 2006. See www.ntwrightpage.com/Wright_War_On_Terror.htm (accessed November 27, 2006).

Wright N.T., *Simply Christian* (London: SPCK, 2006).

Yoder, John Howard, *The Christian Witness to the State* (Scottdale, Pennsylvania: Herald Press, 2002).

Zerner, Ruth, "Bonhoeffer on Discipleship and Community," *Lutheran Forum*, 30 (1996), 35–8.

Public Theology in Cultural Engagement

edited by
Stephen R. Holmes

Public Theology in Cultural Engagement offers foundational and programmatic essays exploring helpful ways to theologise about culture with missional intent. The book opens with three chapters taking steps towards developing a general theology of culture. Part Two explores the contribution of key biblical themes to a theology of culture – creation, law, election, Christology, and redemption. The final section considers theological proposals for engagement with culture past and present with contemporary reflections on nationalism and on drug culture. Contributors include Colin Gunton, Robert Jenson, Stephen Holmes, Colin Greene, Luke Bretherton and Brian Horne.

'This book represents groundbreaking and foundational thinking.' – **David Spriggs**, The Bible Society UK

Stephen R. Holmes is a Baptist minister and Lecturer in Theology at the University of St Andrews in Scotland.

978-1-84227-542-7

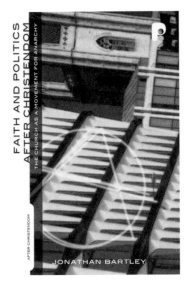

Faith and
Politics
After Christendom

Jonathan
Bartley

For the best part of 1700 years, the institutional church has enjoyed a hand-in-hand relationship with government but in this post-Christendom era the relationship has weakened to the point where the church can no longer claim to play any significant part in government. This book aims to offer perspectives and resources for a church no longer at the centre of society but on the margins. It invites a realistic and hopeful response to challenges and opportunities awaiting the church in twenty-first century politics.

'An important and timely book . . . a compelling read . . . This book provides a very helpful map and compass.' – **David Alton – Lord Alton of Liverpool**, Independent Crossbench Peer

'Jonathan Bartley has made a highly intelligent contribution to a debate which citizens of all creeds, and of none, ought to be following.' – **Bruce Clark**, *The Economist*

'Jonathan Bartley, one of the smartest young evangelicals around, offers compelling insights and suggestions, based on deep thought and clear-headed research.' – **Stephen Bates**, *The Guardian*

'This book should be considered essential reading by all those who care about the role of faith in civil society, whatever their beliefs.' – **Roy McCloughry**, lecturer in ethics, St Johns College Nottingham

Jonathan Bartley is director of the Christian think tank, Ekklesia.

978-1-84227-348-7

A Royal Priesthood

The Use of the Bible Politically and Ethically

Edited by Craig Bartholomew, Jonathan Chaplain, Robert Song and Al Wolters

This book presents a sustained engagement with the hugely important work of Christian ethicist and political theologian Oliver O'Donovan. A team of world class Christian scholars discuss O'Donovan's work in biblical, theological and political perspective. Contributors include N.T. Wright, Walter Moberly, Gordon McConville, Andrew Lincoln, Bruce Wannenwetsch, Christopher Rowland, Jonathan Chaplain and Craig Bartholomew. There is a response to each contribution from Oliver O'Donovan.

> 'Takes the discussion to a new level . . . This is a collection to which scholars in theology, ethics, biblical studies and political theory will return time and again with profit.' – **John Webster**, University of Aberdeen

> 'Extraordinarily illuminating and a model of intellectual engagement . . . Unlike most other collections, the whole is a great deal more than the sum of the parts. First-rate!' – **Nicholas Wolterstorff**, Yale University

> 'It would be difficult to exaggerate the creativity, importance and timeliness of these essays . . . This volume may well signal a constructive agenda for biblical interpretation over the next ten years. I cannot speak too highly of it.' – **Anthony Thiselton**, University of Nottingham

978-1-84227-067-7

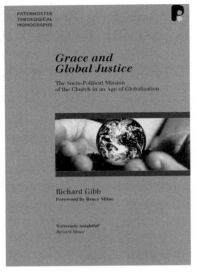

Grace and Global Justice

The Socio-Political Mission of the Church in an Age of Globalisation

Richard Gibb

What does it mean for the twenty-first-century church to conceive of itself as a community defined by the covenant of grace? Grace and Global Justice explores the ramifications of this central Christian doctrine for the holistic mission of the church in the context of a globalized world. Gibb shows how the church can be a voice for justice on behalf of the global poor by affirming its mission as a community of grace.

'Extremely insightful.' – **Richard Mouw**, President and Professor of Theology, Fuller Theological Seminary

'This study is warmly recommended for its theological insights and its careful integration of international political theory and biblical faith.' – **Mark Amstutz**, Professor of Political Science, Wheaton College

'An insightful and pertinent analysis.' – **Alan Torrance**, Professor of Systematic Theology, University of St Andrews

'In much evangelical theology the terms "grace" and "global justice" are rarely teamed together, but it is the basis of Gibb's forceful and richly-resourced argument that they must. This is vigorous theology . . . It provides a model for others to follow.' – **David F. Wright**, Emerutus Professor of Patristic and Reformed Christianity, University of Edinburgh

Richard Gibb is Assistant Minister of Charlotte Chapel, Edinburgh.

978-1-84227-465-1